Fifth Edition

JOURNALS IN PSYCHOLOGY

A Resource Listing For Authors

AMERICAN PSYCHOLOGICAL ASSOCIATION
WASHINGTON, DC

Published by
American Psychological Association
750 First Street, NE
Washington, DC 20002

Copies may be ordered from
American Psychological Association
Order Department
P.O. Box 92984
Washington, DC 20090-2984

In the UK and Europe, copies may be ordered from
American Psychological Association
3 Henrietta Street
Covent Garden, London
WC2E 8LU England

Printer: United Book Press, Inc., Baltimore, MD
Cover Designer: Minker Design, Bethesda, MD
Technical/Production Editor: Olin J. Nettles

ISBN: 1-55798-438-7

Printed in the United States of America

PREFACE

A t the last 11 American Psychological Association (APA) annual conventions, the Publications and Communications Board has sponsored a question and answer session on preparing manuscripts for journal submission. The questions authors ask most often concerned selecting the appropriate journals for their submissions. Considering that *Psychological Abstracts* scans over 1,400 journals in the behavioral and social sciences for articles of interest to psychologists, this is not surprising. Approximately 500 journals contain 20% or more articles written by psychologists. For 300 or so of these journals, psychologists provide more than 50% of the content.

For the author seeking an outlet for a manuscript, finding the appropriate journal obviously can be a significant undertaking. In an effort to assist authors in determining which of the many journals to consider, the American Psychological Association developed *Journals in Psychology*.

This resource is not intended to be a comprehensive listing of all publishing in psychology—it is instead a selective guide to several hundred English-language publications containing more than just an occasional article written by a psychologist. General information is provided on the publisher, editor, editorial policy, manuscript preparation, number of articles published, number of subscribers, and journal frequency. The journals for the 1997 edition were selected first on the basis of English-language publication and, for most, an editor/publisher location in the U.S. The second criterion was content: The editorial policy statement and the tables of contents were required to indicate that psychology was at least a substantial portion of the journal's editorial domain.

This fifth edition of *Journals in Psychology* contains entries for 355 journals. A few publishers are still reluctant to provide information on the number of subscribers, and for new journals of course, that information is not available (NA).

Journals in Psychology

The journals are listed in alphabetical order by title. If you know which journal you are looking for, you can thumb through the listings or check the alphabetical list of titles that starts on page 241. To find journals by specialty, check the classified index that starts on page 247. The index classifies journals by subfield and special interest areas in psychology.

We would appreciate your feedback on the effectiveness of the index and your thoughts on this publication. A reader response sheet is enclosed at the back of this volume. We hope you will take advantage of it to tell us of journals we have omitted and to suggest additional data we might provide to make your selection of a journal easier and more efficient.

Susan Knapp
Director
Publications Program

Acta Psychologica

Publisher: Elsevier Science Publishers B.V.
(Imprint: North-Holland)
P.O. Box 211
1000 AE Amsterdam
The Netherlands

Editor: M.W. van der Molen
Faculteit der Psychologie
Universiteit van Amsterdam
Roetersstraat 15
1018 WB Amsterdam
The Netherlands

Editorial Policy: Under Managing Editor, M. W. van der Molen, the specific fields covered by *Acta Psychologica* are Perception (editor: J. Wagemans); Human Performance (editors: M. W. van der Molen and G. P. van Galen); Learning and Memory (editor: G.Wolters); Judgment and Decision Making (editor: P. Koele); and Cognitive Ergonomics (editor: F. L. van Nes).

Acta Psychologica publishes original papers reporting on experimental studies, as well as theoretical and review articles, in human experimental psychology. Applied work is considered if it is directly related to basic issues in the field. The journal also publishes book reviews and a list of Books Received.

Selective Notes on Submissions: Instructions to authors included in each issue of the journal. Authors are requested to follow the "Guidelines for Nonsexist Use of Language" as stated in the *Publication Manual of the American Psychological Association* (4th ed.). Authors are requested to provide an abstract, conforming to the "Outline for Preparation of Abstracts" in *Psychological Abstracts,* to be printed at the beginning of their paper. Submit four (4) copies of the manuscript to the editor.

Journal Frequency: 9 issues per year

Articles/Pages Published per Year: 30/900

Total Subscribers: NA

Book Reviews Accepted: Yes

Rejection Rate: NA

Addiction

Publisher: Carfax
P.O. Box 25
Abingdon, Oxfordshire
OX14 3UE
England

Editor: Griffith Edwards
National Addiction Centre
4 Windsor Walk
London SE5 8AF
England

Editorial Policy: *Addiction* is a refereed journal. Its goal is to serve international and interdisciplinary scientific and clinical communication, to strengthen links between science and policy, and to stimulate and enhance the quality of debate. Submissions are sought which are not only technically competent, but are original and contain information or ideas of fresh interest to our international readership. Books and major reports may be submitted for review, and material for the News and Notes section is welcomed. We seek to serve the developing as well as the developed world. We aim to handle submissions courteously and promptly, and welcome dialogue with our contributors and readers.

The journal publishes work on alcohol, tobacco and other drugs. We favor rapidly developing research themes where there is a real sense of the cutting edge. We will publish papers dealing with instrument design (but only if they are describing significant advances). We consider ethnographic and qualitative research. We have a strong commitment to publishing historical research. We publish review papers provided they are critical, comprehensive, international in vision, and point to strong, and preferably new conclusions.

Selective Notes on Submissions: Instructions to authors included in each issue of the journal. Authors to prepare manuscripts according to Vancouver or Harvard style. Submit four (4) copies of the manuscript to the editor. Submissions from the U.S.A. should be sent to the regional editor: Thomas F. Babor, University of Connecticut Health Center, Farmington, CT 06030-1410.

Journal Frequency: Monthly

Articles/Pages Published per Year: 96/1800

Total Subscribers: 1,500

Book Reviews Accepted: Yes

Rejection Rate: 66%

Addictive Behaviors

Publisher: Elsevier Science Press
660 White Plains Road
Tarrytown, NY 10591-5153

Editor: Peter M. Miller, PhD
Hilton Head Institute
Valencia Road in Shipyard
     Planta
P.O. Box 7138
Hilton Head Island, SC 29938

Editorial Policy: *Addictive Behaviors* is a professional journal designed to publish original research, theoretical papers, and critical reviews in the area of substance abuse. The journal focuses on alcohol and drug abuse, smoking, and problems associated with eating. Articles represent interdisciplinary endeavors with research in such fields as biochemistry, psychology, sociology, psychiatry, neurology, and pharmacology being represented. While theoretical orientations are diverse, the emphasis of the journal is primarily empirical. That is, sound experimental design combined with objective assessment procedures is a requisite for inclusion of papers. Occasionally, uncontrolled clinical demonstrations or case reports appear in brief form if they are innovative and likely to induce further research in the area. A case report, to be acceptable, must embody one or more of the following: (1) a new and original method; (2) an apparently advantageous variation of a previous method; (3) an observation of considerable interest; (4) an unusually clear account of the use of an accepted method. In all instances, baseline and follow-up quantitative data of no less than six months duration should be presented. Two major types of research reports are encouraged. The first type includes descriptive studies in which functional relationships between a substance abuse and any one of a combination of social, biochemical, cognitive, environmental, attitudinal, emotional, or neurological factors are established. A study in which the relationship between social stress and alcohol consumption were assessed in both alcoholics and social drinkers is included in this category. Descriptive studies which contribute meaningfully to the development and/or modification of clinical treatment strategies are given priority. The second type of study involves clinical outcome data in which treatment or prevention procedures are systematically evaluated either by controlled group research or single-case experimental designs.

Selective Notes on Submissions: Instructions to authors included in each issue of the journal. Authors to prepare manuscripts according to the *Publication Manual of the American Psychological Association* (4th ed.). Submit three (3) copies of the manuscript to the editor.

Journal Frequency: Bimonthly

Articles/Pages Published per Year: 42/600

Total Subscribers: 1,200

Book Reviews Accepted: No

Rejection Rate: 30%

Notes From Publisher: Free sample copy available on request.

Administration and Policy in Mental Health

Publisher: Human Sciences Press, Inc.
233 Spring Street
New York, NY 10013-1578

Editor: Saul Feldman
Bay Area Foundation for Human Resources
850 California Street
San Francisco, CA 94108

Editorial Policy: The aim of *Administration and Policy in Mental Health* is to advance the practice, study, and process of administration in the mental health setting. The journal publishes peer-reviewed original articles and case reports on all aspects of the organization and administration of mental health services and on mental health policy. Topics for articles may include, but need not be limited to, financing mental health services, managed mental health, delivery of services, staffing, leadership, organizational relations and policy, and the like. The journal also publishes reports that are briefer and less research-oriented than the articles that make up the remainder of the journal. Reports need not include references.

Selective Notes on Submissions: Instructions to authors included in each issue of the journal. Authors to prepare manuscripts according to the *Publication Manual of the American Psychological Association* (4th ed.). Submit three (3) copies of the manuscript to the editor.

Journal Frequency: Bimonthly

Articles/Pages Published per Year: 30/360

Total Subscribers: 1,500

Book Reviews Accepted: NA

Rejection Rate: 30%

Adolescence

Publisher: Libra Publishers, Inc.
3089C Clairemont Drive
Suite 383
San Diego, CA 92117

Editor: William Kroll

Editorial Policy: *Adolescence* is an international quarterly devoted to the psysiological, psychological, psychiatric, sociological, and educational aspects of the second decade of human life.

Selective Notes on Submissions: Instructions to authors included in each issue of the journal. Authors to prepare manuscripts according to the *Publication Manual of the American Psychological Association* (4th ed.). Submit two (2) copies of the manuscript to the editor, c/o the publisher. For acknowledgment of receipt, authors should enclose a stamped, self-addressed postcard containing the title of the work. Authors are also requested to enclose a business-size stamped, self-addressed envelope for the report of editorial decisions.

Journal Frequency: Quarterly

Articles/Pages Published per Year: 100/1000

Total Subscribers: 3,000

Book Reviews Accepted: Yes

Rejection Rate: 75%

Aggressive Behavior

Publisher: Wiley-Liss, Inc.
605 Third Avenue
New York, NY 10158

Editor: Ronald Baenninger
Department of Psychology
Temple University
Philadelphia, PA 19122

Editorial Policy: *Aggressive Behavior* will consider manuscripts in the English language which relate to either overt or implied conflict behaviors. Papers concerning mechanisms underlying or influencing behaviors generally regarded as aggressive and the physiological and/or behavioral consequences of being subject to such behaviors also fall within the scope of the journal. Review articles will be considered as well as empirical and theoretical articles.

Selective Notes on Submissions: Instructions to authors included in each issue of the journal. Authors to prepare manuscripts according to the *Publication Manual of the American Psychological Association* (4th ed.). Submit original plus two (2) copies of the manuscript to the editor.

Journal Frequency: Bimonthly

Articles/Pages Published per Year: 24/470

Total Subscribers: 750

Book Reviews Accepted: Yes

Rejection Rate: 50%

Aging, Neuropsychology, and Cognition

Previous Title: Aging and Cognition

Publisher: Swets & Zeitlinger
P.O. Box 825
2160 SZ Lisse
The Netherlands

Editors: David F. Hultsch, PhD
Department of Psychology
University of Victoria
P.O. Box 3050
Victoria, B.C.
Canada V8W 3P5

David W. Loring
Department of Neurology
Medical College of Georgia
Augusta, GA 30912-3275

Editorial Policy: The purposes of *Aging, Neuropsychology, and Cognition* are to (a) publish research on both the normal and dysfunctional aspects of cognitive development in adulthood and aging and (b) promote the integration of theories, methods, and research findings between the fields of cognitive gerontology and neuropsychology.

Selective Notes on Submissions: Authors to prepare manuscripts according to the *Publication Manual of the American Psychological Association* (4th ed.). Submit four (4) copies of the manuscript to the editors. Authors should supply their electronic mail address and fax number, if available.

Journal Frequency: Quarterly

Articles/Pages Published per Year: 400 pp.

Total Subscribers: NA

Book Reviews Accepted: NA

Rejection Rate: NA

AIDS Education and Prevention

Publisher: Guilford Publications, Inc.
72 Spring Street
New York, NY 10012

Editor: Francisco S. Sy
AIDS Education and Prevention
University of South Carolina
School of Public Health
Columbia, SC 29208

Editorial Policy: Until a cure is found, prevention is the only effective weapon against AIDS, and prevention is only possible through education. To that end, this journal privides professionals who deal with AIDS with the state-of-the-art information they need. It offers high-caliber original contributions that highlight existing and theoretical models of AIDS education and prevention, including their development, implementation, and evaluation.

Selective Notes on Submissions: Instructions to authors included in each issue of the journal. Authors to prepare manuscripts according to the *Publication Manual of the American Psychological Association* (4th ed.). Submit four (4) copies of the manuscript to the editor.

Journal Frequency: Bimonthly

Articles/Pages Published per Year: 36/565

Total Subscribers: 1,500

Book Reviews Accepted: Yes

Rejection Rate: 60%

American Annals of the Deaf

Publisher: American Annals of the Deaf
800 Florida Avenue, NE
Washington, DC 20002

Editor: Donald F. Moores, PhD
American Annals of the Deaf
301 East Fowler Hall
Gallaudet University
800 Florida Avenue, NE
Washington, DC 20002

Editorial Policy: *American Annals of the Deaf,* published since 1847, is a prestigious journal for teachers, administrators, and research professionals involved in the education of deaf students. Published jointly by the Conference of Educational Administrators Serving the Deaf and the Convention of American Instructors of the Deaf, the *Annals* publishes original articles by scholars in the field of deafness.

Selective Notes on Submissions: Instructions to authors included in each issue of the journal. Authors to prepare manuscripts according to the *Publication Manual of the American Psychological Association* (4th ed.). Submit three (3) copies of the manuscript to the editor.

Journal Frequency: 5 issues per year

Articles/Pages Published per Year: 40/430

Total Subscribers: 2,600

Book Reviews Accepted: Yes

Rejection Rate: 67%

American Educational Research Journal

Publisher: American Educational Research Association
1230 17th Street, NW
Washington, DC 20036-3078

Editors: Section on Social and Institutional Analysis:
William B. Thomas
University of Pittsburg
5M38, Forbes Quad
Pittsburgh, PA 15260

Section on Teaching, Learning, and Human Development:
Pat Ashton and James Algina
1403 Norman Hall
University of Florida
Gainesville, FL 32611

Editorial Policy: *American Educational Research Journal* (quarterly) features reports of original research, both empirical and theoretical.

Selective Notes on Submissions: Instructions to authors included in each issue of the journal. Authors to prepare manuscripts according to the *Publication Manual of the American Psychological Association* (4th ed.) or the *Chicago Manual of Style*. Submit five (5) copies of the manuscript to the appropriate section editor(s).

Journal Frequency: Quarterly

Articles/Pages Published per Year: 36/960

Total Subscribers: 17,400

Book Reviews Accepted: No

Rejection Rate: 91%

American Indian and Alaska Native Mental Health Research

Publisher: University Press of Colorado
P.O. Box 849
Niwot, CO 80544

Editor: Spero M. Manson, PhD
NCAIANMHR, Psychiatry,
UCHSC
University North Pavilion,
A011-13
4455 East 12th Avenue
Denver, CO 80220

Editorial Policy: *American Indian and Alaska Native Mental Health Research* seeks to publish theoretical as well as empirical work on the broad range of factors (social, economic, political, and cultural) that affect the emotional and psychological well-being of American Indians and Alaska Natives. Special emphasis is given to contributions to diagnosis, assessment, epidemiology, treatment, and prevention of serious psychological dysfunctions and major mental disorders across the developmental life span.

Selective Notes on Submissions: Authors to prepare manuscripts according to the *Publi-*

cation Manual of the American Psychological Association (4th ed.). Submit four (4) copies of the manuscript to the editor.

Journal Frequency: 3 issues per year

Articles/Pages Published per Year: 25/200

Total Subscribers: 400

Book Reviews Accepted: Yes

Rejection Rate: 50%

American Journal of Community Psychology

Publisher: Plenum Publishing Corporation
233 Spring Street
New York, NY 10113-1578

Editor: 1993–1997:
Edison J. Trickett, PhD
Department of Psychology
University of Maryland
College Park, MD 20742

Editorial Policy: The *American Journal of Community Psychology* publishes empirical research and theoretical papers concerned with the relationship between persons and social issues, institutions, and settings. Topics of interest include but are not limited to: individual and community mental and physical health; educational, legal, and work environment processes, policies, and opportunities; social welfare and social justice. Studies of social problems, broadly defined, as well as evaluations of interventions, are welcomed. Both quantitative and qualitative research are appropriate. Quality of conception and methods appropriate to the question asked and to the current state of knowledge are more important than any particular methodology. A variety of levels of analysis are appropriate, including societal, neighborhood, organizational, group, and individual. Papers concerned with prevention of problems in living; promotion of emotional and physical health, well-being, and competence; empowerment of marginal groups; collective social action; social networks; institutional and organizational change; self- and mutual help; and community based interventions such as collaborative research, advocacy, consultation, training, and planning are welcomed. Although not limited to these areas, the *American Journal of Community Psychology* seeks manuscripts concerned with underrepresented populations (such as women, ethnic minorities, and the physically disabled); social policy, innovative programs, and methodologies; and studies which foster interrelationships between law, ecological, environmental, and community psychology. For further information on editorial policies, authors should consult the editorial statement which appears in the April 1988 issue (Volume 16, Number 2). (This is a publication of APA's Division 27.)

Selective Notes on Submissions: Instructions to authors included in each issue of the journal. Authors to prepare manuscripts according to the *Publication Manual of the American Psychological Association* (4th ed.). Submit four (4) copies of the manuscript to the editor.

Journal Frequency: Bimonthly

Articles/Pages Published per Year: 39/914

Total Subscribers: 900

Book Reviews Accepted: No

Rejection Rate: 74%

American Journal of Dance Therapy

Publisher: Plenum Publishing
                 233 Spring Street
                 New York, NY 10013-1578

Editors: Ruthanna Boris,
                 Carrie Green-Zinn,
                 and Susan Coto McKenna

Editorial Policy: The *American Journal of Dance Therapy*, the official publication of the American Dance Therapy Association, is designed to meet the needs of clinicians, researchers, and educators in dance therapy. The journal welcomes articles from dance therapists and related professionals on theory, research, and clinical practice in dance therapy. Selection of articles is based on originality, adequacy of method, significance of findings, contributions to theory, and clarity of presentation.

Selective Notes on Submissions: Instructions to authors included in each issue of the journal. Authors to prepare manuscripts according to the *Publication Manual of the American Psychological Association* (4th ed.). Submit three (3) copies of the manuscript to the editors, c/o ADTA, 2000 Century Plaza, Columbia, MD 21044.

Journal Frequency: Biannually

Articles/Pages Published per Year: 8/140

Total Subscribers: NA

Book Reviews Accepted: NA

Rejection Rate: NA

American Journal on Mental Retardation

Publisher: American Association on Mental
                    Retardation
                    444 North Capitol Street, NW
                    Suite 864
                    Washington, DC 20001

Editor: Stephen R. Schroeder
                University of Kansas
                1052 Dole Human Development
                Center
                Lawrence, KS 66045

Editorial Policy: *American Journal on Mental Retardation* (ISSN 0895-8017) is a scientific and archival journal for reporting original contributions to knowledge of mental retardation, its treatment and prevention. Such contributions include (a) reports of empirical research on characteristics of people with mental retardation, individual differences in and correlates of such characteristics, and factors that alter those characteristics or correlates; (b) systematic reviews and theoretical reinterpretations of relevant research literatures; (c) scholarly reassessments of clinical, historical, legal, philosophical, or other literatures relevant to understanding, treating, or preventing mental retardation or its correlates; and (d) reports of evaluative research on new treatment procedures or programs. Anno-tated bibliographies, anecdotal case reports, descriptions of treatment procedures of programs, and personal accounts are not published.

Each submitted paper is reviewed by experts in the area of the paper's content. To be published, a paper must conform to the highest standards of professional development of the discipline(s) identified with its content. Research papers are judged on the importance of the question(s) asked, soundness of conceptualization and rationale, relevance of research operations to the question(s), reliability of results, logic of conclusions, and clarity and economy of presentation. Literature reviews, theoretical reinterpretations, and scholarly reassessments are judged on relevance of focus, incisiveness with which issues are defined, completeness of coverage of relevant literatures, consistency in the application of evaluative criteria, soundness of inferences and conclusions, and novelty and probable fruitfulness of interpretation. Such papers must include new insights.

Selective Notes on Submissions: Instructions to authors included in each issue of the journal. Authors to prepare manuscripts according to the *Publication Manual of the American Psychological Association* (4th ed.). Submit five (5) copies of the manuscript to the editor.

Journal Frequency: Bimonthly

Articles/Pages Published per Year: 800 pp.

Total Subscribers: 11,600

Book Reviews Accepted: Yes

Rejection Rate: 75%

Notes From Publisher: Complete information for authors available by request from AAMR, Washington, DC.

American Journal of Orthopsychiatry

Publisher: American Orthopsychiatry
                 Association
                 330 Seventh Avenue, 18th Floor
                 New York, NY 10001

Editor: Ellen Bassuk, MD

Editorial Policy: The journal is dedicated to informing public policy, professional practice, and knowledge production relating to mental health and human development, from a multidisciplinary and interprofessional perspective. Clinical, theoretical, research, or expository papers that are essentially synergistic and directed at concept or theory development, reconceptualization of major issues, explanation, and interpretation are especially welcomed for Editorial Board consideration. Selection of articles for publication is based on their originality, adequacy of method, significance of findings, contribution to theory, and clarity and brevity of presentation.

Selective Notes on Submissions: Instructions to authors included in each issue of the journal. Authors to prepare manuscripts according to the *Publication Manual of the American Psychological Association* (4th ed.). Submit four (4) copies of the manuscript to the editor (c/o publisher).

Journal Frequency: Quarterly

Articles/Pages Published per Year: 56/620

Total Subscribers: NA

Book Reviews Accepted: Yes

Rejection Rate: NA

American Journal of Psychoanalysis

Publisher: Human Sciences Press
                 233 Spring Street
                 New York, NY 10013-1578

Editor: Douglas Ingram, MD, Editor
              American Journal of
                 Psychoanalysis
              329 East 62nd Street
              New York, NY 10021

Editorial Policy: The *American Journal of Psychoanalysis* was founded in 1941 and is sponsored by the Association for the Advancement of Psychoanalysis of the Karen Horney Psychoanalytic Institute and Center. Its purpose is to communicate modern concepts of psychoanalytic theory and practice, and related investigation in allied fields. It is addressed to everyone interested in the understanding and therapy of emotional problems.

Selective Notes on Submissions: Instructions to authors included in each issue of the journal. Submit original and three (3) copies of the manuscript to the editor.

Journal Frequency: Quarterly

Articles/Pages Published per Year: 40/400

Total Subscribers: NA

Book Reviews Accepted: Yes

Rejection Rate: NA

The American Journal of Psychology

Publisher: University of Illinois Press
1325 South Oak Street
Champaign, IL 61820

Editor: Donelson E. Dulany
University of Illinois at
Urbana-Champaign
603 East Daniel Street
Champaign, IL 61820

Editorial Policy: *The American Journal of Psychology* (ISSN 002-9556) was founded in the interest of general experimental psychology and is devoted to the basic science of mind. The journal publishes original experimental research, theoretical presentations, combined theoretical and experimental analyses, historical commentaries, shorter notes and discussions, obituaries of prominent psychologists, and in-depth reviews of significant books.

Selective Notes on Submissions: Instructions to authors included in each issue of the journal. Authors to prepare manuscripts according to the *Publication Manual of the American Psychological Association* (4th ed.). Submit four (4) copies of the manuscript to the editor.

Journal Frequency: Quarterly

Articles/Pages Published per Year: 30/700

Total Subscribers: 2,500

Book Reviews Accepted: Y

Rejection Rate: 65%

Notes From Publisher: Average evaluation time is approximately 3 months. Average time from acceptance to publication is approximately one year.

American Psychologist

Publisher: American Psychological
Association
750 First Street, NE
Washington, DC 20002-4242

Editor: Raymond D. Fowler, PhD
Chief Executive Officer
American Psychological
Association
750 First Street, NE
Washington, DC 20002-4242

Editorial Policy: The *American Psychologist* is the official journal of the American Psychological Association and, as such, contains archival documents. It also publishes articles on current issues in psychology as well as empirical, theoretical, and practical articles on broad aspects of psychology.

Selective Notes on Submissions: No style sheet included. Authors to prepare manuscripts according to the *Publication Manual of the American Psychological Association* (4th ed.). Submit three (3) copies of the manuscript to the editor.

Journal Frequency: Monthly

Articles/Pages Published per Year: 160/ 1,000

Total Subscribers: 106,700

Book Reviews Accepted: No

Rejection Rate: 87%

Animal Behaviour

Publisher: Academic Press
24-28 Oval Road
London NW1 7DX
England

Editors: European Editor:
A. K. Turner, Managing Editor
Department of Life Science
University of Nottingham
Nottingham NG7 2RD
England

American Editor:
M. D. Beecher
Animal Behaviour Editorial
   Office
University of Washington
119 Guthrie Hall
Box 351525
Seattle, WA 98195-1525

Editorial Policy: *Animal Behaviour* accepts both original papers and critical reviews. Original papers may be field or laboratory studies and should bear a fundamental relationship to the natural lives of animals. Preference is given to papers that are theoretically based rather than purely descriptive. The material must not have been published or submitted for publication elsewhere. Short communications are also welcomed.

Selective Notes on Submissions: Instructions to authors included in each issue of the

journal. Submit four (4) copies of the manuscript to the editor.

Journal Frequency: Monthly

Articles/Pages Published per Year: 240/ 2000

Total Subscribers: NA

Book Reviews Accepted: Yes

Rejection Rate: NA

Animal Learning and Behavior

Publisher: Psychonomic Society, Inc.
1710 Fortview Road
Austin, TX 78704

Editor: Robert A. Rescorla
Department of Psychology
University of Pennsylvania
3815 Walnut Street
Philadelphia, PA 19104

Editorial Policy: *Animal Learning and Behavior* publishes experimental and theoretical contributions and critical reviews in the areas of investigation encompassed by the title of the journal. Examples are sensation, perception, conditioning, learning, attention, memory, motivation, emotion, development, social behavior, and comparative investigations. Studies involving human subjects will be considered if, in the editor's opinion, they deal with principles of animal learning and behavior that do not apply exclusively to humans. Experimental articles may report the results of a single experiment or a series of related experiments. Theoretical articles should provide interesting and reasonable alternatives to existing ideas, and must reflect familiarity with the existing work in the area of the article. Reviews of the literature should be critical, have an appreciable theoretical content, and not be primarily bibliographic in their impact.

Selective Notes on Submissions: Instructions to authors included in each issue of the journal. Authors to prepare manuscripts according to the *Publication Manual of the American Psychological Association* (4th ed.), except that in the abbreviation of physical units, the style of the American Institute of Physics is followed. Submit four (4) copies of the manuscript to the editor.

Journal Frequency: Quarterly

Articles/Pages Published per Year: 50/450

Total Subscribers: 1,250

Book Reviews Accepted: No

Rejection Rate: NA

Anxiety, Stress, and Coping: An International Journal

Publisher: Harwood Academic Publishers

Editors: Stevan E. Hobfoll
Applied Psychology Center
Kent Hall, Kent State University
Kent, OH 44242-0001
Reinhard Pekrun
Institute of Psychology
University of Regensburg
D-93040 Regensburg
Germany

Editorial Policy: The journal provides a forum for scientific, theoretically important, and clinically significant research reports and conceptual contributions. It deals not only with the assessment of anxiety, stress, and coping, and with experimental and field studies on anxiety dimensions and stress and coping processes, but also with related topics such as the antecedents and consequences of stress and emotions. While the journal will be open to a diversity of articles, it will be interested primarily in (1) well-designed, methodologically sound research reports, (2) theoretical papers, and (3) interpretative literature reviews or meta-analyses. However, case studies, and clinical, therapeutic, and educational articles that contribute to furthering research and theory will also be published.

Selective Notes on Submissions: Instructions to authors included in each issue of the journal. Authors to prepare manuscripts according to the *Publication Manual of the American Psychological Association* (4th ed.). Submit three (3) copies of the manuscript to the editors.

Journal Frequency: Quarterly

Articles/Pages Published per Year: 24\440

Total Subscribers: NA

Book Reviews Accepted: No

Rejection Rate: 85%

Applied Cognitive Psychology

Publisher: John Wiley & Sons, Ltd.
Baffins Lane
Chichester
West Sussex PO19 1UD
England

Editors: North American Editor:
Kathy Pezdek
Department of Psychology
The Claremont Graduate School
Claremont, CA 91711-3955

Graham Davies
Department of Psychology
University of Leicester
University Road
Leicester LE1 7RH
England

Editorial Policy: *Applied Cognitive Psychology* seeks to publish the best papers dealing with psychological analyses of problems of memory, learning, thinking, language, and consciousness as they are reflected in the real world. The journal will publish papers on a wide variety of issues and from diverse theoretical perspectives.

Selective Notes on Submissions: Instructions to authors included in each issue of the journal. Authors to prepare manuscripts according to the *Publication Manual of the American Psychological Association* (4th ed.). Submit three (3) copies of the manuscript to the appropriate editor.

Journal Frequency: Bimonthly

Articles/Pages Published per Year: 42/540

Total Subscribers: 652

Book Reviews Accepted: Yes

Rejection Rate: NA

Applied Psycholinguistics

Publisher: Cambridge University Press
40 West 20th Street
New York, NY 10011-4211

Editors: Catherine E. Snow
Graduate School of Education
Harvard University
Cambridge, MA

John L. Locke
Department of Human
   Communication Sciences
University of Sheffield
Sheffield, England

Editorial Policy: *Applied Psycholinguistics* publishes original articles on the psychological processes involved in language. Articles address the development, use, and impairment of language in all its modalities, including spoken, signed, and written. *Applied Psycholinguistics* is of interest to professionals in a variety of fields, including linguistics, psychology, speech and hearing, reading, language teaching, special education, and neurology. Specific topics featured in the journal include:

• Language development
the development of speech perception and
   production
the acquisition and use of sign language
studies of discourse development
second language learning

• Language disorders in children and adults,
   associated with
brain damage
retardation and autism
specific learning disabilities

hearing impairment
emotional disturbance

• Literacy development
early literacy skills
dyslexia and other reading disorders
writing development and disorders
spelling development and disorders

• Psycholinguistic processing
bilingualism
sentence processing
lexical access

In addition to research reports, theoretical reviews will be considered for publication, as will short notes, discussions of previously published papers, and topics within its purview.

Selective Notes on Submissions: Instructions to authors included in each issue of the journal. Authors to prepare manuscripts according to the *Publication Manual of the American Psychological Association* (4th ed.). Submit four (4) copies of the manuscript. Articles pertaining to early communicative development, phonetics, and phonology, and to pathologies of spoken and written language (including dyslexia) should be sent to John Locke. Articles related to bilingualism, discourse, and preliteracy skills should be sent to Catherine Snow. All other papers may be sent to either editor.

Journal Frequency: Quarterly

Articles/Pages Published per Year: 24/400

Total Subscribers: 1,000

Book Reviews Accepted: NA

Rejection Rate: NA

Applied Psychological Measurement

Publisher: Sage Publications, Inc.
2455 Teller Road
Thousand Oaks, CA 91320

Editor: David J. Weiss
N660 Elliott Hall
University of Minnesota
Minneapolis, MN 55455-0344

Editorial Policy: *Applied Psychological Measurement* publishes empirical research on the application of techniques of psychological measurement to substantive problems in all areas of psychology and related disciplines. The general classes of studies published include: (1) reports on the development and application of innovative measuring techniques; (2) reports of methodological developments in the solution of measurement problems; (3) studies comparing applications of different measurement techniques; (4) studies investigating the limits of applicability of measurement methodologies; (5) empirical studies in the methodology of validation and reliability; and (6) critical reviews of measurement methodology. Reports of the development of new measurement instruments and studies of the validity and reliability of psychological measuring instruments are published only if they have a methodological focus. Methodologically oriented studies in the measurement of ability, aptitude, personality, interests, and social and perceptual variables will be considered, as will studies in test development and unidimensional and multidimensional scaling. This journal does not publish papers which are purely statistical in nature, unless they are demonstrably related to applied measurement problems (e.g., problems in the determination of validity or reliability of measurement techniques). *APM* publishes two types of data-based research papers: regular manuscripts and manuscripts submitted under the Advance Review Option (ARO). Regular manuscripts report on research that has been completed; ARO is designed to provide researchers with advance review of their proposed research before the research is implemented. Brief reports will also be considered for publication. These papers report on exploratory, small-sample, and replication studies, as well as brief technical notes. (*APM* also publishes abstracts of computer programs and book reviews. See journal for instructions on submission.)

Selective Notes on Submissions: Instructions to authors included in each issue of the journal. Authors to prepare manuscripts according to the *Publication Manual of the American Psychological Association* (4th ed.). Submit three (3) copies of the manuscript to the editor. Telephone: (612) 625-0862. Internet: DJWEISS@VX.CIS. UMN.EDU

Journal Frequency: Quarterly

Articles/Pages Published per Year: 35/450

Total Subscribers: 1,000

Book Reviews Accepted: Yes

Rejection Rate: 67%

Notes From Publisher: Authors preparing or planning empirical research should note the Advance Review Option.

Applied Psychology: An International Review

Publisher: Psychology Press
27 Church Road
Hove, East Sussex BN3 2FA
England

Editor: Professor Michael Frese
Applied Psychology
University of Giessen
Department of Psychology
Otto Behaghel-Str. 10, 35394
Giessen
Germany

Editorial Policy: The journal of the IAAP, which is now in its 46th volume, is a forum for scholarly exchange in research findings and reviews in applied psychology. This includes documenting advances in psychological research and discovery in fields such as: work and organizational psychology, environmental issues, health, developmental psychology, gerontology, sport, education, community problems, intergroup relations, and national development. Particularly invited are articles that advance our understanding of applied phenomena across different national and cultural contexts, that stimulate debates and discussions, and that help us to understand communalities that underlie the various areas of applied psychology.

There are the following types of contributions in *Applied Psychology* (all of them freely submitted, except contributions to the special issues): *normal contributions,* freely submitted to the journal and describing an important piece of research or providing a review of a specific issue; *lead articles,* (approximately 35 printed pages), with open peer commentaries (5 printed pages) that should stimulate the international scientific discussion; *international replication notes,* that provide replication of known phenomena within cultural contexts that have not been studied before (5 printed pages); and *special issues,* with guest editors and invited contributions with particular thematic or regional focus. Submissions to the *Review* are invited, and should be sent to the address given. All of the articles are reviewed, and emphasis is placed on maintaining the world-wide scope of the journal.

Selective Notes on Submissions: Instructions to authors included in each issue of the journal. Authors to prepare manuscripts according to the *Publication Manual of the American Psychological Association* (4th ed.). Submit five (5) copies of the manuscript to the editor.

Journal Frequency: Quarterly

Articles/Pages Published per Year: 24/400

Total Subscribers: 2,000

Book Reviews Accepted: No

Rejection Rate: 71–80%

Applied Psychophysiology and Biofeedback

Publisher: Plenum Publishing Corporation
233 Spring Street
New York, NY 10013-1578
in association with

Association for Applied
Psychophysiology
10200 West 44th Avenue, #304
Wheat Ridge, CO 80033

Editor: Frank Andrasik, PhD
Center for Behavioral Medicine
University of West Florida
11000 University Parkway
Pensacola, FL 32514

Editorial Policy: *Applied Psychphysiology and Biofeedback* is an international, interdisciplinary journal devoted to study of the interrelationship of physiological systems, cognition, social and environmental parameters, and health. Priority is given to original research, basic and applied, which contributes to the theory, practice, and evaluation of applied psychophysiology and biofeedback [see Editorial, Applied Psychophysiology and Biofeedback, 1997, 22, (1)]. Although the major emphasis is placed upon empirical research, methodological, conceptual, and theoretical papers, and evaluative reports are welcomed. The journal recognizes that important advances have come about by innovative small-n research and encourages case studies and clinical replication series. Letters to the editor, concerning issues raised in articles previously published in the journal, will appear from time to time. *Applied Psychophysiology and Biofeedback* is the official publication of the Association for Applied Psychophysiology and Biofeedback.

Selective Notes on Submissions: Instructions to contributors and a membership application for AAPB are included in each issue of the journal. Authors to prepare manuscripts according to the *Publication Manual of the American Psychological Association* (4th ed.). Submit five (5) complete sets of the manuscript to the editor.

Journal Frequency: Quarterly

Articles/Pages Published per Year: 25/320

Total Subscribers: 2,500

Book Reviews Accepted: No

Rejection Rate: 60%

Archives of Clinical Neuropsychology

Publisher: Elsevier Science, Inc.
                   660 White Plains Road
                   Tarrytown, NY 10591-5153

Editor: Cecil R. Reynolds
                   Department of Educational
                       Psychology
                   Texas A & M University
                   College Station, TX 77843

Editorial Policy: *Archives of Clinical Neuropsychology,* published 4 issues per annum, is sponsored by the National Academy of Neuropsychologists. The journal publishes original contributions dealing with the psychological aspects of the etiology, diagnosis, and treatment of disorders arising out of dysfunction of the central nervous system. *Archives of Clinical Neuropsychology* will also consider manuscripts involving the established principles of the profession of neuropsychology: (a) delivery and evaluation of services; (b) ethical and legal issues; and (c) approaches to education and training. Preference will be given to empirical reports and key reviews. Brief research reports and commentaries on published articles (not exceeding two printed pages) will also be considered. At the discretion of the editor, rebuttals to commentaries may be invited. Occasional papers of a theoretical nature will be considered.

Selective Notes on Submissions: Instructions to authors included in each issue of the journal. Authors to prepare manuscripts according to the *Publication Manual of the American Psychological Association* (4th ed.). Submit four (4) copies of the manuscript to the editor.

Journal Frequency: Quarterly

Articles/Pages Published per Year: 32/400

Total Subscribers: NA

Book Reviews Accepted: NA

Rejection Rate: NA

Notes From Publisher: Free sample copy available upon request.

Archives of Sexual Behavior

Publisher: Plenum Publishing Corporation
                   233 Spring Street
                   New York, NY 10013-1578

Editor: Richard Green, MD, JD
                   University of Cambridge
                   Institute of Criminology
                   7 West Road
                   Cambridge CB3 9DT
                   England

Editorial Policy: *Archives of Sexual Behavior*, the official publication of the International Academy of Sex Research, has emerged as the leading scholarly publication in the area of human sexuality. The journal reports the latest research trends in the science of human sexual behavior, bringing together high-quality submissions from such diverse fields as psychology, psychiatry, biology, ethology, endocrinology, and sociology. Contributions feature a broad range of subjects, including: clinical research in sexual dysfunctions; neuroendocrine correlates of sexual behavior; the development of masculinity and femininity in children; therapeutic techniques ranging from behavior therapy to psychoanalysis; sexual attitudes and behaviors in special populations; sex education; and cross-cultural studies.

Selective Notes on Submissions: Instructions to authors included in each issue of the journal. Authors to prepare manuscripts according to the *Style Manual for Biological Journals,* published by the American Institute of Biological Sciences. Submit original and three (3) copies of the manuscript to the editor.

Journal Frequency: Bimonthly

Articles/Pages Published per Year: 36/540

Total Subscribers: NA

Book Reviews Accepted: NA

Rejection Rate: NA

Arts in Psychotherapy

Publisher: Elsevier Science, Inc.
655 Avenue of the Americas
New York, NY 10011

Editor: Robert J. Landy, PhD, RDT
Professor and Director
Drama Therapy Program
New York University
New York, NY 10012

Editorial Policy: *Arts in Psychotherapy* is a quarterly, international journal for professionals in the fields of mental health and education. The journal publishes articles (including illustrations) by art, dance/movement, drama, music, and poetry psychotherapists, as well as psychiatrists and psychologists, that reflect the theory and practice of these disciplines. There are no restrictions on philosophical orientation or application. *Arts in Psychotherapy* reports news and commentaries on national and international conferences and current education information relevant to the creative arts in therapy. The journal also includes book reviews, invites letters to the editor, and welcomes dialogue between contributors.

Selective Notes on Submissions: Instructions to authors included in each issue of the journal. Authors to prepare manuscripts according to the *Publication Manual of the American Psychological Association* (4th ed.). Submit three (3) copies of the manuscript to the managing editor: Sylvia M. Halpern, 20 Ridgecrest East, Scarsdale, NY 10583-2012.

Journal Frequency: 5 issues per year

Articles/Pages Published per Year: 32/400

Total Subscribers: NA

Book Reviews Accepted: Yes

Rejection Rate: NA

Notes From Publisher: Free sample copy available upon request.

Assessment

Publisher: Psychological Assessment
Resources, Inc.
P.O. Box 998
Odessa, FL 33556

Editor: Robert P. Archer
Department of Psychiatry and
Behavioral Sciences
Eastern Virginia Medical School
825 Fairfax Avenue (Hofheimer
Hall 730)
Norfolk, VA 23507

Editorial Policy: *Assessment* publishes articles derived from psychometric research, clinical comparisons, or theoretical formulations and literature reviews that fall within the broad domain of clinical and applied assessment. The emphasis of this journal is on the publication of information of direct relevance to the use of assessment measures, including the practical applications of measurement methods, test development and interpretation practices, and advances in the description and prediction of human behavior. The scope of the journal extends from the evaluation of individuals and groups in clinical, counseling, health, forensic, organizational, industrial, and educational settings to the assessment of treatment efficacy, program evaluation, job performance, or the study of behavior outcomes. Papers considered appropriate for publication encompass investigations related to the development, validation, and evaluation of new or established assessment instruments; the application of computer-based technologies to assessment issues; measurement of human characteristics, resources, aptitudes, abilities, or traits; and description of abnormal behavior and diagnosis of mental disorders. Papers that focus on cognitive and neuropsychological assessment, the interface of cognitive, personality, and psycopathology domains, and the definition of traits and behaviors that comprise aspects of normal behavior and the realm of psychopathology are within journal purview.

Articles are invited that target empirical classification of normal and abnormal behaviors and personality characteristics, theory and measurement of diagnostic constructs, identification and clarification of mental disorders, and reliability and validity of clinical diagnoses and judgments. Research subjects may represent diverse age and socioeconomic categories and both clinical and nonclinical populations. Research reviews and methodological papers will be considered, and article format may be varied to accommodate brief reports.

Selective Notes on Submissions: Instructions to authors included in each issue of the journal. Authors to prepare manuscripts according to the *Publication Manual of the American Psychological Association* (4th ed.). Submit four (4) copies of the manuscript to the editor.

Journal Frequency: Quarterly

Articles/Pages Published per Year: 44/400

Total Subscribers: 1,500

Book Reviews Accepted: No

Rejection Rate: 70%

Australian Journal of Psychology

Publisher: Australian Academic Press Pty., Ltd.
32 Jeays Street
Bowen Hills, QLD 4006
Australia

Editor: Professor J. G. O'Gorman
Griffith University
Division of Health & Behavioral Sciences
Nathan, QLD 4111
Australia

Editorial Policy: The *Australian Journal of Psychology* presents articles and book reviews on any topic with a central reference to psychology and an emphasis on academic or archival functions. It publishes experimental studies, reviews of significant issues in the discipline, and papers that make a theoretical contribution. Articles focusing on methodological issues are also appropriate. Articles are published in order of receipt of the finally accepted manuscript. The journal publishes its editorial policy in each issue and details can be found in any of its issues on the journal's editorial policies and reviewing procedures.

Selective Notes on Submissions: Instructions to authors included in each issue of the journal. Authors to prepare manuscripts according to the *Publication Manual of the American Psychological Association* (4th ed.); authors are to use the Macquarie Dictionary for spelling. Submit four (4) copies of the manuscript to the editor.

Journal Frequency: 3 issues per year

Articles/Pages Published per Year: 25/372

Total Subscribers: 6,000

Book Reviews Accepted: Yes

Rejection Rate: NA

Australian and New Zealand Journal of Family Therapy

Publisher: Australian & New Zealand Journal of Family Therapy
P.O. Box 633
Lane Cove, NSW 2066
Australia

Editor: Max Cornwell

Editorial Policy: The *Australian and New Zealand Journal of Family Therapy* promotes the theory and practice of family therapy in Australia and New Zealand. It is designed to meet the needs of therapists working in the field of family therapy, and to act as a forum for discussion of current issues. The journal is keen to publish articles having a major clinical relevance, including case studies, new ideas, theory, techniques, research and commentaries. Original articles are sought that add to existing knowledge, or examine the use of previously stated ideas under the local conditions. Clarity of communication and brevity of style are of great importance in furthering the general aim of making this a journal for the workplace. Book and Video Reviews, Network News, and Story Corner will be regular features, as well as interviews, comment, and education update.

Selective Notes on Submissions: Instructions to authors included in each issue of the journal. Authors to prepare manuscripts according to the *Style Manual for Authors,*

Editors and Printers of Australian Government Publications. Submit three (3) copies of the manuscript to the editor c/o publisher.

Journal Frequency: Quarterly

Articles/Pages Published per Year: 20/272

Total Subscribers: 1,500

Book Reviews Accepted: Yes (by invitation only)

Rejection Rate: NA

Notes From Publisher: All papers anonymously refereed; copies of reports made available to authors.

Australian Psychologist

Publisher: Australian Psychological Society
National Science Center
191 Royal Parade
Parkville, Victoria 3052
Australia

Editor: Christina Lee
Department of Psychology
University of Newcastle
Newcastle, NSW 2308
Australia

Editorial Policy: Submissions should be relevant to professional and applied psychology. Research must be of a high quality and have a demonstrated professional focus and/or application. Reviews should be state-of-the-art in professional areas. Professional comment should address matters of professional and public relevance.

Selective Notes on Submissions: Instructions to authors included in each issue of the journal. Authors to prepare manuscripts according to the *Publication Manual of the American Psychological Association* (4th ed.). Submit three (3) copies of the manuscript to the editor.

Journal Frequency: 3 issue per year

Articles/Pages Published per Year: 36/220

Total Subscribers: 6,500

Book Reviews Accepted: Yes

Rejection Rate: 60%

Basic and Applied Social Psychology

Publisher: Lawrence Erlbaum Associates, Inc.
10 Industrial Avenue
Mahwah, NJ 07430-2262

Editor: Frederick J. Rhodewalt
Department of Psychology
University of Utah
Salt Lake City, UT 84112

Editorial Policy: *Basic and Applied Social Psychology* will publish research articles, literature reviews, criticism, and methodological or theoretical statements spanning the entire range of social psychological issues. The journal is based on the belief that social psychologists can have a part in the understanding and solution of many of the problems of modern life. Thus the journal will publish basic work in areas of social psychology that can be applied to societal problems as well as direct application of social psychology to these problems. The major objectives of the journal are to provide a consolidated place for the publication of basic and applied research from a broad range of disciplines and specialty areas. This includes research on legal and political issues, environmental influences on behavior, organizations, aging, medical and health-related outcomes, sexuality, education, the effects of mass media, gender issues, and population problems. Much of this research has significant implications for basic social processes and may be some of the most exciting work in the field of social psychology. *Basic and Applied Social Psychology* intends to provide a way for social psychologists to communicate with one another across a wide range of problem interests and nontraditional subspecialties. Its goal is not only to provide a forum for a broad mixture of experiments, field studies, and reviews of social psychology, but also to serve as a resource for those specialists interested in the problems that social psychologists study and for investigators interested in the application of complex human experimentation to various problems of health, environment, and society.

Selective Notes on Submissions: Instructions to authors included in each issue of the journal. Authors to prepare manuscripts according to the *Publication Manual of the American Psychological Association* (4th ed.). Submit four (4) copies of the manuscript to the editor.

Journal Frequency: Quarterly

Articles/Pages Published per Year: 28/480

Total Subscribers: 1,000

Book Reviews Accepted: Yes

Rejection Rate: 70–75%

Behavior Genetics

Publisher: Plenum Publishing Corporation
233 Spring Street
New York, NY 10013-1578

Editor: David W. Fulker
Executive Editor

Institute of Behavioral Genetics
University of Colorado
Campus Box 447
Boulder, CO 80309

Editorial Policy: *Behavior Genetics* is published in cooperation with the Behavior Genetics Association. *Behavior Genetics* is a journal dealing with the inheritance and evolution of behavioral characters in man and other species. Papers dealing with the application of the various perspectives of genetics to the study of behavioral characteristics and with the influence of behavioral differences on the genetic structure of populations. In addition to papers reporting original studies, the journal publishes critical reviews and theoretical papers relevant to behavior genetics. Short communications, letters to the editor, and news sections are also included.

Selective Notes on Submissions: Instructions to authors included in each issue of the journal. Authors to prepare manuscripts according to the *Style Manual for Biological Journals,* published by the American

Institute for Biological Sciences. Submit the original and two (2) copies of the manuscript to the editor.

Journal Frequency: Bimonthly

Articles/Pages Published per Year: 48/600

Total Subscribers: NA

Book Reviews Accepted: Yes

Rejection Rate: NA

Notes From Publisher: No page charges.

Behavior, Health, and Aging

Publisher: Springer Publishing Company
536 Broadway
Ney York, NY 10012-9904

Editor: Carl Eisdorfer
Professor and Chairman
Department of Psychiatry
(D-29)
P.O. Box 016960
University of Miami
Miami, FL 33101

Editorial Policy: *Behavior, Health, and Aging* is a refereed journal directed toward professionals and scholars interested in adult development and aging and the health of the aged including gerontologists and geriatricians, psychologists (particularly in behavioral medicine), medical sociologists, psychiatrists, nurses, public policy professionals, social workers, and investigators in any of the related disciplines.

Selective Notes on Submissions: Instructions to authors included in each issue of the journal. Authors to prepare manuscripts according to the *Publication Manual of the American Psychological Association* (4th ed.). Submit four (4) copies of the manuscript to the editor.

Journal Frequency: 3 issues per year

Articles/Pages Published per Year: 15/201

Total Subscribers: NA

Book Reviews Accepted: NA

Rejection Rate: NA

Behavior Modification

Publisher: Sage Publications, Inc.
2455 Teller Road
Newbury Park, CA 91320

Editor: Michel Hersen
Nova University
Center for Psychological Studies
3301 College Avenue
Fort Lauderdale, FL 33314

Alan S. Bellack
The Medical College of
Pennsylvania at EPPI
3300 Henry Avenue
Philadelphia, PA 19129

Editorial Policy: *Behavior Modification* is an interdisciplinary journal designed to publish relevant research and clinical papers in the area of applied behavior modification.

Sufficient detail will be included so that readers will clearly understand what was done, how it was done, and why the particular strategy was selected. Assessment and modification techniques for problems in psychiatric, clinical, education, and rehabilitation settings are all considered to be within the scope of the journal, as are papers describing measurement and modification of behavior in normal populations if the analogue to the applied settings is sufficiently clear. Single-case experimental research and group comparison designs are also considered acceptable if they depart from standard techniques or if the case is of particular clinical interest. Reviews and theoretical discussions, if they contribute substantially to the application of behavioral modification, will also be considered for publication.

Selective Notes on Submissions: Instructions to authors included in each issue of the journal. Authors to prepare manuscripts according to the *Publication Manual of the American Psychological Association* (4th ed.), and submit one original and two (2) copies of the manuscript to either editor.

Journal Frequency: Quarterly

Articles/Pages Published per Year: 28/512

Total Subscribers: 1,676

Book Reviews Accepted: Yes

Rejection Rate: 50%

Behavior and Philosophy

Publisher: Cambridge Center for
                  Behavioral Studies

Publications Department
11 Waterhouse Street
Cambridge, MA 02138

Editors: Professor Max Hocutt, Editor
Department of Philosophy
P.O. Box 870218
University of Alabama
Tuscaloosa, AL 35487

Professor Howard Rachlin,
    Associate Editor
Department of Psychology
State University of New York
Stony Brook, NY 11794

Editorial Policy: The journal welcomes essays and reviews of philosophical interest and import by psychologists, economists, and philosophers: anybody who deals with the science of behavior in a fundamental way. A premium is placed on good, clear writing.

Selective Notes on Submissions: Authors to prepare manuscripts according to the *Publication Manual of the American Psychological Association* (4th ed.). Submit three (3) copies of the manuscript to either of the two editors. (Foreign writers need send only one copy.)

Journal Frequency: Semiannually

Articles/Pages Published per Year: 15/200

Total Subscribers: 600

Book Reviews Accepted: Yes

Rejection Rate: 75%

Behavior Research Methods, Instruments, and Computers

Publisher: Psychonomic Society, Inc.
1710 Fortview Road
Austin, TX 78704

Editor: Robert W. Proctor
Department of Psychological
Science
Purdue University
West Lafayette, IN 47907

Editorial Policy: *Behavior Research Methods, Instruments, and Computers* publishes articles, as its name implies, in the areas of the methods, techniques, instrumentation, and computer applications in research in experimental psychology.

Selective Notes on Submissions: Instructions to authors included in each issue of the journal. Authors to prepare manuscripts according to the *Publication Manual of the American Psychological Association* (4th ed.), except that, in the abbreviation of physical units, the style of the American Institute of Physics is followed. Submit four (4) copies of the manuscript to the editor.

Journal Frequency: Quarterly

Articles/Pages Published per Year: 84/500

Total Subscribers: 1,160

Book Reviews Accepted: NA

Rejection Rate: NA

Behavior Therapy

Publisher: Association for Advancement of
Behavior Therapy
15 West 36th Street
New York, NY 10018

Editor: Frank Andrasik
Center for Behavioral Medicine
University of West Florida
11000 University Parkway
Pensacola, FL 32514

Editorial Policy: *Behavior Therapy* is an international journal devoted to the application of behavioral and cognitive sciences to clinical problems. It primarily publishes original research of an experimental/clinical nature which contributes to the theories, practices and evaluations of behavior therapy, broadly defined [see Editorial, *Behavior Therapy*, 1990, 21, (1) and 1996, 27, (1)]. Although the major emphasis is placed upon empirical research, methodological and theoretical papers as well as evaluative reviews of the literature will also be published. Case studies, where the interventions have not been evaluated experimentally, and clinical replication series will be published [see Announcement, *Behavior Therapy*, 1996, 27, (1)]. The format for publication includes articles, case studies, the clinical replication series, and letters to the editor concerning issues raised in manuscripts previously published in *Behavior Therapy*.

Selective Notes on Submissions: Instructions to authors included in each issue of the journal. Authors to prepare manuscripts according to the *Publication Manual of the American Psychological Association* (4th ed.). Submit five (5) complete sets of the manuscript to the editor.

Journal Frequency: Quarterly

Articles/Pages Published per Year: 40/660

Total Subscribers: 3,400

Book Reviews Accepted: Yes (invited only)

Rejection Rate: 70–75%

Behavioral and Brain Sciences

Publisher: Cambridge University Press
40 West 20th Street
New York, NY 10011-4211

Editor: Steven Harnad
20 Nassau Street, Suite 240
Princeton, NJ 08542

Editorial Policy: *Behavioral and Brain Sciences* (BBS) is an international journal providing a special service called Open Peer Commentary to researchers in any area of psychology, neuroscience, behavioral biology, or cognitive science who wish to solicit, from fellow specialists within and across these BBS disciplines, multiple responses to a particularly significant and controversial piece of work. (See Instructions for Authors and Commentators published in each issue on the inside back cover.) The purpose of this service is to contribute to the communication, criticism, stimulation, and particularly the unification of research in the behavioral and brain sciences, from molecular neurobiology to artificial intelligence and the philosophy of mind. Papers judged by the editors and referees to be appropriate for commentary are circulated to a large number of commentators selected by editors, referees, and authors to provide substantive criticism, interpretation, elaboration, and pertinent complementary and supplementary material from a full cross-disciplinary perspective. The article, accepted commentaries, and the author's response then appear simultaneously in BBS.

Selective Notes on Submissions: Instructions to authors included in each issue of the journal. Authors to prepare manuscripts according to *A Manual of Style,* The University of Chicago Press. Submit original manuscript with eight (8) copies with a diskette in Word or WordPerfect to the editor. Articles must not exceed 14,000 words (and should ordinarily be considerably shorter); commentaries should not exceed 1,000 words.

Journal Frequency: Quarterly

Articles/Pages Published per Year: 700 pp.

Total Subscribers: 2,500

Book Reviews Accepted: NA

Rejection Rate: NA

Behavioral Disorders

Publisher: Council for Children With
Behavioral Disorders
1910 Association Drive
Reston, VA 22091-1589

Editors: Jo M. Hendrickson
and Gary M. Sasso
N259 Lindquist Center
University of Iowa
Iowa City, IA 52242

Editorial Policy: *Behavioral Disorders* is
published four times each year by the Council for Children With Behavioral Disorders,
a division of the Council for Exceptional
Children. Papers published in this journal are
reports of original investigations and theoretical papers that relate to the education of
students with emotional and behavioral
disorders.

Selective Notes on Submissions: Instructions
to authors included in each issue of the
journal.

Journal Frequency: Quarterly

Articles/Pages Published per Year: 35/300

Total Subscribers: 9,000

Book Reviews Accepted: Yes

Rejection Rate: 60%

Notes From Publisher: Reviewer guidelines
available from editor on request. Guest
reviewers invited to apply.

Suggested Index Terms: Emotional disturbance, behavioral problems, special education.

Behavioral Ecology and Sociobiology

Publisher: Springer-Verlag
Tiergartenstr. 17
D-69121 Heidelberg
Germany

Editor: Editorial Manager
Tatiana Czeschlik
Editorial Office
Behavioral Ecology &
Sociobiology
Springer-Verlag
Tiergartenstr. 17
D-69121 Heidelberg
Germany

Editorial Policy: *Behavioral Ecology and
Sociobiology* publishes original contributions dealing with quantitative empirical and
theoretical studies in the field of the analysis
of animal behavior on the level of the individual, population, and community. Special
emphasis is placed on the proximate mechanisms, ultimate functions, and evolution of
ecological adaptations of behavior.

Selective Notes on Submissions: Instructions
to authors included in each issue of the
journal. Submit five (5) copies of the manuscript to the Editorial Manager.

Journal Frequency: Monthly

Articles/Pages Published per Year: 100/800

Total Subscribers: NA

Book Reviews Accepted: NA

Rejection Rate: NA

Behavioral Medicine

Publisher: Heldref Publications
1319 18th Street, NW
Washington, DC 20036-1802

Editors: C. David Jenkins, PhD
            Evan G. Pattishall, Jr., MD, PhD

Editorial Policy: *Behavioral Medicine* is an interdisciplinary journal of research and practice that publishes manuscripts dealing with the many levels of interaction of behavior and health. Included are studies in the basic and clinical medical sciences as well as in the social and behavioral sciences. The journal publishes original controlled research studies both experimental and clinical; evaluation studies; occasional review articles and case reports; articles on stress management; animal studies with clear human implications; and book reviews.

Selective Notes on Submissions: Instructions to authors included in each issue of the journal. Authors to prepare manuscripts according to the Amerian Medical Association style manual. Submit three (3) copies of the manuscript to the Managing Editor c/o the publisher.

Journal Frequency: Quarterly

Articles/Pages Published per Year: 20/200

Total Subscribers: 865

Book Reviews Accepted: Yes

Rejection Rate: 80%

Notes From Publisher: Virtually all articles are based on strong research, both medical and psychological approaches.

Suggested Index Terms: Psychoneuroimmunology, stress, Type A, locus of control, placebo effect, cardiovascular disease, hypertension, posttraumatic stress disorder, social learning, biofeedback.

Behavioral Neuroscience

Publisher: American Psychological
            Association
            750 First Street, NE
            Washington, DC 20002-4242

Editor: Michela Gallagher
            Department of Psychology
            Davie Hall, CB #3270
            University of North Carolina
            Chapel Hill, NC 27599

Editorial Policy: The primary mission of *Behavioral Neuroscience* is to publish original research papers in the broad field of the biological bases of behavior. Occasional review articles and theoretical papers are also acceptable for publication if they are judged to make original and important conceptual contributions to the field. Studies covering the entire range of relevant biological and neural sciences, for example, anatomy, chemistry, physiology, endocrinology, and pharmacology, are considered so long as behavioral variables are measured or manipulated or if the work has clear relevance to behavior. Studies on the genetic, evolutionary, and developmental aspects of behavior are also appropriate, as are behavioral studies, if they have clear implications for biological processes or mechanisms. Single-experiment papers are deemed just as acceptable as multiple-experiment papers. Good experimental design, controls and procedures, importance or significance, and proper scholarship are the major criteria, as indeed they have always been. The journal also publishes a "Brief Communications" section. (Papers for this section should be so labeled and must not exceed 2,000 words of text and 2 figures or tables.)

Selective Notes on Submissions: Instructions to authors included in each issue of the journal. Authors to prepare manuscripts according to the *Publication Manual of the American Psychological Association* (4th ed.). Submit four (4) copies of the manuscript to the editor.

Journal Frequency: Bimonthly

Articles/Pages Published per Year: 118/1200

Total Subscribers: 1,910

Book Reviews Accepted: No

Rejection Rate: 52%

Behavioral Science

Publisher: Behavioral Science
9815 Carroll Canyon Road, Suite 106
San Diego, CA 92131

Editor: James Grier Miller

Editorial Policy: *Behavioral Science* publishes original articles on new theories, experimental research, and applications relating to all levels of living and nonliving systems. The major criterion for acceptance is potential generalizability across two or more levels, i.e., cells, organisms, groups, organizations, societies, and supranational systems. Articles should specifically indicate how they are generalizable. Generalizations of an implied nature are not acceptable.

The editors especially want manuscripts of a theoretical or empirical nature which have broad interdisciplinary implications not found in a journal devoted to a single discipline. Papers should be based on precise observations and quantitative data, and present hypotheses testable at more than one level. Preference is for empirical studies whose findings lead to hypotheses which are testable at various levels. Simulation, modeling, and artificial intelligence manuscripts which can lead to verification of general theories applicable across all levels of living and nonliving systems are particularly welcome. In addition, the editors encourage applications of general systems theory and simulation models or expert systems developed in specific application areas such as health care delivery, social cognitive prcesses, or world modeling. The editors also seek real-life reports of tests of the application of cross-level theory.

Selective Notes on Submissions: Instructions to authors included in each issue of the journal. Authors to prepare manuscripts according to the *Publication Manual of the American Psychological Association* (4th ed.). Submit five (5) copies of the manuscript to the editor. Submit to the editorial office, P.O. Box 8369, La Jolla, CA 92038-8369

Journal Frequency: Quarterly

Articles/Pages Published per Year: 300 pp.

Total Subscribers: NA

Book Reviews Accepted: NA

Rejection Rate: NA

Behavioral Sciences and the Law

Publisher: John Wiley & Sons, Ltd.
Baffins Lane
West Sussex
Chichester IO19 1UD
England

Editor: Alan Tomkins
Law Psychology Program
University of Nebraska
Lincoln, NE 68588

Editorial Policy: *Behavioral Sciences and the Law* will stress important mental health issues within the framework of civil and criminal law. It aims to balance theoretical, clinical, and research writings to provide the broadest perspective on pertinent psycho-legal topics of concern to mental health and legal professionals alike.

Selective Notes on Submissions: Instructions to authors included in each issue of the journal. Authors to prepare manuscripts according to the *Publication Manual of the American Psychological Association* (4th ed.). Submit three (3) copies of the manuscript to the editor. No duplicate submissions to other journals permitted.

Journal Frequency: Quarterly

Articles/Pages Published per Year: 62/600

Total Subscribers: 756

Book Reviews Accepted: NA

Rejection Rate: NA

Behaviour

Publisher: E. J. Brill, Publishers
Postbus 9000
2300 PA Leiden
The Netherlands

Editors: M. Daly
Department of Psychology
McMaster University
1280 Main Street West
Hamilton, Ontario
Canada L8S 4K1

J. G. van Rhijn
Slochterweg 3
9635 TA Noordbroek
The Netherlands

Editorial Policy: *Behaviour* aims to publish substantial contributions to the biological analysis of the causation, ontogeny, function, and evolution of behavior of all animal species, including humans. It is open primarily to reports of original research, but theoretical and other papers will be considered if they clearly promote the experimental study of the subject. Descriptive and methodological papers can only be considered if they illuminate basic biological questions. Physiological, genetic, and ecological aspects of the subject are given their due share of space. The editorial board is currently encouraging papers on causal and ontogenetic problems.

Selective Notes on Submissions: Instructions to authors included in each issue of the journal. Submit three (3) copies of the manuscript to the editor. European, Asian and African authors submit to J. van Rhijn; American (North, South, and Central) , Australian, New Zealand, and Pacific Island authors submit to M. Daly.

Journal Frequency: 8 issues per year

Articles/Pages Published per Year: 1280 pp.

Total Subscribers: 900

Book Reviews Accepted: No

Rejection Rate: 47%

Behaviour Change

Publisher: Australian Academic Press
                 32 Jeays Street
                 Bowen Hills, QLD 4006
                 Australia

Editor: Matthew R. Sanders
                 Department of Psychiatry
                 The University of Queensland
                 Clinical Sciences Building
                 Royal Brisbane Hospital
                 Herston, Q4029
                 Australia

Editorial Policy: *Behavior Change* is devoted to the publication of research involving the application of behavioral and cognitive–behavioral principles and techniques to the assessment and treatment of health, social, organizational, community, and educational problems. It publishes original empirical studies using either single-subject or group-comparison methodologies, review articles, case studies, brief technical and clinical notes, invited book reviews, and special issues dealing with particular topics in depth.

Selective Notes on Submissions: Instructions to authors included in each issue of the journal. Authors to prepare manuscripts according to the *Publication Manual of the*

American Psychological Association (4th ed.). Submit four (4) copies of the manuscript to the editor.

Journal Frequency: Quarterly

Articles/Pages Published per Year: 28/280

Total Subscribers: 1,000

Book Reviews Accepted: Yes (by invitation)

Rejection Rate: NA

Behaviour Research and Therapy

Publisher: Elsevier Science Press
                 1000 AE1 Amsterdam
                 The Netherlands

Editor: Stanley Rachman, PhD
                 Department of Psychology
                 University of British Columbia
                 Vancouver, BC
                 Canada V6T 1Z4

                 Behavioral Assessment section:
                 S. Taylor, Editor
                 Department of Psychiatry
                 2255 Wesbrook Mall
                 Vancouver, BC
                 Canada V6T 2A1

Editorial Policy: In recent years there has been an ever-growing interest in applying modern learning theories to the control of maladaptive behavior and the improvement of learning efficiency. The theories of Hull, Skinner, Mowrer, Spence, and Wolpfe in particular have stimulated a great deal of research into such varied topics as the rational treatment of neuroses, the experimental manipulation of psychotic symptoms, "learning machines," operant conditioning treatment of stammering and other speech defects, the "blanket-and-bell" therapy of enuresis, deconditioning treatment, aversion therapy, "reciprocal inhibition" methods of desensitization behavior therapy, and many others. The application of learning theory and the experimental method to clinical psychology also promises to carry this discipline beyond mere psychometry and close the gap between the laboratory and the clinic. The main conception unifying all these different approaches has been the belief that behavioral disorders of the most divergent type are essentially learned responses, and that modern learning theory has much to teach us regarding the acquisition and extinction of such responses. This conception, cutting across many existing boundary lines which seperate psychiatry, education, clinical psychology, remedial reading, psychotherapy, social work, and psychoanalysis, forms the basis for the appearance of this journal, the main purpose of which is to give direction and focus to this new movement. Contributions will stress equally the application of existing knowledge to psychiatric and and social problems, experimental research into fundamental questions arising from these attempts to relate learning theory and maladaptive behavior, and high-level theoretical attempts to lay more secure foundations for experimental and observational studies along these lines.

Selective Notes on Submissions: Instructions to authors included in each issue of the journal. Authors to prepare manuscripts according to the *Publication Manual of the American Psychological Association* (4th ed.). Submit three (3) copies of the manuscript and a computer disk to the appropriate editor.

Journal Frequency: Monthly

Articles/Pages Published per Year: 120/ 1200

Total Subscribers: 2,000

Book Reviews Accepted: Invited only

Rejection Rate: 70–80%

Notes From Publisher: Free sample copy available upon request.

Behavioural Brain Research

Publisher: Elsevier Science Publishers, B.V.
P.O. Box 211
1000 AE Amsterdam
The Netherlands

Editors: J. P. Huston
Institute of Physiological Psychology
University of Düsseldorf
Universitatstrasse 1
40225 Düsseldorf
Germany

T. E. Robinson
The University of Michigan
Department of Psychology
Biopsychology Program
East Hall
525 East University Street
Ann Arbor, MI 48109-1109

Editorial Policy: *Behavioural Brain Research* is an international, interdisciplinary journal dedicated to the publication of articles in the field of behavioral neuroscience, broadly defined. Contributions from the entire range of disciplines that comprise the neurosciences, behavioral sciences, or cognitive sciences are appropriate, as long as the goal is to delineate the neural mechanisms underlying behavior. Thus, studies may range from neurophysiological, neuroanatomical, neurochemical, or neuropharmacological analysis of brain–behavior relations, including the use of molecular genetic or behavioral genetic approaches, to studies that involve the use of brain imaging techniques, to neuroethological studies. Reports of original research, of major methodological advances, or of novel conceptual approaches are all encouraged. The journal will also consider critical reviews on selected topics as well as compilations of papers dealing with a unitary theme.

Selective Notes on Submissions: Instructions to authors included in each issue of the journal. Submit four (4) copies of the manuscript with a floppy disk in MS-DOS format to one of the editors.

Journal Frequency: Monthly

Articles/Pages Published per Year: 125/ 1440

Total Subscribers: NA

Book Reviews Accepted: No

Rejection Rate: NA

Behavioural and Cognitive Psychotherapy

Publisher: Wisepress Ltd.
                   The Old Church Hall
                   89a Quicks Road
                   Wimbledon, London SW19 1EX
                   England

Editor: Paul M. Salkovskis
                   Department of Psychiatry
                   University of Oxford
                   Warneford Hospital
                   Oxford OX3 7JX
                   England

Editorial Policy: *Behavioural and Cognitive Psychotherapy* is an international multidisciplinary journal for the publication of original research, of an experimental or clinical nature, that contributes to the theory, practice, and evolution of behavior therapy. As such, the scope of the journal is very broad, and articles relevant to most areas of human behavior and human experience, which would be of interest to members of the helping and teaching professions, will be considered for publication.

As an applied science, the concepts, methodology, and techniques of behavioral psychotherapy continue to change. The journal seeks both to reflect and to influence those changes.

While the emphasis is placed on empirical research, articles concerned with important theoretical and methodological issues as well as evaluative reviews of the behavioral literature are also published. In addition, given the emphasis of behavior therapy on the experimental investigation of the single case, the Clinical Section of the journal publishes case studies using single-case experimental designs. For the majority of designs this should include a baseline period with repeated measures; in all instances the nature of the quantitative data and the intervention must be clearly specified.

Exceptionally, the journal will consider case studies where, although the interventions have not been experimentally evaluated, the treatment approach and/or problem dealt with is considered to be of particular importance *and* clear indicators of change are provided. Other types of case report can be submitted for the Brief Clinical Reports section (see below).

The following types of articles are suitable for *Behavioural and Cognitive Psychotherapy*:

1. Reports of original research employing experimental or correlational methods and using within or between subject designs.

2. Review or discussion articles which are based on empirical data and which have important new theoretical, conceptual, or applied implications.

3. Brief reports and systematic investigations in single cases employing innovative techniques and/or approaches.

Articles should concern original material which is neither published nor under consideration for publication elsewhere.

Selective Notes on Submissions: Instructions to authors included in each issue of the journal. Authors to prepare manuscripts according to the *Publication Manual of the American Psychological Association* (4th ed.) or the British Psychological Society. Submit four (4) copies of the manuscript to the editor.

Journal Frequency: Quarterly

Articles/Pages Published per Year: 31/383

Total Subscribers: 2,400

Book Reviews Accepted: Yes

Rejection Rate: 55%

Behavioural Processes

Publisher: Elsevier Science Publishers
1000 AE Amsterdam
The Netherlands

Editor: J. E. R. Staddon
Department of Psychology
Duke University
Durham, NC 27706

Editorial Policy: The journal publishes experimental, theoretical, and review papers dealing with fundamental behavioral processes through the methods of natural science. Experimental papers may deal with any species, from unicellular organisms to human beings. Sample topics are cognition in man and animals; the phylogeny, ontogeny, and mechanisms of learning; animal suffering; and the neuroscientific bases of behavior. Studies using pharmacological, physiological, and biochemical techniques are appropriate provided they address behavioral issues. Theoretical papers can be at any level, from the cellular through top-down modelling of the whole organism, so long as whole-organism behavior is a component. Quantitative treatments, neural-network and other parallel models, and mathematical or computer models are especially appropriate. Review papers should emphasize behavioral data; interdisciplinary topics, especially those that touch on the relations between behavioral and neural properties, are especially welcome. Most book reviews are solicited, but unsolicited are also considered. In addition to full-length papers, short reports (less than 2,000 words) are also considered. In addition to full-length papers, short reports (less than 2,000 words) are also considered. Conference abstracts, reports, and announcements will be published at the editors' discretion.

Selective Notes on Submissions: Instructions to authors included in each issue of the journal. Submit three (3) copies of the manuscript to the editor. Typescripts should be sent to either:

Editorial Secretariat, Behavioural Processes, c/o A. Lempereur, Faculté de Psychologie, Université de Louvain, 10 Place Désiré Mercier, B-1348 Louvain-la-Neuve, Belgium; or

J. E. R. Staddon, Behavioural Processes, Department of Psychology, Duke University, Durham, NC 27706.

Journal Frequency: Monthly

Articles/Pages Published per Year: NA

Total Subscribers: NA

Book Reviews Accepted: Yes

Rejection Rate: NA

Biological Psychology

Publisher: Elsevier Science Publishers, B.V.
P.O. Box 211
1000 AE Amsterdam
The Netherlands

Editor: Dr. Richard Jennings
University of Pittsburgh
Western Psychiatric Institute and Clinic
3811 O'Hara Street
Pittsburgh, PA 15213-2593

Editorial Policy: *Biological Psychology* publishes original scientific papers which relate biological and psychological processes. The biological measures include variables relevant to physiology, biochemistry, endocrinology, and pharmacology. The journal concentrates on work on human subjects but it will accept animal work of particular relevance to human psychology. Papers are frequently in the fields on psychophysiology and behavioral medicine. We encourage the dual submission of any papers with biological and psychological interests. *Biological Psychology* accepts papers on techniques and methodology providing they are relevant to the type of work published in the journal. Review articles are acceptable and short papers of less than 900 words, including case reports, are welcome. Announcements of particular interest to the readership will be included; critical reviews of relevent books only are published.

Selective Notes on Submissions: Instructions to authors included in each issue of the journal. Authors to prepare manuscripts according to the *Publication Manual of the American Psychological Association* (4th ed.). Submit five (5) copies of the manuscript to the editor.

Journal Frequency: Bimonthly

Articles/Pages Published per Year: 50/700

Total Subscribers: 500

Book Reviews Accepted: Yes

Rejection Rate: 35%

Brain and Cognition

Publisher: Academic Press, Inc.
1250 Sixth Avenue
San Diego, CA 92101

Editor: Harry A. Whitaker, PhD
Centre de Research du Centre
    Hospitalier
Côte-des-Neiges
4565, Chemin de la Reine-Marie
Montreal, Quebec
Canada H3W 1W5

Editorial Policy: *Brain and Cognition* publishes original research articles, case histories, theoretical articles, critical reviews, historical articles, and scholarly notes; contributions will be concerned with any aspect of human neuropsychology, other than language. Appropriate topics include movement, perception, praxis, emotion, memory, and cognition, in relationship to brain structure and function. *Brain and Cognition* will publish experimental research papers, clinical case histories, reviews, short notes (limited to under 10 pages typed), and discussion/commentary articles. Book reviews may be submitted for publication and will also be solicited; of particular interest are those book reviews that, in addition to critically summarizing a book's content, make a scholarly contribution in their own right.

Selective Notes on Submissions: Instructions to authors included in each issue of the journal. Submit one original and five (5)

copies of the manuscript to *Brain and Cognition*, Editorial Office, 525 B Street, Suite 1900, San Diego, CA 92101-4495.

Journal Frequency: Bimonthly

Articles/Pages Published per Year: 56/900

Total Subscribers: NA

Book Reviews Accepted: Yes

Rejection Rate: NA

Notes From Publisher: Papers must be written in English. Language data may be given in English when clearly identifiable, otherwise it should be transcribed into the phonetic alphabet of the International Phonetic Association (IPA).

Brain and Language

Publisher: Academic Press, Inc.
1250 Sixth Avenue
San Diego, CA 92101

Editor: Harry A. Whitaker, PhD
Centre de Research du Centre
    Hospitalier
Côte-des-Neiges
4565, Chemin de la Reine-Marie
Montreal, Quebec
Canada H3W 1W5

Editorial Policy: *Brain and Language* publishes original research articles, case histories, theoretical articles, critical reviews, historical studies, and scholarly notes. Each contribution will be concerned with human language or communication (speech, hearing, reading, writing, or nonverbal modalities) related to any aspect of the brain or brain function. Each will have theoretical import, either formulating new hypotheses or supporting or refuting new or previously established ones. The interdisciplinary focus includes the fields of neurology, linguistics, neurophysiology, psychology, neuroanatomy, psychiatry, neurosurgery, speech pathology, philosophy, and computer science. Manuscripts of several different types are solicited: regular articles, single or multiple case history studies, critical reviews of books of interest to the journal's readership, and short (limited to under 10 pages typed) scholarly notes and comments discussing issues of topical interest.

Selective Notes on Submissions: Instructions to authors included in each issue of the journal. Authors to prepare manuscripts according to the *Publication Manual of the American Psychological Association* (4th ed.). Submit one original and five (5) copies of the manuscript to *Brain and Language*, Editorial Office, 525 B Street, Suite 1900, San Diego, CA 92101-4495.

Journal Frequency: 8 issues per year

Articles/Pages Published per Year: 69/1400

Total Subscribers: NA

Book Reviews Accepted: Yes

Rejection Rate: NA

Notes From Publisher: Papers must be written in English. Language data may be given in English when clearly identifiable, otherwise it should be transcribed into the phonetic alphabet of the International Phonetic Association (IPA).

British Journal of Clinical Psychology

Publisher: British Psychological Society
Journals Office
13A Church Lane
East Finchley, London N2 8DX
England

Editor: Dr. Stephen Morley
Department of Psychiatry
Behavioral Science
University of Leeds
England

Editorial Policy: The journal publishes original contributions to knowledge in the applied science of clinical psychology. Topics covered reflect the broad role of the clinical psychologist and include studies of the aetiology, assessment and amelioration of psychological disorders of all kinds, in all settings and among all age groups. Neuropsychology and mental handicaps are included alongside studies of psychiatric populations. The journal also publishes papers relating to behavioral medicine, health psychology and counselling. Brief reports, limited to two printed pages afford rapid publication of research studies, critical or review comments whose essential contribution can be made within a small space.

Selective Notes on Submissions: Instructions to authors included in each issue of the journal. Authors to prepare manuscripts according to the *BPS Style Guide*. Authors may also use the *Publication Manual of the American Psychological Association* (4th ed.). Submit four (4) copies of the manuscript to the editor c/o BPS Journals Office.

Journal Frequency: Quarterly

Articles/Pages Published per Year: 53/646

Total Subscribers: 2,940

Book Reviews Accepted: Yes

Rejection Rate: 80%

British Journal of Developmental Psychology

Publisher: British Psychological Society
Journals Office
13A Church Lane
East Finchley, London N2 8DX
England

Editor: Dr. Paul Harris
University of Oxford

Editorial Policy: The journal aims to publish full-length empirical, conceptual, review and discussion papers, as well as brief reports on work in progress in the following areas: development during childhood and adolescence; early infant perceptual, cognitive and motor development; abnormal development—the problems of handicaps, learning difficulties and childhood autism; educational implications of child development; parent–child interaction; social and moral development; and the effects of aging.

Selective Notes on Submissions: Instructions to authors included in each issue of the journal. Authors to prepare manuscripts according to the *BPS Style Guide.* Authors may also use the *Publication Manual of the American Psychological Association* (4th ed.). Submit four (4) copies of the manuscript to the editor c/o BPS Journals Office.

Journal Frequency: Quarterly

Articles/Pages Published per Year: 32/400

Total Subscribers: 1,272

Book Reviews Accepted: Yes

Rejection Rate: 70%

British Journal of Educational Psychology

Publisher: British Psychological Society
Journals Office
13A Church Lane
East Finchley, London N2 8DX
England

Editor: Michael Youngman
School of Education
University of Nottingham
University Park
Nottingham NG7 2RD
England

Editorial Policy: The journal welcomes contributions covering a wide canvas of educational research. Each issue contains about ten papers and five research notes. It reports on the results of empirical studies involving children or adults in any aspect of education. Occasionally, theoretical papers or symposia in educational psychology are published. The journal also publishes papers about those with special educational needs.

Selective Notes on Submissions: Instructions to authors included in last part of lead volume. It is recommended that contributors consult *Suggestions to Contributors* issued by the Standing Committee on Publications of the British Psychological Society (sample copy available from The BPS, St. Andrew's House, 48 Princess Road East, Leicester LE1 7DR). Submit two (2) copies to the editor c/o BPS Journals Office.

Journal Frequency: Quarterly

Articles/Pages Published per Year: 45/518

Total Subscribers: 3,200

Book Reviews Accepted: Yes

Rejection Rate: 66%

British Journal of Guidance and Counselling

Publisher: Carfax Publishing Company
P.O. Box 25
Abingdon, Oxfordshire OX14 3UE
England

Editor: A. G. Watts
NIC EC, Sheraton House
Castle Park, Cambridge CB3 OAX
England

Editorial Policy: The *British Journal of Guidance and Counselling* exists to communicate theoretical and practical writing of high quality in the guidance and counselling field. Its concern is to promote development in this field by providing a forum for debate between academics, trainers and practitioners on topical and/or controversial issues related to: the theory and practice of guidance and counselling; the provision of guidance and counselling services; and training and professional issues. Empirical studies relating to the practice of guidance and counselling are reported— drawing on a variety of disciplines, encompassing both qualitative and quantitative methodologies, and ranging in scope from large-scale surveys to single case-studies. The *British Journal of Guidance and Counselling* also explores the interface between the various areas of guidance and counselling and their relationship to such cognate fields as education, psychotherapy and social work.

Selective Notes on Submissions: Instructions to authors included in each issue of the journal. Authors to prepare manuscripts according to the *Publication Manual of the American Psychological Association* (4th ed.). Submit four (4) copies of the manuscript to the editor.

Journal Frequency: Quarterly

Articles/Pages Published per Year: 40/512

Total Subscribers: 509

Book Reviews Accepted: Yes

Rejection Rate: 48%

British Journal of Health Psychology

Publisher: British Psychological Society

Editors: Joan Wardle
Health Behaviour Unit
Institute of Psychology
University of London

Andrew Steptoe
Department of Psychology
St. George's Medical School
University of London

Editorial Policy: Researchers and clinicians throughout the world are invited to submit the following type of papers:

• papers reporting original investigations in health psychology

• theoretical papers which may be analyses or commentaries on established theories in health psychology, or presentations of theoretical innovations

• review papers which should aim to provide systematic overviews, evaluations and interpretations of research in a given field of health psychology

• methodological papers dealing with methodological issues of particular relevance to health psychology

Scope includes:

The extended coverage of all areas of psychological factors relating to health and illness across the life span.

• experimental and clinical research on aetiology and the management of acute and chronic illness

• responses to ill health, screening and medical procedures

• research on health behavior

• psychological aspects of prevention

Research carried out at individual, group and community levels.

Particular focus on clinical applications and interventions.

Selective Notes on Submissions: Instructions to authors included in each issue of the journal. Authors to prepare manuscripts according to the British Psychological Society but the *Publication Manual of the American Psychological Association* (4th ed.) is acceptable. Submit four (4) copies of the manuscript to the editor. Send to British Journal of Health Psychology, Journals Office, 13a Church Lane, London N2 8DX, England.

Journal Frequency: Quarterly

Articles/Pages Published per Year: 30/384

Total Subscribers: NA

Book Reviews Accepted: Yes

Rejection Rate: 64%

British Journal of Mathematical and Statistical Psychology

Publisher: British Psychological Society
Journals Office
13A Church Lane
East Finchley, London N2 8DX
England

Editor: Philip T. Smith
University of Reading

Editorial Policy: *The British Journal of Mathematical and Statistical Psychology* publishes articles relating to any area of psychology which have a greater mathematical or statistical or other formal aspect of the argument than is normally acceptable to other journals. Articles which have a clear reference to substantive psychological issues are preferred. New models for psychological processes, new approaches to existing data, critiques of existing models and improved algorithms for estimating the parameters of a model are examples of articles which may be favored.

Selective Notes on Submissions: Instructions to authors included in each issue of the journal. Authors to prepare manuscripts according to the *BPS Style Guide*. Authors may also use the *Publication Manual of the American Psychological Association* (4th ed.). Submit four (4) copies of the manuscript to the editor c/o the BPS Journals Office.

Journal Frequency: Biannual

Articles/Pages Published per Year: 23/400

Total Subscribers: 730

Book Reviews Accepted: NA

Rejection Rate: 60%

British Journal of Medical Psychology

Publisher:　British Psychological Society Journals Office
13A Church Lane
East Finchley, London N2 8DX
England

Editors:　Duncan Cramer
University of Loughborough

Frank Margison
Manchester Health Authority

Editorial Policy: The *British Journal of Medical Psychology* is an international journal with a traditional orientation towards psychodynamic issues. Whilst maintaining a broad theoretical base and insisting upon sound and sensible methodology, it aims to avoid the more simplistic approaches to psychological science. The journal aims to bring together the medical and psychological disciplines and this is reflected in the composition of the editorial team. Collaborative studies between psychologists and psychiatrists are especially encouraged. Original theoretical and research contributions are invited from the fields of psychodynamic and interpersonal psychology, particularly as they have a bearing upon vulnerability to and adjustment to both medical and psychological disorders.

Selective Notes on Submissions: Instructions to authors included in each issue of the journal. Authors to prepare manuscripts according to the *BPS Style Guide*. Authors may also use the *Publication Manual of the American Psychological Association* (4th ed.). Submit four (4) copies of the manuscript to the editor c/o the BPS Journals Office.

Journal Frequency: Quarterly

Articles/Pages Published per Year: 38/400

Total Subscribers: 2,370

Book Reviews Accepted: Yes

Rejection Rate: 74%

British Journal of Psychology

Publisher: British Psychological Society
13A Church Lane
East Finchley, London N2 8DX
England

Editor: Vicki Bruce
University of Sterling

Editorial Policy: The editorial board of the *British Journal of Psychology* is prepared to consider for publication: (a) reports of empirical studies likely to further our understanding of psychology, (b) critical reviews of the literature, and (c) theoretical contributions.

Selective Notes on Submissions: Instructions to authors included in each issue of the journal. Authors to prepare manuscripts according to the *BPS Style Guide.* Authors may also use the *Publication Manual of the American Psychological Association* (4th ed.). Submit four (4) copies of the manuscript to the editor c/o the BPS Journals Office.

Journal Frequency: Quarterly

Articles/Pages Published per Year: 35/560

Total Subscribers: 3,230

Book Reviews Accepted: Yes

Rejection Rate: 75%

British Journal of Psychotherapy

Publisher: Artesian Books
18 Artesian Road
London W2 5AR
England

Editor: Jean Arundale
York Clinic
Guys Hospital
117 Borough High Street
London SE1 1NP
England

Editorial Policy: The *British Journal of Psychotherapy* provides a forum for discussion and debate for the profession as a whole and is not aligned with any one psychotherapy or psychotherapy and psychoanalytic organization. It is, however, sponsored by a majority of the analytically oriented psychotherapy organizations: the Lincoln Clinic and Institute for Psychotherapy, the London Centre for Psychotherapy, the Guild of Psychotherapists, the Arbours Association, the Centre for Analytical Psychotherapy, the Institute of Psychotherapy and Counseling, and the Centre for Attachment-based Psychoanalytic Psychotherapy.

Selective Notes on Submissions: Instructions to authors included in each issue of the journal. Submit five (5) copies of the manuscript to the editor.

Journal Frequency: Quarterly

Articles/Pages Published per Year: 38/576

Total Subscribers: 2,600

Book Reviews Accepted: Yes

Rejection Rate: 80%

British Journal of Social Psychology

Publisher: British Psychological Society
Journals Office
13A Church Lane
East Finchley, London N2 8DX
England

Editor: Dr. Russell Spears
University of Amsterdam

Editorial Policy: The journal publishes original papers in all areas of social psychology,
including attitude and attitude change,
person perception and social cognition,
social interaction between individuals in or
outside group settings, intergroup relations,
applications of social psychological knowledge to social issues or problems, and
individual differences or personality processes insofar as these bear upon social
cognition or behavior. The following types
of papers are invited: (a) papers reporting
original empirical investigations; (b) theoretical papers, which may be analyses or
comments on established theories in social
psychology, or presentations of theoretical
innovations, extensions or integrations; (c)
review papers, which should aim to provide
systematic overviews and evaluations of
research in a given field of social psychology, and identify issues requiring further
research; (d) methodological papers dealing
with any methodological issues of particular
relevance to social psychologists; and (e)
brief reports or comments which are given
accelerated review for quick publication.

Selective Notes on Submissions: Instructions
to authors included in each issue of the
journal. Authors to prepare manuscripts
according to the *BPS Style Guide*. Authors
may also use the *Publication Manual of the*
American Psychological Association (4th
ed.). Submit four (4) copies of the manuscript to the editor c/o the BPS Journals
Office.

Journal Frequency: Quarterly

Articles/Pages Published per Year: 34/470

Total Subscribers: 2,100

Book Reviews Accepted: NA

Rejection Rate: 77%

Canadian Journal of Behavioural Science

Publisher: Canadian Psychological
Association
151 States Street
Suite 205
Ottawa, Ontario
Canada K1P 5H3

Editor: Richard Clément
Ecole de psychologie
Université d'Ottawa
Pavillon Lamoureux, Pièce 342
145, rue Jean-Jacques Lussier
Ottawa, Ontario
Canada K1N 6N5

Editorial Policy: The *Canadian Journal of*
Behavioural Science publishes original
contributions in the applied areas of psychology, including, but not limited to, the following topics: abnormal, behavioral and
psychotherapeutic intervention strategies,
child and developmental, clinical, community, education, environment, organizational

behavior and development, personality, psychometrics, and social. A limited amount of space is also available in the journal for brief reports with theoretical or practical implications. In addition to presenting important case studies, the Brief Reports section can also be used to disseminate Canadian norms or forms for standardized tests, and for summarizing program evaluation studies.

Selective Notes on Submissions: Instructions to authors included in each issue of the journal. Authors to prepare manuscripts according to the *Publication Manual of the American Psychological Association* (4th ed.). Submit four (4) copies of the manuscript to the editor.

Journal Frequency: Quarterly

Articles/Pages Published per Year: 34/480

Total Subscribers: 2,600

Book Reviews Accepted: NA

Rejection Rate: NA

Canadian Journal of Experimental Psychology

Previous Title: *Canadian Journal of Psychology*

Publisher: Canadian Psychological
                 Association
                 151 States Street
                 Suite 205
                 Ottawa, Ontario
                 Canada K1P 5H3

Editor: Colin M. MacLeod
             Division of Life Sciences
             University of Toronto
             Scarborough, Ontario
             Canada M1C 1A4

Editorial Policy: The journal publishes original research papers in the broad field of general experimental psychology. The journal will publish (a) substantial papers reporting on an integrated series of studies that reflect a major research program, (b) theoretical reviews that synthesize major developments in a particular research area and advance new ideas, and (c) short articles that report single experiments deemed to be of special methodological or empirical interest. The limit of short articles is 2,500 words, plus one or two tables or diagrams. From time to time, the journal will publish a book review section that features Canadian authors, as well as new books judged to be of broad interest to the research community.

Selective Notes on Submissions: Instructions to authors included in each issue of the journal. Authors to prepare manuscripts according to the *Publication Manual of the American Psychological Association* (4th ed.). Submit four (4) copies of the manuscript to the editor.

Journal Frequency: Quarterly

Articles/Pages Published per Year: 20/512

Total Subscribers: 2,300

Book Reviews Accepted: Yes

Rejection Rate: NA

Canadian Psychology

Publisher: Canadian Psychological
             Association
             151 States Street
             Suite 205
             Ottawa, Ontario
             Canada K1P 5H3

Editor: Victor Catano
             Psychology Department
             St. Mary's University
             Halifax, NS
             Canada B3H 3C3

Editorial Policy: *Canadian Psychology* is a generalist, professional affairs, and applied journal published by the Canadian Psychological Association. The journal publishes generalist articles in the areas of theory, research, and practice that are of interest to a broad cross-section of psychologists. The journal also publishes professional issues articles addressing issues of relevance to Canadian practitioners and researchers in psychology; De Rerum Novarum articles on new developments in the practice of psychology including program descriptions and case studies illustrative of innovative approaches; invited book reviews of books written primarily by Canadian psychologists; letters to the editor on topical subjects or on matters not justifying a full article.

Selective Notes on Submissions: Instructions to authors included in each issue of the journal. Authors to prepare manuscripts according to the *Publication Manual of the American Psychological Association* (4th ed.). Submit four (4) copies of the manuscript to the editor, three (3) with no author identification.

Journal Frequency: Quarterly

Articles/Pages Published per Year: 48/400

Total Subscribers: 4,700

Book Reviews Accepted: Yes (by invitation)

Rejection Rate: 91%

Child Abuse and Neglect

Publisher: Elsevier Science, Inc.
             660 White Plains Road
             Tarrytown, NY 10591-5153

Editor: Richard D. Krugman, MD
             Kempe National Center
             1205 Oneida Street
             Denver, CO 80220

Editorial Policy: *Child Abuse and Neglect* provides an international, multidisciplinary forum on all aspects of child abuse and neglect, including sexual abuse, with special emphasis on prevention and treatment. The scope extends further to all those aspects of life that either favor or hinder optimal family interaction. The journal publishes a wide range of material, including original, theoretical, and empirical contributions; review articles describing the current situation in specific areas; exchange of ideas; and brief communications.

Selective Notes on Submissions: Instructions to authors included in each issue of the journal. Authors to prepare manuscripts according to the *Publication Manual of the American Psychological Association* (4th ed.). Submit four (4) copies of the manuscript to the editor.

Journal Frequency: Quarterly

Articles/Pages Published per Year: 55/580

Total Subscribers: 1,500

Book Reviews Accepted: NA

Rejection Rate: NA

Notes From Publisher: Free sample copy available on request.

Child Development

Publisher: University of Chicago Press
Child Development Publications
5720 Woodlawn Avenue
Chicago, IL 60637

Editor: Marc H. Bornstein
University of Michigan
300 North Ingalls
10th Floor
Ann Arbor, MI 48109-0406

Editorial Policy: *Child Development* is a publication outlet for reports of empirical research, theoretical articles, and reviews that have theoretical implications for developmental research. As a publication of an interdisciplinary organization, contributions from all disciplines concerned with developmental processes are welcome.

Selective Notes on Submissions: Instructions to authors included in each issue of the journal. Authors to prepare manuscripts according to the *Publication Manual of the American Psychological Association* (4th ed.). Submit five (5) copies of the manuscript to the editor.

Journal Frequency: Bimonthly

Articles/Pages Published per Year: 108/1600

Total Subscribers: 8,500

Book Reviews Accepted: NA

Rejection Rate: NA

The Clinical Neuropsychologist

Previous Title: Clinical Neuropsychologist

Publisher: Swets & Zeitlinger
Heerweg 347
2161 CA Lisse
The Netherlands

Editors: Byron P. Rourke
Department of Psychology
University of Windsor
Windsor, Ontario
Canada N9B 2X1

Kenneth M. Adams
Psychology Service (116B)
VA Medical Center
2215 Fuller Road
Ann Arbor, MI 48105

Editorial Policy: Journal selections include articles on clinical issues, professional issues, education, and training.

Selective Notes on Submissions: Instructions to authors included in each issue of the journal. Authors to prepare manuscripts according to the *Publication Manual of the American Psychological Association* (4th ed.). Submit four (4) copies of the manuscript to the editor.

Journal Frequency: Quarterly

Articles/Pages Published per Year: 600 pp.

Total Subscribers: 2,100

Book Reviews Accepted: Yes

Rejection Rate: 35%

Notes From Publisher: Authors will be asked to contribute to the cost of excessive illustrations and elaborate tables.

Clinical Psychology Review

Publisher: Pergamon Press, Inc.
                 660 White Plains Road
                 Tarrytown, NY 10591-5153

Editors: Allan S. Bellack
                 The Medical College of
                     Pennsylvania at EPPI
                 3200 Henry Avenue
                 Philadelphia, PA 19129

                 Michel Hersen
                 Nova University
                 Center for Psychological
                     Studies
                 3301 College Avenue
                 Fort Lauderdale, FL 33314

Editorial Policy: *Clinical Psychology Review,* now a bimonthly journal, publishes substantive reviews of topics germane to clinical psychology. Its purpose is to help clinical psychologists keep up-to-date on relevant issues outside of their immediate areas of expertise by publishing scholarly but readable reviews. Articles cover diverse issues including psychopathology, psychotherapy, behavior therapy, behavioral medicine, community mental health, assessment, and child development. Reviews on other topics such as psychophysiology, learning therapy, and social psychology often appear if they have a clear relation to research or practice in clinical psychology. Integrative literature reviews and summary reports of innovative ongoing clinical research programs are also sometimes published. Reports on individual research studies are not appropriate.

Selective Notes on Submissions: Instructions to authors included in each issue of the journal. Authors to prepare manuscripts according to the *Publication Manual of the American Psychological Association* (4th ed.). Submit three (3) high quality copies of the manuscript to Allan S. Bellack.

Journal Frequency: 8 issues per year

Articles/Pages Published per Year: 50/1000

Total Subscribers: 6,500

Book Reviews Accepted: NA

Rejection Rate: NA

Notes From Publisher: Free sample copy available on request.

Clinical Psychology: Science and Practice

Publisher: Oxford University Press
                 2001 Evans Road
                 Cary, NC 27513

Editor: Alan E. Kazdin, PhD
Department of Psychology
Yale University
P.O. Box 208205, Yale Station
New Haven, CT 06520-8205

Editorial Policy: *Clinical Psychology: Science and Practice* (ISSN 0969-5893) is published quarterly for the Division of Clinical Psychology (D12) of the American Psychological Association. The journal presents cutting-edge developments in the science and practice of clinical psychology by publishing scholarly topical reviews of research, theory, and application to diverse areas of the field, including assessment, intervention, service delivery, and professional issues.

Selective Notes on Submissions: Instructions to authors included in each issue of the journal. Authors to prepare manuscripts according to the *Publication Manual of the American Psychological Association* (4th ed.). Submit four (4) copies of the manuscript to the editor. Scholarly reviews in any area of clinical psychology and disciplines that interface directly with clinical psychology are welcome. Empirical investigations and surveys are not considered within the domain of the journal.

Journal Frequency: Quarterly

Articles/Pages Published per Year: 24/400

Total Subscribers: 7,500

Book Reviews Accepted: No

Rejection Rate: 75%

Cognition

Publisher: Elsevier Science Publishers B.V.
P.O. Box 211
1000 AE Amsterdam
The Netherlands

Editor: Dr. Jacques Mehler
Laboratoire de Sciences
Cognitives et
Psycholinguistique
54, Boulevard Raspail
75006 Paris
France

Editorial Policy: *Cognition* is an international interdisciplinary journal publishing theoretical and experimental papers covering all aspects of the study of the mind. Contributions include research papers in the fields of psychology, linguistics, neuroscience, ethology, philosophy, and epistemology. Only papers that meet the highest standards of quality in the relevant disciplines are published. The journal includes research papers, short experimental reports, review monographs, discussions, and replies. It also serves as a forum for discussion of every aspect of cognitive science as a field. From time to time, the journal publishes special issues on flourishing research areas such as connectionism, literacy, and the biology of cognition. *Cognition* publishes many of the most important papers in cognitive science and is the premier international and interdisciplinary journal in the field. It is required reading for anyone who wishes to keep up to date in this exciting research area.

Selective Notes on Submissions: Instructions to authors included in each issue of the journal. Authors to prepare manuscripts according to the *Publication Manual of the American Psychological Association* (4th ed.). Submit four (4) copies of the manuscript to the editor.

Journal Frequency: Monthly

Articles/Pages Published per Year: 48/1200

Total Subscribers: NA

Book Reviews Accepted: NA

Rejection Rate: NA

Cognition and Emotion

Publisher: Psychology Press
27 Palmeira Mansions
Church Road
Hove, East Sussex BN3 2FA
England

Editor: W. Gerrod Parrot
Department of Psychology
Georgetown University
Box 571001
Washington, DC 20057-1001

Editorial Policy: This journal is devoted to
the study of emotion, especially those
aspects related to mental processes. It
publishes articles in this rapidly growing
area of research, which involves cognitive,
social, clinical, and developmental psychology, cognitive science, and neuropsychology.

Selective Notes on Submissions: Authors are
to prepare manuscripts according to the
*Publication Manual of the American Psy-
chological Association* (4th ed.). Submit
five (5) copies of the manuscript to the
editor.

Journal Frequency: Bimonthly

Articles/Pages Published per Year: 35/672

Total Subscribers: 536

Book Reviews Accepted: No

Rejection Rate: 72%

Notes From Publisher: Frequent "Special
Issues" published.

Cognitive Development

Publisher: Ablex Publishing Corporation
355 Chestnut Street
Norwood, NJ 07648

Editor: Janet Wilde Astington
Institute of Child Study
45 Wolmer Road
Toronto
Canada M5R 2X2

Editorial Policy: Articles of reasonable length
and of developmental or life span interest on
such topics as perception, memory, language, concepts, thought, problem solving,
intelligence, acquisition of knowledge, and
social cognition are appropriate for *Cognitive Development*. These may be reports of
empirical research, methodological advances, theoretical essays, or critical reviews. Emphasis will be placed on timeliness
and general interest value of the articles
submitted. Book reviews will typically be
done on invitation, but volunteers will be
considered.

Selective Notes on Submissions: Instructions
to authors included in each issue of the
journal. Authors to prepare manuscripts
according to the *Publication Manual of the*

American Psychological Association (4th ed.). Submit three (3) copies of the manuscript to the editor.

Journal Frequency: Quarterly

Articles/Pages Published per Year: 32/500

Total Subscribers: 450

Book Reviews Accepted: Yes

Rejection Rate: NA

Cognitive Neuropsychology

Publisher: Psychology Press
(UK) Taylor & Francis, Ltd.
27 Church Road
Hove, East Sussex BN3 2FA
England

Editor: Max Coltheart
Department of Psychology
Birbeck College
Malet Street
London WC1E 7HX
England

Editorial Policy: *Cognitive Neuropsychology* promotes the study of cognitive processes from a neuropsychological perspective. *Cognitive Neuropsychology* publishes articles in this rapidly growing area of research, which involves the coalescence of interests of clinical neuropsychology and cognitive pathology.

Selective Notes on Submissions: Instructions to authors included in the journal's first issue of each year. Authors to prepare manuscripts according to the *Publication Manual of the American Psychological*

Association (4th ed.). Submit four (4) copies of the manuscript to the Editorial Assistant, c/o the publisher.

Journal Frequency: 8 issues per year

Articles/Pages Published per Year: 24/672

Total Subscribers: 624

Book Reviews Accepted: Yes

Rejection Rate: NA

Cognitive Psychology

Publisher: Academic Press, Inc.
1250 Sixth Avenue
San Diego, CA 92101

Editor: Keith Holyoak
Department of Psychology
UCLA, Franz Hall
405 Hilgard Avenue
Los Angeles, CA 90095-1563

Editorial Policy: *Cognitive Psychology* publishes original empirical, theoretical, and tutorial papers; methodological articles; and critical reviews dealing with memory, language processing, perception, problem solving, and thinking. This journal emphasizes work on human cognition. Papers dealing with relevant problems in such related areas as social psychology, development psychology, linguistics, artificial intelligence, and neurophysiology also are welcomed provided that they are of direct interest to cognitive psychologists and are written so as to be understandable by such readers. There are no maximum or minimum length restrictions for journal articles. Minor or very specialized studies are seldom accepted.

Selective Notes on Submissions: Instructions to authors included in each issue of the journal. Authors to prepare manuscripts according to the *Publication Manual of the American Psychological Association* (4th ed.). Submit five (5) copies of the manuscript to the editor.

Journal Frequency: 9 issues per year

Articles/Pages Published per Year: 24/900

Total Subscribers: NA

Book Reviews Accepted: No

Rejection Rate: NA

Cognitive Therapy and Research

Publisher: Plenum Publishing Corporation
233 Spring Street
New York, NY 10013-1578

Editor: Rick Ingram
Department of Psychology
San Diego State University
San Diego, CA 92182

Editorial Policy: *Cognitive Therapy and Research* is a broadly conceived interdisciplinary journal whose main function is to stimulate and communicate research and theory on the role of cognitive processes in human adaptation and adjustment. It attempts to integrate such diverse areas of

psychology as clinical, cognitive, counseling, developmental, experimental, learning, personality, and social psychology. The journal publishes experimental studies, theoretical articles, review articles, methodological articles, case studies, and brief reports. The majority of publication space is devoted to experimental studies.

Selective Notes on Submissions: Instructions to authors included in each issue of the journal. Authors to prepare manuscripts according to the *Publication Manual of the American Psychological Association* (4th ed.). Submit five (5) copies of the manuscript to the editor.

Journal Frequency: Bimonthly

Articles/Pages Published per Year: 40/700

Total Subscribers: NA

Book Reviews Accepted: NA

Rejection Rate: 80%

Community Mental Health Journal

Publisher: Human Sciences Press
233 Spring Street
New York, NY 10013-1578

Editor: David L. Cutler, MD
Department of Psychiatry
OPO 2
Oregon Health Sciences
University
3181 S.W. Sam Jackson Park
Road
Portland, OR 97201-9979

Editorial Policy: The *Community Mental Health Journal* is sponsored by and is an official publication of the National Council of Community Mental Health Centers, Inc. It is devoted to the broad fields of community mental health theory, practice, and research. Manuscripts are accepted for consideration with the understanding that they represent original material, have not been published elsewhere, and are not being considered for publication in another journal.

Selective Notes on Submissions: Instructions to authors included in each issue of the journal. Authors to prepare manuscripts according to the *Publication Manual of the American Psychological Association* (4th ed.). Submit three (3) copies of the manuscript to the editor.

Journal Frequency: Bimonthly

Articles/Pages Published per Year: 45/600

Total Subscribers: 2,500

Book Reviews Accepted: Invited only

Rejection Rate: 70%

Computers in Human Behavior

Publisher: Elsevier Science Inc.
P.O. Box 211
1000 AE Amsterdam
The Netherlands

Editor: Robert D. Tennyson
Department of Educational
Psychology
211a Burton Hall

University of Minnesota
178 Pillsbury Drive, SE
Minneapolis, MN 55455

Editorial Policy: *Computers in Human Behavior* is a scholarly journal dedicated to examining the use of computers from a psychological perspective. Original theoretical work, research reports, literature reviews, software reviews, book reviews, and announcements are published. The journal addresses both the use of computers in psychology, psychiatry, and related disciplines as well as the psychological impact of computer use on individuals, groups, and society. The former category includes articles exploring the use of computers for professional practice, training, research, and theory development. The latter category includes articles dealing with the psychological effects of computers on phenomena such as human development, learning, cognition, personality, and social interactions. The journal addresses human interactions with computers, not computers per se. The computer is discussed only as a medium through which human behaviors are shaped and expressed. The primary message of most articles involves information about human behavior. Therefore, professionals with an interest in the psychological aspects of computer use, but with limited knowledge of computers, will find this journal of interest.

Selective Notes on Submissions: Instructions to authors included in each issue of the journal. Authors to prepare manuscripts according to the *Publication Manual of the American Psychological Association* (4th ed.). Submit three (3) high-quality-bond copies of the manuscript to the editor.

Journal Frequency: Quarterly

Articles/Pages Published per Year: 25/300

Total Subscribers: NA

Book Reviews Accepted: Yes

Rejection Rate: NA

Notes From Publisher: Free sample copy available on request.

Consciousness and Cognition

Publisher: Academic Press
              6277 Sea Harbor Drive
              Orlando, FL 32887-4900

Editors: Bernard J. Baars
            Wright Institute
            2728 Durant Avenue
            Berkeley, CA

            William P. Banks
            Pomona College
            Claremont, CA 91711

Editorial Policy: *Consciousness and Cognition* provides a forum for a natural-science approach to the issues of consciousness, voluntary control, and self. The journal will feature empirical research (in the form of regular articles and short reports) and theoretical articles. Book reviews, intergrative theoretical and critical literature reviews, and tutorial reviews will also be published. Any article may be chosen for peer commentary with author response, normally published in the same issue as the article. Authors are invited to suggest possible commentators when submitting their manuscripts. The journal aims to be both scientifically rigorous and open to novel contributions.

Topics of interest include but are not limited to:

- Implicit memory

- Selective and directed attention

- Priming, subliminal or otherwise

- Neuroelectric correlates of awareness and decision-making

- Assessment of awareness; protocol analysis

- The properties of automaticity in perception and action

- Relations between awareness and attention

Selective Notes on Submissions: Instructions to authors included in each issue of the journal. Authors to prepare manuscripts according to the *Publication Manual of the American Psychological Association* (4th ed.). Submit four (4) copies of the manuscript to the editor. Submit to: Editorial Office, 525 B Street, Suite 1900, San Diego, CA 92101-4495

Journal Frequency: Quarterly

Articles/Pages Published per Year: NA

Total Subscribers: NA

Book Reviews Accepted: Yes

Rejection Rate: NA

Consulting Psychology Journal: Practice and Research

Publisher: Educational Publishing
Foundation
750 First Street, NE
Washington, DC 20002-4242

Editor: Skipton Leonard, PhD
11741 Bowman Green Drive
Reston, VA 22090

Editorial Policy: The mission of *Consulting Psychology Journal: Practice and Research* is to facilitate the exchange of knowledge and ideas regarding the field of consultation to the community of psychologists and others interested in consultation. The journal publishes articles in the following areas: (a) theoretical/conceptual articles with implications for application to consulting; (b) original research regarding consultation; (c) in-depth reviews of research and literature in specific areas of consultation practice; (d) case studies that demonstrate the application of innovative consultation methods/strategies, that highlight critical or often overlooked issues for consultation, or that have unusual features that would be of general interest to other consultants; (e) articles on consultation practice development; and (f) articles addressing the unique issues encountered by consulting psychologists in applying their knowledge and skill to the problems of clients. The journal also publishes special topic issues with guest editors on a regular basis. Topics for these issues are suggested by the members of Division 13.

Selective Notes on Submissions: Instructions to authors included in each issue of the journal. Authors to prepare manuscripts according to the *Publication Manual of the*

American Psychological Association (4th ed.). Submit three (3) copies of the manuscript to the editor, c/o the publisher, along with a 5 1/4" or 3 1/2" DOS-formatted floppy disk.

Journal Frequency: Quarterly

Articles/Pages Published per Year: 28/232

Total Subscribers: 1,000

Book Reviews Accepted: No

Rejection Rate: 17%

Contemporary Educational Psychology

Publisher: Academic Press, Inc.
1250 Sixth Avenue
San Diego, CA 92101

Editor: James M. Royer
Department of Psychology
University of Massachusetts
Amherst, MA 01003

Editorial Policy: *Contemporary Educational Psychology* publishes articles dealing with empirical research and theory in psychology as related to the educational process. Since the process of education is a lifelong one, materials reflect the several life phases from neonatal to senescence and death; however, these stages are reflected in an educational framework. Articles and reviews must show a clear relationship to the process in topic, data, and theory. Specifically, the journal contains articles that demonstrate the application of psychological methods and skills to the educational process. Both classroom and laboratory experimentation are relevant, particularly as they emphasize problem-solving. Instructional techniques may be reported, if adequate controls are used to demonstrate the validity of the findings. Theoretical contributions may include issues, comparisons, analyses, and the like as appropriate content.

Selective Notes on Submissions: Instructions to authors included in each issue of the journal. Authors to prepare manuscripts according to the *Publication Manual of the American Psychological Association* (4th ed.). Submit four (4) copies of the manuscript to the editor.

Journal Frequency: Quarterly

Articles/Pages Published per Year: 36/495

Total Subscribers: NA

Book Reviews Accepted: Yes

Rejection Rate: 75%

Contemporary Psychoanalysis

Publisher: W. A. White Institute
                 20 W. 74th Street
                 New York, NY 10023

Editor: Arthur H. Feiner, PhD
              W. A. White Institute
              20 W. 74th Street
              New York, NY 10023

Editorial Policy: *Contemporary Psychoanalysis* is dedicated to the publication of significant contributions to the understanding of personality and behavior. Manuscripts that are original, innovative and challenging in the field of contemporary psychoanalytic theory and practice are solicited. While the William Alanson White Institute and the William Alanson White Psychoanalytic Society represent the interpersonal frame of reference in psychoanalysis, this journal welcomes all points of view.

Selective Notes on Submissions: Instructions to authors included in each issue of the journal. Submit three (3) copies of the manuscript to the editor.

Journal Frequency: Quarterly

Articles/Pages Published per Year: 40/680

Total Subscribers: 1,700

Book Reviews Accepted: No

Rejection Rate: 75%

Counseling Psychologist

Publisher: Sage Publications, Inc.
                 2455 Teller Road
                 Newbury Park, CA 91320

Editor: P. Paul Heppner, PhD
              Department of Psychology
              210 McAlester Hall
              University of Missouri-Columbia
              Columbia, MO 65211

Editorial Policy: The *Counseling Psychologist* is the official publication of the Division of Counseling Psychology (Division 17) of the American Psychological Association. Each issue includes a major article or set of articles on a specific theme of importance to the theory, research, and practice of counseling psychology. Additionally, beginning in 1986 most issues have included included an invited review of empirical research on a focused topic within the four broad domains of counseling, career psychology, normal development/student development, and training/supervision. (Guidelines for submitting proposals for both major articles and research reviews are provided in Volume 13, Number 1.) The professional, scientific, international, and special populations forums include brief position papers, reports of professional surveys, and illustrations of innovative techniques or the research and service activities of counseling psychology. Comments and letters to the editor are published on a space-available basis. In order to ensure timeliness, comments should be submitted no later than three months after the date of the issue containing the article on which the comment is made.

Selective Notes on Submissions: Instructions to authors included in each issue of the journal. Authors to prepare manuscripts according to the *Publication Manual of the American Psychological Association* (4th ed.). Submit three (3) copies of the manuscript to the editor.

Journal Frequency: Quarterly

Articles/Pages Published per Year: 49/750

Total Subscribers: 5,600

Book Reviews Accepted: No

Rejection Rate: 68%

Counselling Psychology Quarterly

Publisher: Carfax Publishing Company
P.O. Box 25
Abingdon, OX14 3UE
England

Editors: W. J. Alladin
U.K. Counselling Service
Queensway Business Centre
Dunlop Way
Scunthorpe, North Lincolnshire
    DN16 3RT
England

North American Editor:
E. Thomas Dowd
Department of Psychology
118 Kent Hall
Kent State University
Kent, OH 44242

Editorial Policy: *Counselling Psychology Quarterly* is an international journal reporting on practice, research, and theory. The journal is particularly keen to encourage and publish papers that will be of immediate practical relevance to counselling, clinical, occupational, and medical psychologists throughout the world. Original, independently refereed contributions will be included on practice, research, and theory (especially articles that integrate these three areas) from whatever methodological or theoretical standpoint. The journal will also include regular international peer review commentaries on major issues.

Selective Notes on Submissions: Instructions to authors included in each issue of the journal. Authors to prepare manuscripts according to the *Publication Manual of the American Psychological Association* (4th ed.). Submit three (3) copies of the manuscript to the appropriate editor.

Journal Frequency: Quarterly

Articles/Pages Published per Year: 28/400

Total Subscribers: 400

Book Reviews Accepted: Yes

Rejection Rate: 50%

Counselor Education and Supervision

Publisher: American Association for
                  Counseling and Develop-
                  ment
                  5999 Stevenson Avenue
                  Alexandria, VA 22304

Editor: Martin H. Ritchie
                  Counselor and Human Services
                      Education
                  Snyder Memorial
                  University of Toledo
                  Toledo, OH 43606-3390

Editorial Policy: *Counselor Education and Supervision* invites articles concerned with research, theory, development, or program applications pertinent to counselor education and supervision. The journal is concerned with matters relevant to the preparation or supervision of counselors in agency and school settings, in colleges and universities, or at local, state, and federal levels. *Counselor Education and Supervision* is the official publication of the Association for Counselor Education and Supervision (ACES), a member of the American Counseling Association (ACA).

Selective Notes on Submissions: Instructions to authors included in each issue of the journal. Authors to prepare manuscripts according to the *Publication Manual of the American Psychological Association* (4th ed.). Submit four (4) copies of the manuscript to the editor.

Journal Frequency: Quarterly

Articles/Pages Published per Year: 32/400

Total Subscribers: 4,500

Book Reviews Accepted: Yes, unsolicited

Rejection Rate: 82%

Creativity Research Journal

Publisher: LEA
                  10 Industrial Avenue
                  Mahwah, NJ 07430-2262

Editor: Mark A. Runco
                  California State University
                  EC 105
                  Fullerton, CA 92634

Editorial Policy: The *Creativity Research Journal* publishes high-quality scholarly research. Preference is given to reports from carefully designed empirical studies. Theoretical papers are also published. Literature reviews are only published if they offer an explicit integration or significant contribution to theory. Special care is taken to capture the full range of approaches to the study of creativity (e.g., behavioral, clinical, cognitive, cross-cultural, developmental, educational, personological, psychoanalytic, psychometric, social); but all published articles will focus on creativity.

Selective Notes on Submissions: Authors to prepare manuscripts according to the *Publication Manual of the American Psychological Association* (4th ed.). Submit five (5) copies of the manuscript to the editor.

Journal Frequency: Quarterly

Articles/Pages Published per Year: 40/400

Total Subscribers: NA

Book Reviews Accepted: NA

Rejection Rate: NA

Criminal Behaviour and Mental Health

Publisher: Whurr Publishers, Ltd.
19b Compton Terrace
London N1 2UN
England

Editors: John Gunn, Pamela Taylor, and
David Farrington

Editorial Policy: *Criminal Behaviour and Mental Health* brings together material relevant to the interface among psychiatry, psychology, crime, and the law. It contains chiefly research papers on the causes of crime and delinquency, the treatment of mentally abnormal offenders, the police, the probation services, the courts, the legal process, and the social services. Discussion papers are also published from time to time. Most of the papers are submitted by psychiatrists and psychologists, but papers from other disciplines are encouraged. Although the journal is intended primarily for psychia-

trists and psychologists who work with mentally abnormal offenders or violent patients or who are engaged in research or teaching on crime or the criminal justice sytem, it is also of interest to lawyers, criminologists, sociologists, and other social scientists.

Selective Notes on Submissions: Instructions to authors included in each issue of the journal. Submit four (4) copies of the manuscript to John Gunn, c/o Institute of Psychiatry, De Crespigny Park, Denmark Hill, London SE5 8AF, England

Journal Frequency: Quarterly

Articles/Pages Published per Year: 30/320

Total Subscribers: NA

Book Reviews Accepted: Yes

Rejection Rate: 50%

Criminal Justice and Behavior

Publisher: Sage Publications, Inc.
2455 Teller Road
Thousand Oaks, CA 91320

Editor: Curt R. Bartol
Department of Psychology
Castleton State College
Castleton, VT 05735

Editorial Policy: *Criminal Justice and Behavior* seeks contributions examining psychological and behavioral aspects of the juvenile and criminal justice systems. The concepts "criminal justice" and "behavior" should be interpreted broadly to include analyses of the etiology of delinquent or criminal behavior, the process of law violation, of victimology, offender classification and treatment, deterrence, and incapacitation. The journal will include analyses of both clientel and employees in the justice systems; and it will include analyses of the effects of differing sanctions or programs. The journal emphasizes reports of original empirical research, theoretical contributions, development and testing of innovative programs and practices, and critical reviews of literature or theory on central topics of criminal justice and behavior. Articles dealing with behavioral aspects of juvenile or criminal justice are welcomed from throughout the world.

Selective Notes on Submissions: Instructions to authors included in each issue of the journal. Authors to prepare manuscripts according to the *Publication Manual of the American Psychological Association* (4th ed.). Submit three (3) copies of the manuscript to the editor.

Journal Frequency: Quarterly

Articles/Pages Published per Year: 32/500

Total Subscribers: 2,170

Book Reviews Accepted: Yes; send to Anne M. Bartol, PhD, Book Review Editor, c/o the Editor.

Rejection Rate: 86%

Cultural Diversity and Mental Health

Publisher: John Wiley & Sons
                      605 Third Avenue
                      New York, NY 10158

Editor: Lillian Comas-Díaz, PhD
                      Transcultural Mental Health
                         Institute
                      1301 20th Street, NW,
                         Suite 711
                      Washington, DC 20036

Editorial Policy: Ethnosociocultural factors, including age, ethnicity, gender, race, sexual orientation, socioeconomic status, language, religion, and political and social ideology can have a significant impact on the process and outcome of mental health treatment. *Cultural Diversity and Mental Health* provides psychologists, social workers, psychiatrists, counselors, and other mental health professionals with the knowledge base and therapeutic tools to effectively assess and treat clients from diverse backgrounds. This periodical features lively topical articles, comprehensive reviews, clinically relevant research reports, and timely book reviews. In addition, the journal includes case reports reflecting the ethnocultural and social factors clinicians should be aware of when treating specific groups of clients.

Selective Notes on Submissions: Instructions to authors included in each issue of the journal. Authors to prepare manuscripts according to the *Publication Manual of the American Psychological Association* (4th ed.). Submit four (4) copies of the manuscript to the editor.

Journal Frequency: 3 issues per year

Articles/Pages Published per Year: 21/210

Total Subscribers: NA

Book Reviews Accepted: NA

Rejection Rate: NA

Current Psychology

Publisher: Transaction Publishers
Department 3094
Rutgers, The State University of
New Jersey
New Brunswick, NJ 08903

Editors: Noel P. Sheehy
Queens University
10 Lennoxvale,
Malone Row
Belfast BT7 1NN,
Northern Ireland

Nathaniel J. Pallone
Rutgers University
1111 Newhouse Center for Law
and Justice
15 Washington Street
Newark, NJ 07102

Editorial Policy: An international forum for rapid dissemination of information at the cutting edge of psychology. Significant empirical contributions from all areas of psychology including social psychology; small groups and personality; human development; sensation, perception, and cognition; clinical and abnormal psychology; and methodology and field research.

Selective Notes on Submissions: Instructions to authors included in each issue of the journal. Authors to prepare manuscripts according to the *Publication Manual of the American Psychological Association* (4th ed.). Submit three (3) copies of the manuscript to the editor. Tables, figures, graphs, and other artwork should be provided camera-ready on separate pages. To facilitate "blind review" name(s) of author(s) should appear only on a detachable cover page. No simultaneous submissions.

Journal Frequency: Quarterly

Articles/Pages Published per Year: 384 pp.

Total Subscribers: 550

Book Reviews Accepted: No

Rejection Rate: NA

Death Studies

Publisher: Taylor & Francis
1101 Vermont Avenue, NW
Suite 200
Washington, DC 20005-3521

Editor: Robert A. Neimeyer, PhD
Department of Psychology
University of Memphis
Memphis, TN 38152

Editorial Policy: *Death Studies* publishes refereed papers in the areas of bereavement and loss, grief therapy, death attitudes, suicide, and death education. It provides an interdisciplinary, international forum for a variety of professionals contributing research reports on all aspects of death, dying, and bereavement, as well as papers dealing with ethical, legal, and professional controversies related to death and terminal care. Applied papers outlining concrete techniques and procedures for use in clinical and pedagogic settings are also appropriate.

Selective Notes on Submissions: Authors to prepare manuscripts according to the *Publication Manual of the American Psychological Association* (4th ed.). Submit four (4) copies of the manuscript to the editor. All accepted manuscripts, artwork, and photographs become the property of the publisher.

Journal Frequency: Bimonthly

Articles/Pages Published per Year: 42/600

Total Subscribers: NA

Book Reviews Accepted: Yes

Rejection Rate: 80%

Development and Psychopathology

Publisher: Cambridge University Press
40 W. 20th Street
New York, NY 10011

Editors: Dante Cicchetti, Director
Department of Psychology
Mt. Hope Family Center
University of Rochester
187 Edinburgh Street
Rochester, NY 14608

Barry Nurcombe
Bradley Hospital
Brown University

Editorial Policy: This multidisciplinary journal is devoted to the publication of original empirical, theoretical, and review papers which address the interrelationship of normal and pathological development in adults and children. It is intended to serve and integrate the emerging field of developmental psychopathology, which strives to understand patterns of adaptation and maladaptation throughout the life span. Explorations of abnormal functioning in the social, emotional, cognitive, linguistic, and biological domains help to clarify normal developmental processes. Reciprocally, elucidations of principles of normal development help to broaden our understanding of psychopathological conditions. Contributions are from a wide array of disciplines because an effective developmental approach to psychopathology necessitates a broad synthesis of knowledge. Contributions may also be on the processes underlying the adaptive outcomes in populations "at risk" for psychopathology. This journal is of vital interest to psychologists, psychiatrists, social scientists, neuroscientists, pediatricians, and researchers.

Selective Notes on Submissions: Instructions to authors included in each issue of the journal. Authors to prepare manuscripts according to the *Publication Manual of the American Psychological Association* (4th ed.). Submit four (4) copies of the manuscript to the editor.

Journal Frequency: Quarterly

Articles/Pages Published per Year: 50/900

Total Subscribers: NA

Book Reviews Accepted: NA

Rejection Rate: NA

Developmental Neuropsychology

Publisher: Lawrence Erlbaum Associates, Inc.
365 Broadway
Hillsdale, NJ 07642

Editor: Dennis L. Molfese
Department of Behavioral and Social Sciences, 6517
Southern Illinois University
Carbondale, IL 62901-6517

Editorial Policy: *Developmental Neuropsychology* is devoted to exploring the relationships which exist between brain and behavior across the life span. The journal will publish scholarly papers on the appearance and development of behavioral functions such as language, perception, and cognitive processes as they relate to brain functions and structures. Some examples of subjects that would be appropriate for publication are studies of early cognitive behaviors in normal and brain-damaged children, plasticity and recovery of function after early brain damage, the development of complex cognitive and motor skills, and specific and nonspecific disturbances such as learning disabilities, mental retardation, schizophrenia, stuttering, and developmental aphasia and so forth. Appropriate gerontologic topics include neuropsychological analyses of normal age-related changes in brain and behavioral functions (e.g., in sensory, motor, cognitive, and adaptive abilities), studies of age-related diseases of the nervous system, and recovery of function in later life. Empirical studies, research reviews, case reports, critical commentary, and book reviews will be published. By publishing both basic and clinical studies of the developing and the aging brain, the editors hope to encourage scholarly work that advances the understanding of developmental neuropsychology.

Selective Notes on Submissions: Instructions to authors included in each issue of the journal. Authors to prepare manuscripts according to the *Publication Manual of the American Psychological Association* (4th ed.). Submit four (4) copies of the manuscript to the editor.

Journal Frequency: Quarterly

Articles/Pages Published per Year: 35/682

Total Subscribers: 549

Book Reviews Accepted: Yes

Rejection Rate: 45%

Developmental Psychobiology

Publisher: John Wiley & Sons, Inc.
605 Third Avenue
New York, NY 10158

Editor: William P. Smotherman
Department of Psychology
Binghamton University
Vestal Parkway East
Binghamton, NY 13902-6000

Editorial Policy: *Developmental Psychobiology* will publish original reports of research that contribute to understanding behaviorally related developmental processes. The submission of manuscripts whose focus is on behavioral development, whether in the embryo, fetus, neonate, or juvenile animal are welcome. Anatomical, physiological, biochemical, hormonal, pharmacological, genetic, and evolutionary approaches are also appropriate; in fact, the journal strongly supports such multidisciplinary work when the relationship to behavioral development is clear. Experimental and descriptive studies, whether carried out in the laboratory or field and irrespective of the particular species being studied, are considered to be equally meritorious. The submission of studies using invertebrates, humans, or any other animal is encouraged. Workers in all fields of psychology, biology, medicine, and neuroscience involved in ontogenetic studies of behavior are invited to submit manuscripts to *Developmental Psychobiology*.

Selective Notes on Submissions: Brief reports or papers merely describing techniques are discouraged. *Developmental Psychobiology* will also publish comments, consisting of short discussions of issues and problems of interest to other researchers, as well as book reviews. Authors should consult the editors on the preparation and appropriateness of such contributions. Instructions to authors included in each issue of the journal. Submit three (3) copies of the manuscript to the editor.

Journal Frequency: 8 issues per year

Articles/Pages Published per Year: 56/900

Total Subscribers: 900

Book Reviews Accepted: Yes

Rejection Rate: NA

Notes From Publisher: The official journal of the International Society for Developmental Psychobiology.

Developmental Psychology

Publisher:　American Psychological Association
750 First Street, NE
Washington, DC 20002-4242

Editor:　Carolyn Zahn-Waxler, PhD
4305 Dresden Street
Kensington, MD 20895

Editorial Policy: *Developmental Psychology* publishes articles that advance knowledge and theory about human development across the life span. Although most papers address directly the issues of human development, studies of other species are appropriate if they have important implications for human development. The journal includes significant empirical contributions to the study of growth and development and, occasionally, scholarly reviews, theoretical articles, and social policy papers. Studies of any variables that affect human psychological development—whether proximal or distal causes, whether efficient, final, or formal causes— are considered. In the case of laboratory experimental studies, preference is given to reports of series of studies, and the external validity of such studies is a major consideration. Field research, cross-cultural studies, research on gender and ethnicity, and research on other socially important topics are especially welcome.

Selective Notes on Submissions: Instructions to authors included in each issue of the journal. Authors to prepare manuscripts according to the *Publication Manual of the American Psychological Association* (4th ed.). Submit five (5) copies of the manuscript to the editor.

Journal Frequency: Bimonthly

Articles/Pages Published per Year: 90/992

Total Subscribers: 5,500

Book Reviews Accepted: No

Rejection Rate: 77%

Developmental Review

Publisher: Academic Press, Inc.
1250 Sixth Avenue
San Diego, CA 92101

Editor: Grover J. Whitehurst
Department of Psychology
State University of New York
at Stony Brook
Stony Brook, NY 11794

Editorial Policy: *Developmental Review,* an international and interdisciplinary journal, publishes original articles that bear on conceptual issues in psychological development. Appropriate papers include (1) theoretical statements, (2) reviews of literature, (3) summaries of programmatic research, (4) empirical findings that are provocative and of particular relevance for developmental theory, (5) integrated collections of papers on a single theme, (6) analyses of social policy as it affects human development, (7) historical analyses, (8) essays on major books, (9) analyses of method and design. Discussions and commentaries are welcomed. Subject matter may be from the disciplines of psychology, sociology, education, or pediatrics, may be basic or applied, and may be drawn from any species or age range as long as it speaks to issues of psychological development.

Selective Notes on Submissions: Instructions to authors included in each issue of the journal. Authors to prepare manuscripts according to the *Publication Manual of the American Psychological Association* (4th ed.). Submit three (3) copies of the manuscript to the editor.

Journal Frequency: Quarterly

Articles/Pages Published per Year: 16/450

Total Subscribers: NA

Book Reviews Accepted: Yes

Rejection Rate: NA

Dissociation: Progress in the Dissociative Disorders

Publisher: International Society for the
Study of Dissociation
5700 Old Orchard Road,
First Floor
Skokie, IL 60077-1057

Editor: Richard P. Kluft, MD
Institute of Pennsylvania
Hospital
111 North 49th Street
Philadelphia, PA 19139

Editorial Policy: *Dissociation: Progress in the Dissociative Disorders,* provides a forum for scientific and clinical communication about dissociation as a phenomenon and about the dissociative disorders. Despite the growing importance of dissociation and the dissociative disorders in the mental health sciences, the controversy that frequently has surrounded these subjects has often made it difficult for most communications about them to find a suitable place in the more general mental health literature. *Dissociation* is interested in publishing articles that demonstrate theoretical models and inquiries, basic research, clinical research, and clinical findings and methods. It is equally open to the researcher and the clinician. Occasional articles on anthropological, sociological and philosophical studies of dissociation are also published.

Selective Notes on Submissions: Instructions to authors included in each issue of the journal. Authors to prepare manuscripts according to the *Publication Manual of the American Psychological Association* (4th ed.). Submit four (4) copies of the manuscript to the editor. Submit disk as well.

Journal Frequency: Quarterly

Articles/Pages Published per Year: 32/268

Total Subscribers: 3,000

Book Reviews Accepted: Yes

Rejection Rate: 50%

Dreaming: Journal of the Association for the Study of Dreams

Publisher:　　Human Sciences Press
　　　　　　　　233 Spring Street
　　　　　　　　New York, NY 10013-1578

Editor:　　　Donald Kuiken
　　　　　　　　Department of Psychology
　　　　　　　　P-220 Biological Sciences
　　　　　　　　　　Building
　　　　　　　　University of Alberta
　　　　　　　　Edmonton, Alberta
　　　　　　　　Canada T6G 2E9

Editorial Policy: *Dreaming: Journal of the Association for the Study of Dreams* is a multidisciplinary journal, the only professional journal devoted specifically to dreaming. The journal publishes scholarly articles related to dreaming from any discipline and viewpoint. This includes biological aspects of dreaming and sleep/dream laboratory research; psychological articles of any kind related to dreaming; clinical work on dreams regardless of theoretical perspective (Freudian, Jungian, existential, eclectic, etc.); anthropological, sociological, and philosophical articles related to dreaming; and articles about dreaming from any of the arts and humanities. All papers undergo peer review by three to six referees, both within and outside the discipline of the author.

Selective Notes on Submissions: Instructions to authors included in each issue of the journal. Submit four (4) copies of the manuscript to the editor.

Journal Frequency: Quarterly

Articles/Pages Published per Year: 24/280

Total Subscribers: 950

Book Reviews Accepted: No

Rejection Rate: NA

Drug and Alcohol Dependence

Publisher: Elsevier Science, Inc.
660 White Plains Road
Tarrytown, NY 10591-5153

Editor: Chris-Ellen Johnson
Wayne State University
School of Medicine
2761 East Jefferson Avenue
Detroit, MI 48207

Editorial Policy: *Drug and Alcohol Dependence* is an international journal devoted to publishing original research, scholarly reviews, commentaries, and policy analyses in the area of drug and alcohol abuse and dependence. Articles range from studies of the chemistry of substances of abuse, their actions at molecular and cellular sites, in vitro and in vivo investigations of their biochemical, pharmacological and behavioral actions, laboratory-based and clinical research in humans, substance abuse treatment and prevention research, and studies employing methods of epidemiology, sociology, and economics. The rationale for this extensive coverage is the conviction that drug and alcohol abuse/dependence cannot be understood in their entirety from a single perspective and that without an understanding of other areas of research, studies by individual investigators may be limited. The goal of the journal is to provide researchers, clinicians, and policy makers-access to material from all perspectives in a single journal in a format that is understandable and which has recieved rigorous editorial review. The hope of its editors is to promote mutual understanding of the many facets of drug abuse to the benefit of all investigators involved in drug and alcohol research, and to facilitate the transfer of scientific findings to successful treatment and prevention practices.

Selective Notes on Submissions: Instructions to authors included in each issue of the journal. Authors to prepare manuscripts according to Harvard style. Submit four (4) copies of the manuscript to the editor.

Journal Frequency: Monthly

Articles/Pages Published per Year: 72/920

Total Subscribers: 500

Book Reviews Accepted: No

Rejection Rate: 50%

Early Childhood Research Quarterly

Publisher: Ablex Publishing Corporation
355 Chestnut Street
Norwood, NJ 07648

Editor: Dr. Marion Hyson
ECRQ
University of Delaware
111 Alison West
Newark, DE 19716

Editorial Policy: *Early Childhood Research Quarterly* is intended to complement the services provided by NAEYC's current journal, *Young Children,* by providing significant research and scholarship related to the care and education of children from birth through 8 years. Reviewed by a distinguished panel of consulting editors, contents offer in-depth treatment of research and scholarship on all topics in the field and reflect the interdisciplinary nature of NAEYC and its membership. In addition to addressing a wide range of subjects, each issue contains the column "From ERIC/EECE." This column serves to alert readers to recent ERIC document acquisitions related to the topics appearing in each issue, and includes news of interest from the ERIC Clearinghouse on Elementary and Early Childhood Education and other ERIC clearinghouses. Periodically a section of brief reports on topics identified as novel, unusual, or "on the growing edge" of the field is presented and occasional special issues appear under the guest editorship of prominent researchers. The *Quarterly* is an important source of research and scholarship with clear relevance to application and practice in working with young children. As such, the journal is of importance not only to scholars and researchers but also to practitioners, parents, and others interested in the scholarly treatment of issues.

Selective Notes on Submissions: Instructions to authors included in each issue of the journal. Authors to prepare manuscripts according to the *Publication Manual of the American Psychological Association* (4th ed.). Submit four (4) copies of the manuscript to the editor.

Journal Frequency: Quarterly

Articles/Pages Published per Year: 24/520

Total Subscribers: 1,200

Book Reviews Accepted: NA

Rejection Rate: NA

Ecological Psychology

Publisher: Lawrence Erlbaum
                   Associates, Inc.
                   10 Industrial Avenue
                   Mahwah, NJ 07430

Editor: William M. Mace
                   Department of Psychology
                   Trinity College
                   Hartford, CT 06106

Editorial Policy: *Ecological Psychology,* the journal of the International Society of Ecological Psychology, publishes original articles that contribute to the understanding of psychological and behavioral processes as they occur within the ecological constraints of animal–environment systems. Uniting research previously spread over numerous journals and disciplines, *Ecological Psychology* emphasizes research based on animal–environment systems and encourages progress on problems in psychology that would not be made through investigations from individual disciplines. *Ecological Psychology* focuses on problems of perception, action, cognition, communication, learning, development, and evolution in all species, to the extent that those problems derive from a consideration of whole animal–environment systems rather than animals or their environments in isolation from each other.

Selective Notes on Submissions: Instructions to authors included in each issue of the journal. Authors to prepare manuscripts according to the *Publication Manual of the American Psychological Association* (4th ed.). Submit four (4) copies of the manuscript to the editor.

Journal Frequency: Quarterly

Articles/Pages Published per Year: 16/384

Total Subscribers: 500

Book Reviews Accepted: Yes

Rejection Rate: 50%

Education and Treatment of Children

Publisher: The Pressley Ridge Schools
530 Marshall Avenue
Pittsburgh, PA 15214

Editors: R.F. Dickie
California University of
Pennsylvania
California, PA

Daniel E. Hursh
West Virginia University
Morgantown, WV

Editorial Policy: *Education and Treatment of Children* is devoted to the dissemination of information concerning the development and improvement of services for children and youth. Various types of material are appropriate for publication, including original experimental research, experimental replications, adaptations of previously reported research, research reviews, procedure or program descriptions, issue-oriented papers, and brief reader communications and inquiries. All nonexperimental papers will concentrate on the manner in which the described procedure, program, issue, etc., may be applied or related to practical concerns of professionals in the field.

Selective Notes on Submissions: Instructions to authors included in each issue of the journal. Authors to prepare manuscripts according to the *Publication Manual of the American Psychological Association* (4th ed.). Submit five (5) copies of the manuscript to the editors or to Managing Editor Bernie Fabray, Pressley Ridge School, 530 Marshall Avenue, Pittsburgh, PA 15214

Journal Frequency: Quarterly

Articles/Pages Published per Year: 40/384

Total Subscribers: 500

Book Reviews Accepted: Yes

Rejection Rate: 50%

Educational Assessment

Publisher: Lawrence Erlbaum
Associates, Inc.
10 Industrial Avenue
Mahwah, NJ 07430-2262

Editor: Robert C. Calfee
School of Education
Stanford University
Stanford, CA 94305-3096

Editorial Policy: *Educational Assessment* publishes original research and scholarship on the assessment of individuals, groups, and programs in educational settings. Its coverage encompasses a broad range of issues related to theory, empirical research, and practice in the appraisal of educational achievements by students and teachers, young children and adults, and novices and experts. The journal also reports on studies of conventional testing practices, discusses alternative approaches, presents scholarship on classroom practice, and debates on national assessment issues. *Educational Assessment's* stated purpose is to provide a forum for integrating conceptual and technical domains with the arenas of practice and policy and for unifying a literature that is presently scattered over a variety of disciplines and outlets.

Selective Notes on Submissions: Instructions to authors included in each issue of the journal. Authors to prepare manuscripts according to the *Publication Manual of the American Psychological Association* (4th ed.). Submit four (4) copies of the manuscript to the editor.

Journal Frequency: Quarterly

Articles/Pages Published per Year: 20/420

Total Subscribers: NA

Book Reviews Accepted: No

Rejection Rate: 50%

Educational and Psychological Measurement

Publisher: Sage Publications, Inc.
                   2455 Teller Road
                   Thousand Oaks, CA 91320

Editors: Main Section:
                   Bruce Thompson
                   Department of Psychology
                   Texas A & M University
                   College Station, TX 77843-4225

Validity Studies:
Larry G. Daniel
University of Southern
    Mississippi
Southern Station Box 5027
Hattiesburg, MS 39406-5027

Editorial Policy: The journal is open to: (1) discussions of problems in the field of the measurement of individual differences, (2) reports of research on the development and use of tests and measurements in education, industry, and government, (3) descriptions of testing programs being used for various purposes, and (4) reports which are pertinent to the measurement field, such as suggestions of new types of items or improved methods of treating test data. Authors are granted permission to have reprints made of their own articles for their own use at their own expense.

Selective Notes on Submissions: Instructions to authors included in each issue of the journal. Authors to prepare manuscripts according to the *Publication Manual of the American Psychological Association* (4th ed.). Submit four (4) copies of the manuscript to the appropriate editor.

Journal Frequency: Bimonthly

Articles/Pages Published per Year: 108/1080

Total Subscribers: 2,500

Book Reviews Accepted: Yes

Rejection Rate: NA

Educational Psychologist

Publisher: Lawrence Erlbaum Associates
365 Broadway
Hillsdale, NJ 07642

Editor: Paul Pintrich, PhD
Editor, *Educational Psychologist*
University of Michigan
1400 School of Education Building
Ann Arbor, MI 48109

Editorial Policy: The *Educational Psychologist* publishes scholarly essays, reviews, critiques, and articles of a theoretical/conceptual nature that contribute to our understanding of the issues, problems, and research associated with the field of educational psychology. Articles representing all aspects of educational psychology are encouraged. This journal, however, does not publish articles whose primary purpose is to report the method and results of an empirical study. (The *Educational Psychologist* is an APA Division 15 publication.)

Selective Notes on Submissions: Instructions to authors included in each issue of the journal. Authors to prepare manuscripts according to the *Publication Manual of the American Psychological Association* (4th ed.). Submit an original and four (4) copies of the manuscript to the editor.

Journal Frequency: Quarterly

Articles/Pages Published per Year: 30/232

Total Subscribers: 2,500

Book Reviews Accepted: No

Rejection Rate: 85%

Educational Psychology Review

Publisher: Plenum Publishing Corporation
233 Spring Street
New York, NY 10013-1578

Editor: Stephen L. Benton
College of Education
Kansas State University
369 Bluemont Hall
Manhattan, KS 66506

Editorial Policy: *Educational Psychology Review* is an international forum for the publication of peer-reviewed integrative state-of-the-art review papers in the field of general educational psychology (i.e., the application of psychology to education) covering topics such as learning, cognition (e.g., memory, problem solving, creativity, reading), measurement, motivation, individual differences, school-related counseling, and development. In addition, the journal publishes papers on the history of educational psychology, reviews on aspects of educational psychology as a profession, briefer reviews, commentaries, and special thematic issues from time to time. The journal provides breadth of coverage appropriate to a wide readership in educational psychology, yet each review is of sufficient depth to inform specialists in that area.

Selective Notes on Submissions: Instructions to authors included in each issue of the journal. Submit four (4) copies of the manuscript to the editor.

Journal Frequency: Quarterly

Articles/Pages Published per Year: 16/425

Total Subscribers: NA

Book Reviews Accepted: Yes

Rejection Rate: NA

Environment and Behavior

Publisher: Sage Publications, Inc.
2455 Teller Road
Newbury Park, CA 91320

Editor: Robert B. Bechtel
Environmental Psychology
    Program
University of Arizona
Tucson, AZ 85721

Editorial Policy: *Environment and Behavior* is an interdisciplinary journal designed to report rigorous experimental and theoretical work focusing on the influence of the physical environment on human behavior at the individual, group, and institutional levels. Articles are sought in the following areas: (1) Theoretical work on the interrelationships between human environments and behavioral systems. Methodological papers will be considered, provided the primary focus concerns the environment–behavior relationship. (2) Reports on research relating to evaluation of environments designed to accomplish specific objectives (e.g., the social effects of different kinds of living accommodations or the effectiveness of hospital treatment areas). (3) Studies relat-ing to the beliefs, meanings, values, and attitudes of individuals or groups concerning various environments (e.g., the meanings and values attached to neighborhoods, cities, transport routes and devices, or recreational areas). (4) studies concerning physical environments whose human mission is largely implicit or socially underdeveloped. (5) Studies of planning, policy, or political action aimed at controlling environments or behavior.

Selective Notes on Submissions: Instructions to authors included in each issue of the journal. A detailed style sheet is available upon request from the editor or publisher. Submit an original and two (2) copies of the manuscript to the editor.

Journal Frequency: Bimonthly

Articles/Pages Published per Year: 28/768

Total Subscribers: 1,650

Book Reviews Accepted: Yes

Rejection Rate: 78%

Ethics and Behavior

Publisher: Lawrence Erlbaum Associates
365 Broadway
Hillsdale, NJ 07642

Editor: Gerald P. Koocher, PhD
Department of Psychiatry
Children's Hospital
300 Longwood Avenue
Boston, MA 02115

Editorial Policy: *Ethics and Behavior* publishes articles on an array of topics pertaining to various moral issues and conduct. These topics may include, but are not restricted to, the exercise of social and ethical responsibility in human behaviors, ethical dilemmas or professional misconduct in health and human service delivery, the conduct of research involving human and animal participants, fraudulence in the management or reporting of scientific research, and public policy issues involving ethical problems. Date-based, theoretical and particularly instructive case analyses as well as brief summaries of problem cases (approximately 500 words) are also welcome submissions for inclusion in our special Forum section.

Selective Notes on Submissions: Instructions to authors included in each issue of the journal. Authors to prepare manuscripts according to the *Publication Manual of the American Psychological Association* (4th ed.). Submit three (3) copies of the manuscript to the editor.

Journal Frequency: Quarterly

Articles/Pages Published per Year: 24/400

Total Subscribers: NA

Book Reviews Accepted: Yes

Rejection Rate: 65%

European Journal of Cognitive Psychology

Publisher: Psychology Press
27 Church Road
Hove, East Sussex BN3 2FA
England

Editor: Lars: Göran Nilsson
Department of Psychology
Stockholm University
Stockholm S-10691
Sweden

Editorial Policy: Focus on articles of either a theoretical or a review nature in order to provide an integrated rather than empirical approach. Standard reports of research findings including applied research having theoretical implications for "mainstream" cognitive psychology will also be published.

Selective Notes on Submissions: Instructions to authors included in each issue of the journal. Authors to prepare manuscripts according to the *Publication Manual of the American Psychological Association* (4th ed.). Submit four (4) copies of the manuscript to the publisher.

Journal Frequency: Quarterly

Articles/Pages Published per Year: 24 articles

Total Subscribers: 400

Book Reviews Accepted: NA

Rejection Rate: NA

Notes From Publisher: Official journal of the European Society for Cognitive Psychology.

European Journal of Personality

Publisher: John Wiley & Sons, Ltd.
Baffins Lane
Chichester PO19 1UD
England

Editor: Peter Borkenau
Department of Psychology
Martin-Luther University
Postfach 1108
Halle D-06099
Germany

Editorial Policy: The *European Journal of Personality* is intended to reflect all areas of current personality psychology. The journal will emphasize (a) human individuality as manifested in cognitive processes, emotional and motivational functioning, and personal ways of interacting with the environment; (b) individual differences in personality structure and dynamics; and (c) studies of intelligence and interindividual differences in cognitive functioning. Articles will be encouraged that reflect a European tradition in personality psychology.

Selective Notes on Submissions: Instructions to authors included in each issue of the journal. Authors to prepare manuscripts according to the Harvard style manual. Submit four (4) copies of the manuscript to the editor.

Journal Frequency: 5 issue per year

Articles/Pages Published per Year: 25/450

Total Subscribers: 300

Book Reviews Accepted: Yes

Rejection Rate: NA

European Journal of Psychological Assessment

Publisher: Hogrefe & Huber Publishers
P.O. Box 2487
Kirkland, WA 98083-2487

Länggass-Strasse 76
CH-Bern 9
Switzerland

Editors: Professor Rocío Fernández-
Ballesteros
Facultad de Psicologia
Universidad Autonoma de
Madrid
E-28049 Madrid
Spain

Professor Fernando Silva
Facultad de Psicologia
Universidad Complutense de
Madrid
E-28223 Madrid
Spain

Editorial Policy: The journal is the official organ of the *European Association of Psychological Assessment* (EAPA) and includes the Bulletin of the *International Test Commision* (ITC). The EAPA was founded to promote the practice and study of psychological assessment in Europe as well as to foster the exchange of information on this discipline around the world. The ITC is an association of national psychological societies, test commissions, test publishers, and other organizations committed to promoting proper test development and use.

Selective Notes on Submissions: Instructions to authors included in each issue of the journal. Authors to prepare manuscripts according to the *Publication Manual of the American Psychological Association* (4th ed.). Submit three (3) copies of the manuscript to the editor. Manuscripts submitted to two/three referees.

Journal Frequency: 3 issues per year

Articles/Pages Published per Year: 27/250

Total Subscribers: 420

Book Reviews Accepted: Yes

Rejection Rate: 60%

European Journal of Social Psychology

Publisher: John Wiley & Sons, Ltd.
Baffins Lane
Chichester, West Sussex PO19
1UD
England

Editor: Eddy Van Avermaet
L.E.S.P.
Tiensestraat 102
B-3000 Leuven
Belgium

Editorial Policy: The Journal is sponsored by the European Association of Experimental Social Psychology. EJSP welcomes contributions in any area of social psychology. For these purposes social psychology is broadly defined as concerning the relations between individuals and their social environments. The journal publishes research papers but also papers on theory and literature reviews. Major articles as well as short research notes are featured. Consult issue 3, 1994, for the most recent editorial policy statement. Despite the journal title, there are no restrictions as to the origins of contributions; the principal criteria for publication are the scientific merit of the work submitted and its relevance to fundamental issues in social psychology.

Selective Notes on Submissions: Instructions to authors included in each issue of the journal. No style sheet included. Submit five (5) copies of the manuscript to the editor.

Journal Frequency: Bimonthly

Articles/Pages Published per Year: 50/720

Total Subscribers: 1,385

Book Reviews Accepted: No

Rejection Rate: 70%

Notes From Publisher: Decisions normally given on submissions within 12–14 weeks of receipt by editor.

European Psychologist

Publisher: Hogrefe & Huber Publishers
Rohnsweg 25
D-37085 Gottingen
Germany

Editor: Kurt Pawlik
Department of Psychology I
University of Hamburg
Von-Melle-Park 11
D-20146 Hamburg
Germany

Editorial Policy: The *European Psychologist,* the English language voice of psychology in Europe, integrates across all specializations in psychology and provides a general platform for communication and cooperation among psychologists throughout Europe and worldwide. The *European Psychologist* accepts four kinds of contribution for peer-reviewed publication:

1. *Original Articles* form an essential section of the journal. Not necessarily focused on European aspects, these present important new findings and ideas, and are written for a nonspecialist, general readership in psychology.

2. *Contemporary Reviews* provide carefully written state-of-the-art papers on trends and developments within psychology, with possible reference to European perceptions or fields of specialization.

3. *Reports* inform readers about the work of major research and other institutions of psychology in Europe, multicenter studies, as well as European projects and issues in psychology.

4. *Commentaries and News:* The journal will act as a central source of information on important legal, regulatory, ethical, and administrative events of interest to psychologists working throughout Europe.

Selective Notes on Submissions: Instructions to authors included in each issue of the journal. Authors to prepare manuscripts according to the *Publication Manual of the American Psychological Association* (4th ed.). Submit three (3) copies of the manuscript to the editor.

Journal Frequency: Quarterly

Articles/Pages Published per Year: 24/320

Total Subscribers: NA

Book Reviews Accepted: NA

Rejection Rate: 70%

Notes From Publisher: U.S. Distributor: Educational Publishing Foundation c/o APA, 750 First Street, NE, Washington, DC 20002-4242.

Evaluation and Program Planning

Publisher: Elsevier Science Press
1000 AE Amsterdam
The Netherlands

Editor: Jonathan A. Morell
Industrial Technology Institute
P.O. Box 1485
Ann Arbor, MI 48106

Editorial Policy: *Evaluation and Program Planning* is based on the principle that the techniques and methods of evaluation and planning transcend the boundaries of specific fields and that relevant contributions to these areas come from people representing many different positions, intellectual traditions, and interests. In order to further the development of evaluation and planning, we publish articles from the private and public sectors in a wide range of areas: organizational development, planning, human resource development, public health, mental health, social service, public action, mental retardation, corrections, substance abuse, and education. The primary goals of the journal are to assist evaluators and planners to better the practice of their profession, to develop their skills, and to improve their knowledge base.

Selective Notes on Submissions: Instructions to authors included in each issue of the journal. Authors to prepare manuscripts according to the *Publication Manual of the American Psychological Association* (4th ed.). Submit three (3) copies of the manuscript to the editor.

Journal Frequency: Quarterly

Articles/Pages Published per Year: 45/400

Total Subscribers: 700

Book Reviews Accepted: NA

Rejection Rate: 55%

Evaluation Review

Publisher: Sage Publications, Inc.
2455 Teller Road
Newbury Park, CA 91320

Editor: Richard A. Berk
Department of Sociology
University of California,
Los Angeles
Los Angeles, CA 90024

Editorial Policy: *Evaluation Review* is the forum for researchers, planners, and policymakers engaged in the development, implementation, and utilization of studies aimed at the betterment of the human condition. The editors invite submission of papers reporting the findings of evaluation studies in such fields as child development, health, education, income security, manpower, mental health, criminal justice, and the physical and social environments. In addition, the journal will contain articles on methodological developments, discussions of the state of the art, and commentaries on issues related to the application of research results. Special features will include periodic review essays, "research briefs" (reports on ongoing or completed studies), and "craft reports" (focused on innovative applications of specific evaluation research techniques, concepts, and ideas).

Selective Notes on Submissions: Instructions to authors included in each issue of the journal. Authors to prepare manuscripts according to the *Chicago Manual of Style*. Submit three (3) copies of the manuscript to the editor.

Journal Frequency: Bimonthly

Articles/Pages Published per Year: 36/700

Total Subscribers: 2,538

Book Reviews Accepted: No

Rejection Rate: NA

Evolution and Human Behavior

Previous Title: *Ethology and Sociobiology*

Publisher: Elsevier Science, Inc.
655 Avenue of the Americas
New York, NY 10010

Editors: Martin Daly and Margo Wilson
Department of Psychology
McMaster University
Hamilton, Ontario
Canada L8S 4K1

Editorial Policy: *Evolution and Human Behavior* is the official journal of the interdisciplinary Human Behavior and Evolution Society. The journal publishes primary reports of empirical research, review papers that synthesize and interpret other scientists' publications, and papers that present novel theorizing. Although *Evolution and Human Behavior* is primarily a scientific journal, submissions from scholars in the humanities are also invited.

Selective Notes on Submissions: Instructions to authors included in each issue of the journal. Submit three (3) copies of the manuscript to the editor.

Journal Frequency: 6 issues per year

Articles/Pages Published per Year: 480 pp.

Total Subscribers: 1,100

Book Reviews Accepted: Yes

Rejection Rate: 70%

Experimental Aging Research

Publisher:　Taylor & Francis
　　　　　　　1101 Vermont Avenue
　　　　　　　Suite 200
　　　　　　　Washington, DC 20005

Editor:　　Jeffrey W. Elias, PhD
　　　　　　　Department of Psychology
　　　　　　　Texas Tech University
　　　　　　　P.O. Box 4100
　　　　　　　Lubbock, TX 79409-0005

Editorial Policy: *Experimental Aging Research* publishes articles dealing with age and aging at any point in development across the adult life span. Articles of behavior or biobehavioral significance are appropriate: psychology, health psychology, biopsychology, medicine, neurology, psychiatry, epidemiology, anthropology, work research and ergonomics, and behavioral medicine research. Authors should consult the last issue of each volume for editorial policy.

Selective Notes on Submissions: Authors to prepare manuscripts according to the *Publication Manual of the American Psychological Association* (4th ed.). Submit three (3) copies of the manuscript and the original to the editor.

Journal Frequency: Quarterly

Articles/Pages Published per Year: 28/400

Total Subscribers: NA

Book Reviews Accepted: No

Rejection Rate: NA

Experimental and Clinical Psychopharmacology

Publisher:　American Psychological
　　　　　　　Association
　　　　　　　750 First Street, NE
　　　　　　　Washington, DC 20002-4242

Editor:　　Charles R. Schuster
　　　　　　　Wayne State University School
　　　　　　　of Medicine
　　　　　　　University Psychiatric Center
　　　　　　　2751 East Jefferson
　　　　　　　Detroit, MI 48207

Editorial Policy: One goal of the journal is to foster basic research and the development of theory in psychopharmacology. Another is to encourage the integration of basic and applied research, the development of better treatments for drug abuse, and more effective pharmacotherapeutics. To this end, the journal publishes original empirical research involving animals or humans that spans (a) behavioral pharmacology research on social, behavioral, cognitive, emotional, physiological, and neurochemical toxicity; (b) descriptive and experimental studies of drug abuse, including its etiology, progression, adverse effects, and behavioral and pharmacological treatment; and (c) controlled clinical trials that, in addition to improving the effectiveness, range, or depth of application, will increase our understanding of psychological functions or their drug modulation. The journal also publishes theoretical and integrative analyses and reviews that promote our understanding and further systematic research in psychopharmacology. Although case studies are not appropriate, occasional small sample experiments with special populations may be considered. The journal is intended to be informative and useful to both basic and applied researchers and to practitioners operating in varied settings.

Selective Notes on Submissions: Instructions to authors included in each issue of the journal. Authors to prepare manuscripts according to the *Publication Manual of the American Psychological Association* (4th ed.). Submit five (5) copies of the manuscript to the editor.

Journal Frequency: Quarterly

Articles/Pages Published per Year: 54/480

Total Subscribers: 1,450

Book Reviews Accepted: No

Rejection Rate: 31%

Family Process

Publisher: Family Process, Inc.
P.O. Box 460
Vernon, NJ 07462

Editor: Peter Steinglass, MD
c/o Family Process
149 East 78th Street
New York, NY 10021

Editorial Policy: *Family Process* is a multidisciplinary journal that publishes clinical research, training, and theoretical contributions in the broad area of family therapy.

Selective Notes on Submissions: Instructions to authors included in each issue of the journal. Submit five (5) double-spaced copies of the manuscript to the editor.

Journal Frequency: Quarterly

Articles/Pages Published per Year: 40/600

Total Subscribers: 10,000

Book Reviews Accepted: No

Rejection Rate: 75%

Family Relations

Publisher: National Council on Family
Relations
3989 Central Avenue, NE
Suite 550
Minneapolis, MN 55421-3921

Editors: Timothy H. Brubaker
Family Relations
Family and Child Studies Center
Miami University
Oxford, OH 45056

Jeff W. Dwyer
Institute of Gerontology
Wayne State University
226 Knapp Building
87 East Ferry Street
Detroit, MI 48202

Editorial Policy: *Family Relations* is directed toward practitioners serving the family field through education, counseling, and community services. It disseminates reports of experiences in these areas, provides leads for others to explore, evaluates work using innovative methods, and discusses the application of research and theory to practice.

Selective Notes on Submissions: Manuscripts for possible publication should be submitted directly to the editor in triplicate, and should be prepared according to manuscript specifications obtainable from the editor or in the January issue of each volume. For acknowledgment of receipt, include a stamped, self-addressed postcard with manuscript title.

Journal Frequency: Quarterly

Articles/Pages Published per Year: 74/500

Total Subscribers: 6,000

Book Reviews Accepted: NA

Rejection Rate: 75–80%

Notes From Publisher: Turn-around time on new submissions is 10–12 weeks. Manuscript processing fee: $15.

Family Therapy

Publisher: Libra Publishers, Inc.
3089C Clairemont Drive
Suite 383
San Diego, CA 92117

Editor: Martin G. Blinder, MD
50 Idalia Road
San Anselmo, CA 94960

Editorial Policy: The editor welcomes succinct, well-written papers within the broad field of family and marital therapy. Clinical articles devoted to techniques, and richly endowed with illustrative dialogue, are most highly regarded.

Selective Notes on Submissions: Instructions to authors included in each issue of the journal. Authors to prepare manuscripts according to the *Publication Manual of the American Psychological Association* (4th ed.). Manuscripts must be typewritten, double-spaced, on one side of the page, and in duplicate. For acknowledgment of receipt, authors should enclose a stamped, self-addressed postcard containing the title of the work. Authors are also requested to enclose a business-size, stamped, self-addressed envelope for the report of editorial decisions. Submit directly to the publisher.

Journal Frequency: Triannually

Articles/Pages Published per Year: 24/300

Total Subscribers: 1,500

Book Reviews Accepted: Yes

Rejection Rate: 60%

Feminism and Psychology

Publisher: Sage Publications, Ltd.
6 Bonhill Street
London EC2A 4PU
England

Editor: Sue Wilkinson
Department of Social Sciences
Loughborough University
Loughborough
Leicestershire LE11 3TU
England

Editorial Policy: *Feminism and Psychology* aims to provide an international forum for debate at the interface between feminism and psychology. The principal aim of the journal is to foster the development of theory and practice in psychology and to represent the concerns of women in a wide range of contexts across the academic/ applied "divide." It publishes high-quality, original research and debates that acknowledge gender and other social inequalities and consider their psychological effects; studies of sex differences are published only when set in this critical context. Contributions should consider the implications of "race," class, sexuality, and other social inequalities where relevant. The journal seeks to maintain a balance of theoretical and empirical papers and to integrate research, practice, and broader social concerns.

Selective Notes on Submissions: Instructions to authors included in each issue of the journal. Authors to prepare manuscripts according to the Harvard style manual. Submit four (4) copies of the manuscript to the editor.

Journal Frequency: Quarterly

Articles/Pages Published per Year: 18/450

Total Subscribers: NA

Book Reviews Accepted: Yes

Rejection Rate: NA

Suggested Index Terms: Women's studies

Free Associations: Psychoanalysis, Groups, Politics, Culture

Publisher: Process Press
26 Freegrove Road
London N7 9RQ
England

Editor: Robert M. Young
c/o Process Press

Editorial Policy: *Free Associations: Psychoanalysis, Groups, Politics, Culture* is the leading English-speaking journal offering a broader perspective on psychodynamic approaches to human nature, culture, and society. The editors provide an international forum for critical thinking across the analytical tradition and believe it a constructive trend to see authors of different perspectives writing for the same journal. Because clinical experience has a unique contribution in restoring subjectivity to it, the journal shows that psychoanalysis must itself open outward to its broader culture.

Selective Notes on Submissions: Submit three (3) double-spaced copies of the manuscript (with approximate word count) to the editor.

Journal Frequency: Quarterly

Articles/Pages Published per Year: 24/640

Total Subscribers: 1,000

Book Reviews Accepted: Yes

Rejection Rate: NA

Genetic, Social, and General Psychology Monographs

Publisher: Heldref Publications
                 1319 18th Street, NW
                 Washington, DC 20036-1802

Editor: John E. Horrocks
                 Ohio State University

Editorial Policy: *Genetic, Social, and General Psychology Monographs* accepts articles of monograph length, shorter versions of which would be appropriate for publication in either the *Journal of Genetic Psychology,* the *Journal of Social Pathology,* the *Journal of General Psychology,* or the *Journal of Psychology.* As is the case with these four journals, *Genetic, Social, and General Psychology Monographs* is devoted to research and theory. Typically a *Monographs* article exceeds 35 typed pages; makes an outstanding contribution to the field of psychology; and may well present a series of research studies, a new theory, or an in-depth criticism of a recognized existing theory. Innovative research and new approaches are particularly encouraged. Monographs may deal with the biological as well as the behavioral and social aspects of psychology.

Selective Notes on Submissions: Instructions to authors included in each issue of the journal. Authors to prepare manuscripts according to the *Publication Manual of the American Psychological Association* (4th ed.). Submit the original typewritten version and one (1) copy of the manuscript to Managing Editor, *Genetic, Social, and General Psychology Monographs,* 1319 18th Street, NW, Washington, DC 20036-1802.

Journal Frequency: Quarterly

Articles/Pages Published per Year: 21/576

Total Subscribers: 830

Book Reviews Accepted: No

Rejection Rate: 50%

Notes From Publisher: Typesetting charges to author of $50/table, $20/figure, and $25 for the heavy use of statistics.

Group Analysis

Publisher: Sage Publications, Ltd.
                 6 Bonhill Street
                 London EC2A 4PU
                 England

Editor: Malcolm Pines
                 Institute of Group Analysis
                 138 Bramley Road
                 London NI4 4HU
                 England

Editorial Policy: *Group Analysis,* first published in 1967, is the journal of the Group-Analytic Society (London) and covers the theory, practice, and experience of analytic group psychotherapy. This form of psychotherapy brings together concepts derived from psychoanalytic psychology, social psychology, group dynamics, sociology, and anthropology. It uses the integrative approach pioneered by S. H. Foulkes, based on the view that we are all primarily group beings.

The journal fosters international exchange and provides a forum for dialogue among practitioners, theoreticians, and researchers from all of the above disciplines. The journal is a meeting point for these disciplines and accepts articles derived from any of them that relate to group analysis or that bring findings to the attention of group analysts. It particularly welcomes articles on research in the field of group psychotherapy and group dynamics. The journal aims to bring together differing approaches within the field of psychodynamics and does not represent one exclusive approach to group psychotherapy. Articles are also accepted that deal with the direct application of group-analytic principles of work with both small and large groups in the wider context of institutions: medical, nursing, and other health case services; education; and training in group work.

The journal welcomes commentaries on its published articles and aims to stimulate dialogue through correspondence.

Selective Notes on Submissions: Instructions to authors included in each issue of the journal. Submit four (4) copies of the manuscript to the editor.

Journal Frequency: Quarterly

Articles/Pages Published per Year: 44/520

Total Subscribers: NA

Book Reviews Accepted: Yes

Rejection Rate: NA

Suggested Index Terms: Counseling, psychotherapy

Group Dynamics: Theory, Research, and Practice

Publisher: Educational Publishing
                   Foundation
                   750 First Street, NE
                   Washington, DC 20002-4242

Editor: Donelson R. Forsyth, PhD
                   1605 Hanover Avenue
                   Richmond, VA 23220

Editorial Policy: *Group Dynamics* is the official journal of Division 49 (Group Psychology and Group Psychotherapy) of the American Psychological Association. *Group Dynamics* publishes original empirical articles, theoretical analyses, literature reviews, and brief reports dealing with basic and applied topics in the field of group research and application. The journal seeks manuscripts that examine social psychological analyses of group processes, groups in organizational settings, and the dynamics of therapeutic groups. Theoretically driven studies of hypotheses that have implications for understanding and improving groups in organizational, educational, and therapeutic settings are particularly encouraged.

Selective Notes on Submissions: Instructions to authors included in each issue of the journal. Authors to prepare manuscripts according to the *Publication Manual of the American Psychological Association* (4th ed.). Submit four (4) copies of the manuscript to the editor.

Journal Frequency: Quarterly

Articles/Pages Published per Year: NA

Total Subscribers: NA

Book Reviews Accepted: No

Rejection Rate: NA

Health Psychology

Publisher: American Psychological
                  Association
                  750 First Street, NE
                  Washington, DC 20002-4242

Editor: David S. Krantz
                  Department of Medical &
                     Clinical Psychology
                  Uniformed Services University
                     of the Health Sciences
                  4301 Jones Bridge Road
                  Bethesda, MD 20814-4799

Editorial Policy: *Health Psychology* is a scholarly journal devoted to furthering an understanding of scientific relationships between behavioral principles on the one hand and physical health and illness on the other. The readership has a broad range of backgrounds, interests, and specializations, often interdisciplinary in nature. The major type of manuscript being solicited for *Health Psychology* is the report of empirical research. Such papers should have significant theoretical or practical import for an understanding of relationships between behavior and health. Integrative papers that address themselves to a broad constituency are particularly welcome. Suitable topics for submission include, but are not restricted to, the role of environmental, psychosocial, or sociocultural factors that may contribute to disease or its prevention; behavioral methods used in the diagnosis, treatment, or rehabilitation of individuals having physical disorders; and techniques that could reduce disease risk by modifying health beliefs, attitudes, or behaviors including decisions about using professional services. Interventions used may be at the individual, group, multicenter, or community level. *Health Psychology* also encourages the submission of relevant, concise, authoritative reviews, methodological papers, and didactic articles as well as reviews of books and other media presentations. Analyses of health policy from a psychological perspective are appropriate. Scientifically based criticisms of articles appearing in the journal together with the authors' replies shall also be considered. (This is a publication of APA's Division 38.)

Selective Notes on Submissions: Instructions to authors included in each issue of the journal. Authors to prepare manuscripts according to the *Publication Manual of the American Psychological Association* (4th ed.). Submit five (5) copies of the manuscript to the editor.

Journal Frequency: Bimonthly

Articles/Pages Published per Year: 76/592

Total Subscribers: 9,000

Book Reviews Accepted: No

Rejection Rate: 84%

Hispanic Journal of Behavioral Sciences

Publisher: Sage Publications, Inc.
2455 Teller Road
Thousand Oaks, CA 91320

Editor: Amado M. Padilla, PhD
Center for Education Research
Stanford University
Stanford, CA 94305

Editorial Policy: The *Hispanic Journal of Behavioral Sciences* publishes research articles, case histories, critical reviews, and scholarly notes related to Hispanic populations that are of theoretical interest or that deal with methodological issues related to Hispanic populations. The multidisciplinary focus includes the fields of anthropology, economics, education, linguistics, political science, psychology, psychiatry, public health, and sociology. Special Issues on timely topics are also published periodically. Arrangements for Special Issues are done directly with the Editor. Material is accepted only in English that has not been published elsewhere and is not currently under review by other publications.

Selective Notes on Submissions: Instructions to authors included in each issue of the journal. Authors to prepare manuscripts according to the *Publication Manual of the American Psychological Association* (4th ed.). Submit three (3) copies of the manuscript to the editor.

Journal Frequency: Quarterly

Articles/Pages Published per Year: 35/550

Total Subscribers: 1,250

Book Reviews Accepted: Yes

Rejection Rate: 78%

Hormones and Behavior

Publisher: Academic Press, Inc.
1250 Sixth Avenue
San Diego, CA 92101

Editors: Robert W. Goy
Wisconsin Regional Primate
Research Center
1223 Capitol Court
Madison, WI 53715-1299

Editorial Policy: *Hormones and Behavior* publishes a broad range of original articles dealing diversely with behavioral systems known to be hormonally influenced. The scope extends from studies of the evolutionary significance of hormone–behavior relations to those dealing with cellular and molecular mechanisms of hormonal actions on neural tissues and other tissues relevant to behavior. The use of behavior as a major dependent or independent variable is not essential, although such studies continue to be welcome in the journal.

Selective Notes on Submissions: Instructions to authors included in each issue of the journal. Submit four (4) copies of the manuscript to: Editorial Office, Hormones and Behavior, Department of Biology, Boston University, 5 Cummington Street, Boston, MA 02215.

Journal Frequency: Quarterly

Articles/Pages Published per Year: 45/600

Total Subscribers: NA

Book Reviews Accepted: No

Rejection Rate: NA

Human Communication Research

Publisher: Sage Publications, Inc.
                2455 Teller Road
                Thousand Oaks, CA 91320

Editor: Cindy Gallois
           University of Queensland
           Department of Psychology
           Queensland 4072
           Australia

Editorial Policy: *Human Communication Research* is devoted to advancing knowledge and understanding about human symbolic activities. Manuscripts reporting original research, methodologies relevant to the study of human communication, critical syntheses of research, and theoretical and philosophical perspectives on human communicative activity are encouraged. The journal maintains a broad behavioral and social scientific focus but reflects no particular methodological or substantive biases.

Selective Notes on Submissions: Instructions to authors included in each issue of the journal. Authors to prepare manuscripts according to the *Publication Manual of the American Psychological Association* (4th ed.). Submit four (4) copies of the manuscript to the editor. E-mail abstract to editor (cg@psy.ug.oz.au).

Journal Frequency: Quarterly

Articles/Pages Published per Year: 640 pp.

Total Subscribers: 3,300

Book Reviews Accepted: No

Rejection Rate: 80%

Human Development

Publisher: S. Karger AG
           P.O. Box CH-4009
           Basel
           Switzerland

Editor: Dr. Barbara Rogoff
           Social Science II
           Room 277
           University of California
           Santa Cruz, CA 95064

Editorial Policy: NA

Selective Notes on Submissions: Instructions to authors included in each issue of the journal. Submit four (4) copies of the manuscript to the editor.

Journal Frequency: Bimonthly

Articles/Pages Published per Year: 36/360

Total Subscribers: 1,950

Book Reviews Accepted: NA

Rejection Rate: NA

Human Factors

Publisher: Human Factors and Ergonomics
Society
Box 1369
Santa Monica, CA 90406-1369

Editor: William C. Howell, PhD
Science Directorate
American Psychological
Association
750 First Street, NE
Washington, DC 20002-4242

Editorial Policy: *Human Factors*, the quarterly journal of the Human Factors and Ergonomics Society, publishes original articles about people in relation to machines and environments. Evaluative reviews of the literature, definitive articles on methodology, quantitative and qualitative approaches to theory, and empirical articles reporting original research will be considered for publication. Papers that have been published elsewhere will not, in general, be accepted. Three general categories of publication are included. Regular articles, review articles, and brief reports (12 ms pages or less), are considered. *Human Factors* also publishes special issues that focus on topics of significant current interest in human factors.

Selective Notes on Submissions: Instructions to authors included in each issue of the journal. Authors to prepare manuscripts according to the *Author's Guide* from the Human Factors and Ergonomics Society office. Submit five (5) copies of the manuscript to the editor.

Journal Frequency: Quarterly

Articles/Pages Published per Year: 60/768

Total Subscribers: 6,700

Book Reviews Accepted: No

Rejection Rate: 80%

Human Movement Science

Publisher: Elsevier Science Publishers B.V.
P.O. Box 211
1000 AE Amsterdam
The Netherlands

Editor: Dr. H. T. A. Whiting and
M. G. Whiting
Department of Psychology
University of York
Helsington, York Y01 5DD
England

Editorial Policy: *Human Movement Science* provides an interdisciplinary forum for the publication of both theoretical and empirical papers on the topic of human movement. Recognizing the fast changing nature of the field, editorial policy is sensitive to new lines of approach and to innovative theories as well as to traditional, well-established paradigms. This standpoint is reflected both in the composition of the editorial boards and the focus of special issues and target articles. Animal studies, insofar that their significance to human movement is made clear, are equally acceptable. Particular topics likely to pervade successive issues are motor control, motor learning, and coordination.

Human Movement Science contains: (a) reports of empirical work on human and animal movement; (b) overview articles on human movement that are likely to be of interest to a number of related disciplines; (c) methodological articles that focus on recording and analytical techniques for the study of movement; (d) special issues and "target" articles on topics of current importance; (e) book reviews; (f) announcements of meetings, conferences, seminars, new research programs, and staff vacancies within its field of concern.

Selective Notes on Submissions: Instructions to authors included in each issue of the journal. Authors to prepare manuscripts according to the *Publication Manual of the American Psychological Association* (4th ed.). Submit three (3) copies of the manuscript to the editor.

Journal Frequency: 6 issues per year

Articles/Pages Published per Year: 35/736

Total Subscribers: 350

Book Reviews Accepted: No

Rejection Rate: NA

Human Performance

Publisher: Lawrence Erlbaum Associates
              365 Broadway
              Hillsdale, NJ 07642

Editor: Joyce Hogan
            Department of Psychology
            University of Tulsa
            Tulsa, OK 74104

Editorial Policy: *Human Performance* publishes research on the nature of performance in the workplace and in applied settings, and encourages submission of papers that go beyond the study of traditional job behavior.

Submissions to *Human Performance* will be evaluated according to several different criteria: significance, adequacy of design and of execution of study, integrity of analyses, quality of introduction and discussion, clarity of expression, and extent to which the manuscript addresses the emphasis of the journal. Under certain circumstances, we will accept replications and studies in which the null hypothesis is not rejected.

Selective Notes on Submissions: Instructions to authors included in each issue of the journal. Authors to prepare manuscripts according to the style manual of the BPS or the *Publication Manual of the American Psychological Association* (4th ed.). Submit four (4) copies of the manuscript to the editor.

Journal Frequency: Quarterly

Articles/Pages Published per Year: 16/400

Total Subscribers: NA

Book Reviews Accepted: No

Rejection Rate: NA

Human Relations

Publisher: Plenum Publishing Corporation
              233 Spring Street
              New York, NY 10013-1578

Editor: Ray Loveridge
Tavistock Institute of Human
Relations
120 Belsize Lane
London NW3 5BA
England

Editorial Policy: *Human Relations* is founded
on the belief that social scientists in all fields
should work toward integration in their
attempts to understand the complexities of
human problems. Understanding must be
translated into action by linking theory and
practice. We wish to attract manuscripts
from a wide range of contributors who may
be working within their own discipline in a
way which is yet transcendent of it, or
deliberately crossing disciplinary boundaries.
We also wish to attract manuscripts from a
number of different countries. Our intent is
to reflect a broad spectrum of problems and
approaches toward the integration of the
social sciences. Authors may present theoretical developments, new methods, or
review articles, as well as reports of empirical research which may include both qualitative and quantitative data. As an interdisciplinary journal, we accept that there can be
no single convention in research design,
method, and presentation. We wish to
emphasize our openness to innovative
contributions in emerging fields of work,
particularly if these fall outside traditional
areas and approaches.

Selective Notes on Submissions: Instructions
to authors included in each issue of the
journal. Submit three (3) copies of the
manuscript to the editor.

Journal Frequency: Monthly

Articles/Pages Published per Year: 72/1000

Total Subscribers: NA

Book Reviews Accepted: NA

Rejection Rate: NA

Humanistic Psychologist

Publisher: Division 22
c/o Department of Psychology
University of West Georgia
Carrolton, GA 30118

Editor: Christopher M. Aanstoos, PhD
Department of Psychology
University of West Georgia
Carrolton, GA 30118

Editorial Policy: *Humanistic Psychologist*
welcomes all kinds of manuscripts, especially articles, reviews, comments, and
reports that explicate a humanistic perspective on psychotherapy, education, social
responsibility, organization and management, existential phenomenological philosophical foundations, or human science
research.

Selective Notes on Submissions: Instructions
to authors included in each issue of the
journal. Authors to prepare manuscripts
according to the *Publication Manual of the
American Psychological Association* (4th
ed.). Submit two (2) copies of the manuscript to the editor.

Journal Frequency: 3 issues per year

Articles/Pages Published per Year: 18/360

Total Subscribers: 1,200

Book Reviews Accepted: Yes

Rejection Rate: 70%

Humor: International Journal of Humor Research

Publisher: Mouton de Gruyter/Walter
                  de Gruyter, Inc.
                  Postfach 110240
                  D-1000
                  Berlin 11
                  Germany

Editor: Victor Raskin
                  Department of English
                  Purdue University
                  West Lafayette, IN 47907

Editorial Policy: *Humor* was established as an international interdisciplinary forum for the publication of high-quality research papers on humor as an important and universal human faculty. Humor research draws on a wide range of academic disciplines including anthropology, computer science, history, linguistics, literature, mathematics, medicine, philosophy, psychology, and sociology. At the same time, humor research often sheds light on the basic concepts, ideas, and methods of many of these disciplines. The Editorial Board and Board of Consulting Editors are composed of prominent humor researchers who specialize in these disciplines.

Selective Notes on Submissions: Instructions to authors included in each issue of the journal. Submit four (4) copies of the manuscript to the editor.

Journal Frequency: Quarterly

Articles/Pages Published per Year: 28/460

Total Subscribers: 500

Book Reviews Accepted: Yes

Rejection Rate: 87%

Imagination, Cognition and Personality

Publisher: Baywood Publishing Company,
                  Inc.
                  26 Austin Avenue
                  P.O. Box 337
                  Amityville, NY 11701

Editors: Kenneth S. Pope, PhD, and
                  Jerome L. Singer, PhD

Editorial Policy: This journal presents thoughtful explorations of the flow of images, fantasies, memory fragments and anticipations, which constitute our moment-to-moment experience of awareness. It presents original scientific research examining the relationship of consciousness to brain structure and function, to sensory process, to human development, to aesthetic experience, and to the flow of life events.

Selective Notes on Submissions: Instructions to authors included in each issue of the journal. Submit four (4) copies of the manuscript to Jerome L. Singer, PhD, Yale University, Box 208205 Yale Station, New Haven, CT 06520.

Journal Frequency: Quarterly

Articles/Pages Published per Year: 40–48/ 400

Total Subscribers: NA

Book Reviews Accepted: Yes

Rejection Rate: 80%

Individual Psychology

Publisher: University of Texas Press
P.O. Box 7819
Austin, TX 78713

Editor: Gerald J. Mozdzierz
Psychology Service (116B)
Department of Veterans Affairs
Edward Hines, Jr. Hospital
Hines, IL 60141

Editorial Policy: *Individual Psychology: The Journal of Adlerian Theory, Research, and Practice* follows the natural evolution of two earlier journals, *The Individual Psychologist* and *The Journal of Individual Psychology*. The new journal will continue the traditions established by these two earlier journals by publishing contributions to Adlerian practices, principles, and theoretical development as well as techniques, skills, strategies, and procedures in all fields of application.

Selective Notes on Submissions: Instructions to authors included in each issue of the journal. Authors to prepare manuscripts according to the *Publication Manual of the American Psychological Association* (4th

ed.). Submit four (4) copies of theory and research manuscripts to the editor. Submit four (4) copies of practice and application manuscripts to Jon Carlson, Route #4, Box 860, Lake Geneva, WI 53147.

Journal Frequency: Quarterly

Articles/Pages Published per Year: 36/570

Total Subscribers: 720

Book Reviews Accepted: NA

Rejection Rate: NA

Infant Behavior and Development

Publisher: Ablex Publishing Corporation
355 Chestnut Street
Norwood, NJ 07648

Editor: Carolyn Rovee-Collier
Department of Psychology
Rutgers University
Busch Campus
New Brunswick, NJ 08903

Editorial Policy: *Infant Behavior and Development* is an international, interdisciplinary journal, and publishes full-length articles and brief reports of work which makes a substantial contribution to an understanding of infancy. Both human and animal research is acceptable. Theoretical notes and commentaries will be considered, if appropriate, but preference will be given to original research.

Selective Notes on Submissions: Instructions to authors included in each issue of the journal. Authors to prepare manuscripts according to the *Publication Manual of the American Psychological Association* (4th ed.). Submit four (4) copies of the manuscript to the editor. Dot-matrix is not acceptable.

Journal Frequency: Quarterly

Articles/Pages Published per Year: 40/500

Total Subscribers: 1,200

Book Reviews Accepted: NA

Rejection Rate: NA

Notes From Publisher: Authors should retain original artwork until manuscript is formally accepted.

Infant Mental Health Journal

Publisher: John Wiley & Sons
605 Third Avenue
New York, NY 10158

Editor: Joy D. Osofsky
Division of Child Psychiatry
Louisiana State University
    Medical School
1524 Tulane Avenue
New Orleans, LA 70112-2822

Editorial Policy: *Infant Mental Health Journal* publishes research articles, literature reviews, program evaluations, intervention programs, clinical studies, and book reviews that focus on infant social–emotional development, caregiver–infant interactions, contextual and cultural influences on infant

and family development, and all conditions that place infants and/or their families at risk for less-than-optimal development.

Selective Notes on Submissions: Instructions to authors included in each issue of the journal. Authors to prepare manuscripts according to the *Publication Manual of the American Psychological Association* (4th ed.). Submit four (4) copies of the manuscript to the editor.

Journal Frequency: Quarterly

Articles/Pages Published per Year: 32/480

Total Subscribers: 980

Book Reviews Accepted: Yes

Rejection Rate: 68%

Intelligence

Publisher: Ablex Publishing Corporation
355 Chestnut Street
Norwood, CA 07648

Editor: Douglas K. Detterman
Department of Psychology
Case Western Reserve
    University
10900 Euclid Avenue
Cleveland, OH 44106-7123

Editorial Policy: The journal *Intelligence* publishes papers reporting work which makes a substantial contribution to an understanding of the nature and function of intelligence. Varied approaches to the problem will be welcomed. Theoretical and review articles will be considered, if appropriate, but preference will be given to original research. In general, studies concerned with application will not be considered appropriate unless the work also makes a contribution to basic knowledge.

Selective Notes on Submissions: Instructions to authors included in each issue of the journal. Authors to prepare manuscripts according to the *Publication Manual of the American Psychological Association* (4th ed.). Submit four (4) copies of the manuscript to the editor.

Journal Frequency: Bimonthly

Articles/Pages Published per Year: 24/600

Total Subscribers: 650

Book Reviews Accepted: NA

Rejection Rate: NA

International Forum for Logotherapy: Journal of Search for Meaning

Publisher: Viktor Frankl Institute
          of Logotherapy

Editor: R. R. Hutzell
          VA Medical Center
          P.O. Drawer 112
          Knoxville, IA 50138-0112

Editorial Policy: The *Forum* publishes meaning-oriented existential articles relevant to the philosophy and therapy developed by Viktor Frankl. The *Forum* accepts original manuscripts that describe research, theoretical papers, innovative logotherapeutic techniques, case studies, and experiential reports.

Selective Notes on Submissions: Authors to prepare manuscripts according to the *Publication Manual of the American Psychological Association* (4th ed.). Submit two (2) copies of the manuscript to the editor. There are no page costs, membership requirements, etc. The *Forum* is abstracted in Psych Abstracts, Index Medicus, and elsewhere.

Journal Frequency: 2 issues per year

Articles/Pages Published per Year: 24/128

Total Subscribers: 300

Book Reviews Accepted: Yes

Rejection Rate: 40%

International Journal of Aging and Human Development

Publisher: Baywood Publishing Company,
          Inc.
          26 Austin Avenue
          P.O. Box 337
          Amityville, NY 11701

Editor: Robert Kastenbaum
          Department of Communication
          Arizona State University
          Tempe, AZ 85287-1205

Editorial Policy: Under what conditions does "development" end? Under what conditions does "aging" begin? Can these conditions themselves be modified by intervention at the psychological, social, or biological levels? To what extent are patterns of development and aging attributable to biological factors? To psychological factors? How can the social and behavioral sciences contribute to the actualization of human potential throughout the entire life span? What are the implications of gerontological research for our understanding of the total development of the human organism?

These are some of the broad questions with which the *International Journal of Aging and Human Development* is concerned. Emphasis is on psychological and social studies of aging and the aged. However, the journal also publishes research that introduces observations from other fields that illuminate the "human" side of gerontology or utilize gerontological observations to illuminate problems in other fields.

Selective Notes on Submissions: Instructions to authors included in each issue of the journal. Authors to prepare manuscripts according to the *Publication Manual of the American Psychological Association* (4th ed.). Submit three (3) copies of the manuscript to the editor. Theory and discussion articles are welcome.

Journal Frequency: 8 issues per year

Articles/Pages Published per Year: 40/640

Total Subscribers: NA

Book Reviews Accepted: No

Rejection Rate: 80%

International Journal of Aviation Psychology

Publisher: Lawrence Erlbaum Associates
365 Broadway
Hillsdale, NJ 17642

Editor: Richard S. Jensen
OSU Aviation Program
164 West 19th Avenue
Ohio State University
Columbus, OH 43210

Editorial Policy: The *International Journal of Aviation Psychology* will publish scholarly articles developed within this increasingly important field of study. The impetus for this journal, the Biennial International Symposium on Aviation Psychology, described aviation psychology as the development and management of safe, effective aviation systems from the standpoint of the human operators. Four divergent academic disciplines that have continually offered support to the study of aviation psychology are expected to contribute heavily to the contents of the journal, making it truly interdisciplinary. These fields are engineering and computer science, psychology, education, and physiology.

Selective Notes on Submissions: Instructions to authors included in each issue of the journal. Authors to prepare manuscripts according to the *Publication Manual of the American Psychological Association* (4th ed.). Submit three (3) copies of the manuscript to the editor.

Journal Frequency: Quarterly

Articles/Pages Published per Year: 24/400

Total Subscribers: NA

Book Reviews Accepted: Yes

Rejection Rate: 50%

International Journal of Behavioral Development

Publisher: Psychology Press
27 Church Road
Hove, East Sussex BN3 2FA
England

Editor: Rainer K. Silbereisen
IJBD Office
Department of Developmental
Psychology
Friedrich Schiller University
of Jena
Am Steiger 3/1, D-07743
Germany

Editorial Policy: Official journal of the International Society for the Study of Behavioral Development. As a forum for the respected international society, this journal promotes the discovery and application of knowledge about developmental processes at all stages of the lifespan, from infancy through old age. Each issue reports interdisciplinary research in behavioral development, including original research, theoretical reviews, book reviews, and regional research.

Selective Notes on Submissions: Instructions to authors included in each issue of the journal. Authors to prepare manuscripts according to the *Publication Manual of the American Psychological Association* (4th ed.). Submit four (4) copies of the manuscript to the editor.

Journal Frequency: Quarterly

Articles/Pages Published per Year: 32/512

Total Subscribers: 892

Book Reviews Accepted: Yes

Rejection Rate: NA

Notes From Publisher: Book reviews can be submitted to the editor.

International Journal of Behavioral Medicine

Publisher: Lawrence Erlbaum Associates
10 Industrial Avenue
Mahwah, NJ 07430-2262

Editor: Neil Schneiderman
Department of Psychology
University of Miami
Coral Gables, FL 33124

Editorial Policy: This scholarly journal is devoted to furthering an understanding of scientific relations between sociocultural, psychosocial, and behavioral principles on the one hand and biological processes, physical health, and illness on the other. Its readership has a broad range of backgrounds, interests and specializations. The journal's makeup emphasizes original research on such topics as the role of environmental, psychosocial, or sociocultural factors that may contribute to disease or its prevention; animal behavior studies that provide insight into pathophysiological processes; and behavioral methods used in the diagnosis, treatment, or rehabilitation of individuals having physical disorders. All material has significant theoretical or practical import for an understanding of behavioral medicine. [International Society of Behavioral Medicine]

Selective Notes on Submissions: Instructions to authors included in each issue of the journal. Authors to prepare manuscripts according to the *Publication Manual of the American Psychological Association* (4th ed.). Submit five (5) copies of the manuscript to the editor. Contact editor concerning requirements.

Journal Frequency: Quarterly

Articles/Pages Published per Year: NA

Total Subscribers: 1,000

Book Reviews Accepted: No

Rejection Rate: 70%

International Journal of Clinical and Experimental Hypnosis

Publisher: Sage Publications, Inc.
2455 Teller Road
Thousand Oaks, CA 91320

Editor: Fred H. Frankel, MBChB, DPM
Department of Psychiatry
Beth Israel Deaconess
    Medical Center
330 Brookline Avenue
Boston, MA 02215

Editorial Policy: Official publication of the Society for Clinical and Experimental Hypnosis. Publishes only original research papers dealing with hypnosis in psychology, psychiatry, the medical and dental specialties, and allied areas of science. Articles include clinical and experimental studies, answers to clinical questions in a master-class section, discussions of theory, significant historical and cultural material, and related data.

Selective Notes on Submissions: Instructions to authors included in each issue of the journal. Authors to prepare manuscripts according to the style of the journal (references according to the *Publication Manual of the American Psychological Association,* 4th ed.). Submit original (typed on a 10-pitch, letter quality printer or typewriter) and three (3) copies of the manuscript to the editor. Dot matrix not acceptable.

Journal Frequency: Quarterly

Articles/Pages Published per Year: 16/448

Total Subscribers: 2,700

Book Reviews Accepted: Yes

Rejection Rate: NA

Notes From Publisher: Contributors need not be members of the Society.

International Journal of Eating Disorders

Publisher: John Wiley & Sons, Inc.
605 Third Avenue
New York, NY 10158

Editor: Michael Strober, PhD
Neuropsychiatric Institute
University of California
760 Westwood Plaza
Los Angeles, CA 90024

Editorial Policy: The journal publishes basic research, clinical, and theoretical articles of scholarly substance on a variety of aspects of anorexia nervosa, bulimia, obesity, and other atypical patterns of eating behavior and body weight regulation in clinical and normal populations. Full-length articles of brief reports addressing psychological, biological, psychodynamic, sociocultural, epidemiologic, or therapeutic correlates of these clinical phenomena are welcome. Manuscripts submitted should represent a significant addition to our knowledge, or a significant review and synthesis of existing literature.

Selective Notes on Submissions: Instructions to authors included in each issue of the journal. Authors to prepare manuscripts according to the *Publication Manual of the American Psychological Association* (4th ed.). Submit three (3) copies of the manuscript to the editor.

Journal Frequency: 8 issues per year

Articles/Pages Published per Year: 85/800

Total Subscribers: 1,100

Book Reviews Accepted: No

Rejection Rate: NA

International Journal of Group Psychotherapy

Publisher: Guilford Publications, Inc.
72 Spring Street
New York, NY 10012

Editor: William E. Piper, PhD
Department of Psychology
8440-112th Street
University of Alberta
Edmonton, Alberta
Canada T6G 2B7

Editorial Policy: Devoted to reporting and interpreting the theory, research, training, and practice of group psychotherapy, this journal reflects the diversity of work being done and promotes appropriate validation. By serving as a forum for the exchange of ideas and experience, as well as reviews of appropriate books, it aims to clarify and expand knowledge about group technique.

Selective Notes on Submissions: Instructions to authors included in each issue of the journal. Authors to prepare manuscripts according to the *Publication Manual of the American Psychological Association* (4th ed.). Submit six (6) copies of the manuscript to the American Group Psychotherapy Association, 25 East 21st Street, 6th Floor, New York, NY 10010.

Journal Frequency: Quarterly

Articles/Pages Published per Year: 32/575

Total Subscribers: 6,500

Book Reviews Accepted: Yes

Rejection Rate: 60%

International Journal of Offender Therapy and Comparative Criminology

Publisher: Sage Publications
2455 Teller Road
Thousand Oaks, CA 91320

Editor: Edward M. Scott, PhD
Professor Emeritus of Psychiatry
Oregon Health Sciences
University
254 Gaines Hall
840 SW Gaines Road
Portland, OR 97201-2985

Editorial Policy: *International Journal of Offender Therapy and Comparative Criminology* continues to provide an international forum for research, discussion, and treatment of the variables associated with crime and deliquency, placing an emphasis on theoretical and practical issues related to the treatment of offenders.

Selective Notes on Submissions: Submit two (2) copies of the manuscript along with the original, double spaced, with an abstract of not more than 150 words, to the editor.

Journal Frequency: Quarterly

Articles/Pages Published per Year: 39/386

Total Subscribers: 700

Book Reviews Accepted: Yes

Rejection Rate: NA

International Journal of Play Therapy

Publisher: Association for Play Therapy, Inc.
c/o California School of
Professional Psychology
5130 East Clinton Way
Fresno, CA 93727

Editor: Cynthia K. Bromberg
Veterans' Administration
Medical Center
Fresno, CA

Editorial Policy: The *International Journal of Play Therapy* publishes reports of original research, case studies, theoretical articles, and substantive reviews of topics germane to play therapy. Its purpose is to provide information and ideas about the complete spectrum of clinical interventions used in play therapy to the community of practitioners who employ it. This community includes clinical, counseling, and educational psychologists; clinical social workers; guidance counselors; marriage and family therapists; and teachers.

Play therapists espouse many different theoretical orientations. Papers may be expected to represent any of these diverse points of view and will be considered appropriate if they integrate an underlying theory with play therapy applications.

Selective Notes on Submissions: Instructions to authors included in each issue of the journal. Authors to prepare manuscripts according to the *Publication Manual of the American Psychological Association* (4th ed.). Submit four (4) copies of the manuscript to the publisher.

Journal Frequency: 2 issues per year

Articles/Pages Published per Year: 10/140

Total Subscribers: 5,000

Book Reviews Accepted: No

Rejection Rate: NA

International Journal of Psychology

Publisher: Psychology Press
27 Church Road
Hove, East Sussex BN3 2FA
England

Editor: Dr. François Y. Doré
Ecole de psychologie
Pavillon F.A. Savard, Université
    Laval
Quebec
Canada G1K 7P4

Editorial Policy: The *International Journal of Psychology* is the journal of the International Union of Psychological Science (IUPsyS) and is edited by the IUPsyS. Its purpose is to circulate scientific information within and among subdisciplines of psychology and to foster the development of psychological science around the world.

The main part of each issue is devoted to empirical and theoretical papers in various fields of scientific psychology. Fields covered include general psychology (perception, learning, cognitive processes, language, etc.), neuropsychology, and developmental psychology, as well as social, biological, and cross-cultural psychology. The journal emphasizes basic research and theory rather than technical and applied problems. With the aim of overcoming local limitations in psychology, the journal is also devoted to international discussions of theories and methods on which psychologists from various countries and regions may differ.

Many of *IJP*'s issues include a second section, the *International Platform for Psychologists,* which provides an opportunity to exchange news and opinions on psychology as an academic and applied profession. This section also contains information about the IUPsyS, about major international meetings, and about the activities of the National Psychological Societies. Finally it offers an opportunity to express opinions and to discuss internationally significant psychological issues.

Selective Notes on Submissions: Instructions to authors included in each issue of the journal. Authors to prepare manuscripts according to the *Publication Manual of the American Psychological Association* (4th ed.). Submit four (4) copies of the manuscript to the editor.

Journal Frequency: 6 issues per year

Articles/Pages Published per Year: 36/650

Total Subscribers: 700

Book Reviews Accepted: Yes

Rejection Rate: 70%

Notes From Publisher: Material for the International Platform Section should be submitted to one of the following Associate Editors: Dr. Bruce Overmier, Psychology Department, University of Minnesota, 75 East River Road, Minneapolis, MN 55455; Dr. Pierre Ritchie, School of Psychology, University of Ottawa, Ottawa, Ontario K1N 6N5, Canada

International Journal for the Psychology of Religion

Publisher: Lawrence Erlbaum Associates
365 Broadway
Hillsdale, NJ 07642

Editors: L. B. Brown
Alister Hardy Research Centre
Westminster College
Oxford OX2 9AT
England

Ralph W. Hood, Jr.
Department of Psychology
University of Tennessee
Chattanooga, TN 37403

H. Newton Malony
Fuller Theological Seminary

Editorial Policy: The *International Journal for the Psychology of Religion* is a world journal devoted to psychological studies of religious processes and phenomena in all religious traditions. It provides a means for sustained discussion of psychologically relevant issues that can be examined empirically and that concern religion in the most general sense. Work should be of interest to those in the social sciences and those with theological or more general interests in this broad field. Therefore, the journal aims to disseminate psychological theory and research that relates to religion across the national and cultural traditions.

Selective Notes on Submissions: Instructions to authors included in each issue of the journal. Authors to prepare manuscripts according to the *Publication Manual of the American Psychological Association* (4th ed.). Submit four (4) copies of the manuscript to any editor.

Journal Frequency: Quarterly

Articles/Pages Published per Year: 24/240

Total Subscribers: NA

Book Reviews Accepted: Yes

Rejection Rate: NA

International Journal of Short-Term Psychotherapy

Publisher: John Wiley & Sons, Inc.
605 Third Avenue
New York, NY 10158

Editors: Jean-Michel Gaillard
2 Chemin du Petit Bel-Air
CH1225 Chene-Bourg
Geneva
Switzerland

Tewfik Said
Department of Psychiatry
Montreal General Hospital
1650 Cedar Avenue
Montreal, Quebec
Canada H3G 2A4

Editorial Policy: The *International Journal of Short-Term Psychotherapy* is dedicated to providing both researchers and practitioners access to the ongoing clinical work and research in the whole spectrum of short-term psychotherapy; publishes an average of 15–20 articles per year in many systems of short-term psychotherapy such as short-term dynamic psychotherapy, short-term group therapy, and short-term cognitive therapy, as they apply to the wide range of emotional disorders. Each article is about 30 to 40 typed pages, APA standard.

Selective Notes on Submissions: Instructions to authors included in each issue of the journal. Authors to prepare manuscripts according to the *Publication Manual of the American Psychological Association* (4th ed.). Submit three (3) copies of the manuscript to one of the editors.

Journal Frequency: Quarterly

Articles/Pages Published per Year: 18/600

Total Subscribers: 650

Book Reviews Accepted: NA

Rejection Rate: NA

International Journal of Sport Psychology

Publisher: Edizione Luigi Pozzi
Via Panama 68
00198 Roma
Italy

Editors: Alberto Cei
via Panama 68
00198 Roma
Italia

John H. Salmela
University of Ottawa
School of Human Kinetics
125 University
Ottawa, Ontario
Canada KIN 6NS

Editorial Policy: An official journal of the International Society of Sports Psychology.

Selective Notes on Submissions: Instructions to authors included in each issue of the journal. Authors to prepare manuscripts according to the *Publication Manual of the American Psychological Association* (4th ed.). Submit four (4) copies of the manuscript to the editor. Authors from the Americas, submit papers to John H. Salmela.

Journal Frequency: Quarterly

Articles/Pages Published per Year: 30/110

Total Subscribers: 1,100

Book Reviews Accepted: Yes

Rejection Rate: 55%

Irish Journal of Psychology

Publisher: Psychological Society of Ireland

Editors: Ken Brown and
Carol McGuinness, Editors
School of Psychology
The Queens University
Belfast BT7 1NN
Northern Ireland

Editorial Policy: The Editorial Board of the *Irish Journal of Psychology* will consider for publication critical reviews of the literature and original articles dealing with theory, methodology or empirical findings in any branch of pure or applied psychology. In addition, the journal publishes book reviews and the abstracts of theses for which higher degrees in psychology have been awarded by Irish universities. There is no restriction to Irish authors; contributions are welcome from throughout the world. However, only articles submitted in English can be considered. Occasionally, whole issues may be devoted to a special theme. In these instances a Guest Editor may be invited to coordinate contributions.

Selective Notes on Submissions: Instructions to authors included in each issue of the journal. Authors to prepare manuscripts according to the *Publication Manual of the American Psychological Association* (4th ed.). Submit three (3) copies plus a disk copy of the manuscript to the editor.

Journal Frequency: Quarterly

Articles/Pages Published per Year: 400/500

Total Subscribers: 1,200

Book Reviews Accepted: Yes

Rejection Rate: 20–30%

Israel Journal of Psychiatry and Related Sciences: The Official Publication of the Israel Psychiatric Association

Publishers: International Universities Press, Inc.
59 Boston Post Road
P.O. Box 1524
Madison, CT 06443

Gefen Publishing
P.O. Box 6056
Jerusalem 91060
Israel

Editor: Dr. David Greenberg
Jerusalem Mental Health Center
Herzog Hospital
P.O. Box 35300
Jerusalem 91351
Israel

Editorial Policy: The *Israel Journal of Psychiatry and Related Sciences* is the official publication of the Israel Psychiatric Association. Articles are presented on topics of interest to the practicing clinician. Both biologic and psychodynamic approaches are well represented.

Selective Notes on Submissions: Please send manuscripts to the editor.

Journal Frequency: Quarterly

Articles/Pages Published per Year: 32/300

Total Subscribers: 1,000

Book Reviews Accepted: Yes

Rejection Rate: NA

Issues in Mental Health Nursing

Publisher: Taylor & Francis
1101 Vermont Avenue, NW
Suite 200
Washington, DC 20005

Editor: Mary Swanson Crockett
School of Nursing
University of Texas at Austin
1700 Red River
Austin, TX 78701-1499

Editorial Policy: *Issues in Mental Health Nursing* is a refereed journal designed to expand the literature on the psychosocial and mental health aspects of nursing care currently available to students, educators, and practitioners. The journal's main emphasis is on new, innovative approaches to client care, analysis of current issues, and nursing research findings.

Because clinical research is the primary vehicle for the development of nursing science, the journal presents articles that report research findings and lists studies conducted by nurses that focus on the caretaking process. The journal also presents articles that address the application of the nursing process to clients and families for the purpose of mental health promotion, prevention of psychosocial dysfunction, and the resolution or amelioration of existing problems.

A holistic approach to mental health emphasizes the need to acknowledge the mutual interaction and influence between the client and the environment. Families, caretakers, the proximate milieu, and society are significantly influential dimensions of this environment that nurses need to understand. Articles covering current social issues that either directly or indirectly influence the practice of mental health nursing are welcome.

Selective Notes on Submissions: Instructions to authors included in each issue of the journal. Authors to prepare manuscripts according to the *Publication Manual of the American Psychological Association* (4th ed.). Follow Webster's *Third New International Dictionary* for spelling and *Dorland's Illustrated Medical Dictionary* for medical terms. Submit three (3) copies of the manuscript to the editor. Send book reviews to

Elizabeth Leaman Ruefli, University of Texas at Austin, 1700 Red River, Austin, TX 78701.

Journal Frequency: Bimonthly

Articles/Pages Published per Year: 35/600

Total Subscribers: NA

Book Reviews Accepted: Yes

Rejection Rate: NA

Issues in Psychoanalytic Psychology

Previous Title: *Issues in Ego Psychology*

Publisher: Washington Square Institute for Psychotherapy and Mental Health
41 East 11th Street
New York, NY 10003

Editor: Edward Hoberman

Editorial Policy: Washington Square Institute considers for publication manuscripts from readers dealing with theoretical or clinical issues relevant to the field of psychodynamic theory and practice. Manuscripts should be addressed to the editor and accompanied by a brief professional vita suitable for inclusion among the contributors.

Selective Notes on Submissions: No style sheet included. Submit two (2) copies of the manuscript to the editor in care of the publisher.

Journal Frequency: Semiannually

Articles/Pages Published per Year: 250 pp.

Total Subscribers: 300

Book Reviews Accepted: Yes

Rejection Rate: NA

Journal of Abnormal Child Psychology

Publisher: Plenum Publishing Corporation
233 Spring Street
New York, NY 10013-1578

Editor: Donald K. Routh
Department of Psychology
University of Miami
P.O. Box 248185
Coral Gables, FL 33124

Editorial Policy: The *Journal of Abnormal Child Psychology* is devoted to studies of behavioral pathology in childhood and adolescence. The journal publishes papers on research and theory concerned with psychopathology in childhood and adolescence. Priority is given to empirical investigations in etiology, assessment, treatment in the community and correctional institutions, prognosis and follow-up, epidemiology, remediation in the educational setting, pharmacological intervention, and studies related to ecology of abnormal behavior. The target populations comprise subjects exhibiting a variety of neurotic and organic disorders, delinquency, psychosomatic conditions, and disorders of behavior in

mental retardation. Although the journal emphasizes original experimental and correlational research, significant case studies and brief reports detailing meaningful results of ongoing projects are also published.

Selective Notes on Submissions: Instructions to authors included in each issue of the journal. Authors to prepare manuscripts according to the *Publication Manual of the American Psychological Association* (4th ed.). Submit three (3) copies of the manuscript to the editor at P.O. Box 24-8074, Coral Gables, FL 33124.

Journal Frequency: Bimonthly

Articles/Pages Published per Year: 60/750

Total Subscribers: NA

Book Reviews Accepted: NA

Rejection Rate: NA

Journal of Abnormal Psychology

Publisher: American Psychological Association
750 First Street, NE
Washington, DC 20002-4242

Editor: Milton E. Strauss
Department of Psychology
Case Western Reserve University
10900 Euclid Avenue
Cleveland, OH 44106-7123

Editorial Policy: The *Journal of Abnormal Psychology* publishes articles on basic research and theory in the broad field of abnormal behavior, its determinants, and its correlates. The following general topics fall within its area of major focus: (a) psychopathology—its etiology, development, symptomatology, and course; (b) normal processes in abnormal individuals; (c) pathological or atypical features of the behavior of normal persons; (d) experimental studies, with human or animal subjects, relating to disordered emotional behavior or pathology; (e) sociocultural effects on pathological processes, including the influence of gender and ethnicity; and (f) tests of hypotheses from psychological theories that relate to abnormal behavior. Thus, studies of patient populations, analyses of abnormal behavior and motivation in terms of modern behavior theories, case histories, experiments, on the nature of hypnosis and the mechanisms underlying hypnotic phenomena, and theoretical papers of scholarly substance on deviant personality and emotional abnormality would all fall within the boundaries of the journal's interests. Each article should represent an addition to knowledge and understanding of abnormal behavior either in its etiology, description, or change. In order to improve the use of journal resources, it has been agreed by the two editors concerned that the *Journal of Abnormal Psychology* will not consider articles dealing with the diagnosis or treatment of abnormal behavior, and the *Journal of Consulting and Clinical Psychology* will not consider articles dealing with etiology or descriptive pathology of abnormal behavior. Articles that appear to have a significant contribution to both of these broad areas may be sent to either journal for editorial decision.

Selective Notes on Submissions: Instructions to authors included in each issue of the journal. Authors to prepare manuscripts according to the *Publication Manual of the American Psychological Association* (4th ed.). Submit five (5) copies of the manuscript to the editor.

Journal Frequency: Quarterly

Articles/Pages Published per Year: 73/688

Total Subscribers: 8,800

Book Reviews Accepted: No

Rejection Rate: 74%

Journal of Adolescent Research

Publisher: Sage Publications, Inc.
2455 Teller Road
Thousand Oaks, CA 91320

Editor: E. Ellen Thornburg
10030 North Roxbury Drive
Tucson, AZ 85737

Editorial Policy: The *Journal of Adolescent Research* is a peer-reviewed journal that publishes articles on the psychological, cognitive, and physical development of individuals between 10 and 20 years of age. Studies of normal and disturbed adolescents are appropriate. The primary aim of the journal is to publish the results of empirical investigations, but reviews of literature and theoretical articles will be published.

Selective Notes on Submissions: Instructions to authors included in each issue of the journal. Authors to prepare manuscripts according to the *Publication Manual of the*

American Psychological Association (4th ed.). Submit five (5) copies of the manuscript to the editor.

Journal Frequency: Quarterly

Articles/Pages Published per Year: 32/480

Total Subscribers: 1,075

Book Reviews Accepted: No

Rejection Rate: NA

Journal of Affective Disorders

Publisher: Elsevier Science Publishers, B.V.
P.O. Box 2759
1000 CT Amsterdam
The Netherlands

Editor: C. Katona
University College London
    Medical School
Department of Psychiatry
Wolfson Building
Middlesex Hospital
Riding House Street
London W1N 8AA
England

Editorial Policy: The *Journal of Affective Disorders* publishes papers concerned with affective disorders in the widest sense: depression, mania, anxiety, and panic. It is interdisciplinary and aims to bring together different approaches for a diverse readership. High quality papers will be accepted dealing with any aspect of affective disorders, including biochemistry, pharmacology, endocrinology, genetics, statistics, epidemi-

ology, psychodynamics, classification, clinical studies, and studies of all types of treatment.

Selective Notes on Submissions: Instructions to authors included in each issue of the journal. Authors to prepare manuscripts according to the Harvard style manual. Submit three (3) copies of the manuscript.

Journal Frequency: Monthly

Articles/Pages Published per Year: 108/724

Total Subscribers: NA

Book Reviews Accepted: Yes

Rejection Rate: NA

Journal of Aging and Health

Publisher: Sage Publications, Inc.
2455 Teller Road
Thousand Oaks, CA 91320

Editor: Kyriakos S. Markides, PhD
Department of Preventative
    Medicine and Community
    Health
University of Texas Medical
    Branch
Galveston, TX 77555-1153

Editorial Policy: The *Journal of Aging and Health* is an interdisciplinary forum for the presentation of research findings and scholarly exchange in the area of aging and health. Manuscripts are sought that deal with social and behavioral factors related to health and aging. Disciplines represented include: the behavioral and social sciences, public health, epidemiology, demography, health services research, nursing, social work, medicine and related disciplines. Although preference is given to manuscripts presenting the findings of original research, review and methodological pieces will also be considered. Authors of review papers are encouraged to contact the editor before submission.

Selective Notes on Submissions: Instructions to authors included in each issue of the journal. Authors to prepare manuscripts according to the *Publication Manual of the American Psychological Association* (4th ed.). Submit four (4) copies of the manuscript to the editor.

Journal Frequency: Quarterly

Articles/Pages Published per Year: 26/600

Total Subscribers: 1,400

Book Reviews Accepted: No

Rejection Rate: 80%

Notes From Publisher: First issue February 1989.

Journal of Aging Studies

Publisher: JAI Press, Inc.
55 Old Post Road, No. 2
P.O. Box 1678
Greenwich, CT 06836-1678

Editor: Jaber F. Gubrium
Department of Sociology
University of Florida
Gainesville, FL 32611-7330

Editorial Policy: The *Journal of Aging Studies* features scholarly papers offering new interpretations and challenging existing theory and empirical work. Articles need not deal with the field of aging as a whole but with any defensibly relevant topic pertinent to the aging experience and related to the broad concerns and subject matter of the social and behavioral sciences and the humanities. The journal highlights innovation and critique (new directions in general) regardless of theoretical and methodological orientation or academic discipline. Critical, empirical, and theoretical contributions are welcome.

Selective Notes on Submissions: Instructions to authors included in each issue of the journal. Authors to prepare manuscripts according to the *Publication Manual of the American Psychological Association* (4th ed.). Submit four (4) copies of the manuscript to the editor.

Journal Frequency: Quarterly

Articles/Pages Published per Year: NA

Total Subscribers: NA

Book Reviews Accepted: No

Rejection Rate: 80%

Journal of the American Academy of Psychoanalysis

Publisher: Guilford Publications, Inc.
                   72 Spring Street
                   New York, NY 10012

Editor: Jules Bemporad, MD
                   415 Toni Lane
                   Mamaroneck, NY 10543

Editorial Policy: We welcome any material (articles, clinical notes, book reviews, letters to the editor) specifically related to psycho-analytic theory or therapy. Our authors have included psyichiatrists, psychologists, social workers, sociologists, anthropologists, historians, political scientists, professors of literature, etc.

Selective Notes on Submissions: Instructions to authors included in each issue of the journal. Submit four (4) copies of the manuscript to the editor.

Journal Frequency: Quarterly

Articles/Pages Published per Year: 40–45/720

Total Subscribers: 1,500

Book Reviews Accepted: Yes

Rejection Rate: NA

Journal of the American Psychoanalytic Association

Publisher: The Analytic Press
                   309 East 49th Street
                   New York, NY 10017

Editor: Theodore Shapiro, MD

Editorial Policy: The *Journal of the American Psychoanalytic Association* offers the newest and most significant findings in clinical and theoretical psychoanalysis. It presents both practitioners and scholars with the cutting edge of current psychoanalytic thinking, rounding scholarly and clinical issues. Although most articles are clinical and theoretical, also included are applied psychoanalytic contributions and statistical empirical studies on psychoanalytic method and practice.

Selective Notes on Submissions: Instructions to authors included in each issue of the journal. Only articles submitted solely to the *Journal* can be considered for publication. All manuscripts should conform with the style of the *Journal*. Manuscripts may not be returned.

Journal Frequency: Quarterly

Articles/Pages Published per Year: 42/1350

Total Subscribers: 7,500

Book Reviews Accepted: Yes

Rejection Rate: NA

Journal of the American Society for Psychical Research

Publisher: American Society for Psychical
Research
5 West 73rd Street
New York, NY 10023

Editor: Rhea A. White
414 Rockledge Road
New Bern, NC 28562

Editorial Policy: The purpose and scope of the society is (a) The investigation of telepathy, clairvoyance, precognition, veridical hallucinations and dreams, psychometry, and other forms of paranormal cognition; of phenomena bearing upon the hypothesis of survival of bodily death; of claims of paranormal psychical phenomena such as psychokinesis and poltergeists; the study of automatic writing, trance speech, alterations of personality, and other subconscious processes insofar as they may be related to paranormal processes; in short, all types of phenomena called parapsychological or paranormal. (b) The collection, classification, study, and publication of reports dealing with the above phenomena. Readers are asked to report incidents and cases. Names and places must be given, but on request will be treated as confidential. (c) The maintenance of a library on psychical research and related subjects. Contributions of books and periodical files will be welcomed.

Selective Notes on Submissions: Correspondence relating to the journal should be addressed to the editor. All material offered for publication should be in quadruplicate and typewritten (double-spaced). Tables, footnotes, and references should be in the form used in the journal.

Journal Frequency: Quarterly

Articles/Pages Published per Year: 18/410

Total Subscribers: 2,000

Book Reviews Accepted: Solicited only

Rejection Rate: 45%

Journal of Analytical Psychology

Publisher: Routledge
ITP Journals
2-6 Boundary Row
London SE1 8HN
England

Editors: Coline Covington,
Barbara Wharton (UK),
John Beebe (US)

Editorial Policy: Papers dealing with any aspect of analytical psychology are invited, but preference will be given to those having a direct bearing on its clinical application.

Selective Notes on Submissions: Instructions to authors included in each issue of the journal. Submit two (2) copies of the manuscript to the editor. Send manuscripts to the editors at: 1 Daleham Gardens, London, NW3 5BY, U.K.

Journal Frequency: Quarterly

Articles/Pages Published per Year: 24/600

Total Subscribers: NA

Book Reviews Accepted: NA

Rejection Rate: NA

Journal of Anxiety Disorders

Publisher: Elsevier Science Ltd.
                   660 White Plains Road
                   Tarrytown, NY 10591-5153

Editors: Cynthia G. Last, PhD, and
                   Michael Herson, PhD
                   Department of Psychology
                   Nova Southeastern University
                   311 University Drive, Suite 307
                   Coral Springs, FL 33065

Editorial Policy: *Journal of Anxiety Disorders* is an interdisciplinary journal that publishes research papers dealing with all aspects of anxiety disorders for all age groups (child, adolescent, adult, and geriatric). Areas of focus include traditional, behavioral, cognitive, and biological assessment; diagnosis and classification; psychosocial and psychopharmacological treatment; genetics; epidemiology; and prevention. Theoretical and review articles will be considered for publication if they contribute substantially to current knowledge in the field. The journal also contains sections for clinical reports (singe-case experimental designs and preliminary but innovative case series) and book reviews on all aspects of anxiety disorders.

Selective Notes on Submissions: Instructions to authors included in each issue of the journal. Authors to prepare manuscripts according to the *Publication Manual of the American Psychological Association* (4th ed.). Submit three (3) high-quality copies of the manuscript to the editor.

Journal Frequency: Bimonthly

Articles/Pages Published per Year: 30/400

Total Subscribers: NA

Book Reviews Accepted: NA

Rejection Rate: NA

Notes From Publisher: Free sample copy available on request.

Journal of Applied Behavior Analysis

Publisher: Society for the Experimental
                   Analysis of Behavior, Inc.
                   Department of Psychology
                   Indiana University
                   Bloomington, IN 47405

Editor: David P. Wacker
                   251 University Hospital School
                   University of Iowa
                   Iowa City, IA 52242

Editorial Policy: The *Journal of Applied Behavior Analysis* is primarily for the original publication of reports of experimental research involving application of the experimental analysis of behavior to problems of social importance. It will also publish technical articles relevant to such research and discussion of issues arising from behavioral applications.

Selective Notes on Submissions: Instructions to authors included in each issue of the journal. Authors to prepare manuscripts according to the *Publication Manual of the American Psychological Association* (4th ed.). Submit five (5) copies of the manuscript to the editor.

Journal Frequency: Quarterly

Articles/Pages Published per Year: 44/456

Total Subscribers: 5,613

Book Reviews Accepted: Yes

Rejection Rate: 70%

Journal of Applied Behavioral Science

Publisher: Sage Publications, Inc.
2455 Teller Road
Thousand Oaks, CA 91320

Editor: Clayton P. Alderfer
Rutgers University
Graduate School of Applied and
    Professional Psychology
P.O. Box 819
Piscataway, NJ 08855-0819

Editorial Policy: NA

Selective Notes on Submissions: Instructions to authors included in each issue of the journal. Authors to prepare manuscripts according to the *Publication Manual of the American Psychological Association* (4th ed.). Submit five (5) copies of the manuscript to the editor.

Journal Frequency: Quarterly

Articles/Pages Published per Year: 25/400

Total Subscribers: 2,650

Book Reviews Accepted: Yes, infrequently

Rejection Rate: 75%

Journal of Applied Developmental Psychology

Publisher: Ablex Publishing Corporation
355 Chestnut Street
Norwood, NJ 07648

Editors: Irving E. Sigel and
Rodney R. Cocking

Editorial Policy: The *Journal of Applied Developmental Psychology* is intended as a forum for communication between researchers and practitioners working in life span human development fields. Articles describing application of empirical research from social and behavioral disciplines bearing on human development are appropriate. Conceptual and methodological reviews and position papers which facilitate application of research results to such settings as educational, clinical, and the like are also welcome. Recommendations for intervention or for policy are appropriate when data based.

Selective Notes on Submissions: Instructions to authors included in each issue of the journal. Authors to prepare manuscripts according to the *Publication Manual of the American Psychological Association* (4th ed.). Submit three (3) copies of the manuscript to Irving Sigel or Rodney R. Cocking, Educational Testing Service, Rosedale Road, Mail Stop 06-R, Princeton, NJ 08541.

Journal Frequency: Quarterly

Articles/Pages Published per Year: 30/400

Total Subscribers: 400

Book Reviews Accepted: NA

Rejection Rate: NA

Journal of Applied Psychology

Publisher: American Psychological Association
750 First Street, NE
Washington, DC 20002-4242

Editor: Kevin R. Murphy
Department of Psychology
Colorado State University
Fort Collins, CO 80523

Editorial Policy: The *Journal of Applied Psychology* is devoted primarily to original investigations that contribute new knowledge and understanding to any field of applied psychology except clinical psychology. The journal considers quantitative investigations of interest to psychologists doing research or working in such settings as universities, industry, government, urban affairs, police and correctional systems, health and educational institutions, transportation and defense systems, and consumer affairs. A theoretical or review article may

be accepted if it represents a special contribution to an applied field.

Selective Notes on Submissions: Instructions to authors included in each issue of the journal. Authors to prepare manuscripts according to the *Publication Manual of the American Psychological Association* (4th ed.). Submit five (5) copies of the manuscript to the editor.

Journal Frequency: Bimonthly

Articles/Pages Published per Year: 60/707

Total Subscribers: 5,900

Book Reviews Accepted: No

Rejection Rate: 88%

Journal of Applied Social Psychology

Publisher: V. H. Winston and Sons, Inc.
7961 Eastern Avenue
Silver Spring, MD 20910

Editor: Andrew Baum, PhD
Behavioral Medicine & Oncology
University of Pittsburgh
3600 Forbes Avenue, Suite 405
Pittsburgh, PA 15213

Editorial Policy: The *Journal of Applied Social Psychology* will disseminate findings from behavioral science research which have applications to current problems of society. By publishing relevant research and emphasizing excellence of experimental design, as well as potential applicability of experimental results, the journal intends to bridge the theoretical and applied areas of social research. The *Journal of Applied Social Psychology* will serve as a means of communication among scientists, as well as between researchers and those engaged in the task of solving social problems. Preference is given to manuscripts reporting laboratory and field research in areas such as health, race relations, discrimination, group processes, population growth, crowding, accelerated cultural change, violence, poverty, environmental stress, helping behavior, effects of the legal system on society and the individual, political participation and extremism, cross-cultural differences, communication, cooperative problem solving, negotiations among nations, socioeconomics, social aspects of drug action and use, organizational and industrial issues, behavioral medicine, and environmental psychology. Reports of both laboratory and field research are accepted. Suggestions for application of research findings should be included. Theoretical papers are acceptable in limited numbers. Papers of theoretical scope should whenever possible include some research data. Reviews of the pertinent literature should be made with applicability in mind. The journal will publish reviews of selected books on relevant topic areas.

Selective Notes on Submissions: All manuscripts submitted to this journal should follow the style and method of presentation of APA journals. Authors to prepare manuscripts according to the *Publication Manual of the American Psychological Association* (4th ed.). Submit three (3) copies of the manuscript to the editor.

Journal Frequency: Bimonthly

Articles/Pages Published per Year: 92/1962

Total Subscribers: 1,100

Book Reviews Accepted: No

Rejection Rate: 80%

Journal of Applied Sport Psychology

Publisher: Association for the Advancement of Applied Sport Psychology
c/o P.O. Box 1897
Lawrence, KS 66044-8897

Editor: Joan L. Duda
Department of HKLS
Lambert Gymnasium
Purdue University
West Lafayette, IN 47907

Editorial Policy: The *Journal of Applied Sport Psychology* is designed to advance thought, theory, and research on applied aspects of sport psychology. Submissions such as position papers, reviews, theoretical developments specific to sport and/or exercise, and applied research conducted in these settings or having significant applied implications to sport and exercise are appropriate content for the journal.

Selective Notes on Submissions: Authors to prepare manuscripts according to the *Publication Manual of the American Psychological Association* (4th ed.). Submit four (4) copies of the manuscript to the editor.

Journal Frequency: Semiannually

Articles/Pages Published per Year: 12/190

Total Subscribers: NA

Book Reviews Accepted: NA

Rejection Rate: NA

Journal of Behavior Therapy and Experimental Psychiatry

Publisher: Elsevier Science, Inc.
1000 AE Amsterdam
The Netherlands

Editor: Joseph Wolpe, MD
Department of Psychology
Pepperdine University
400 Corporate Pointe
Culver City, CA 90230

Editorial Policy: The *Journal of Behavior Therapy and Experimental Psychiatry* is one of the leading international journals in behavior therapy. It is the only journal that has a special concern for the practice of behavior therapy in clinical psychiatry. In addition to original papers, the journal publishes material intended to provide training in behavior therapy for psychiatrists. It publishes case reports, and from time to time transcriptions of interviews to illustrate how target behaviors are identified and methods selected, how difficulties are handled and progress evaluated. Thus it includes descriptions of therapeutic methods, with technical details sometimes not found in textbooks. The research articles include descriptions of new procedures, analyses of theory of behavior disorders and of behavior change in general, and accounts of experimental studies relating to change in neurotic, psychotic and psychopathic behavior. Because of the didactic emphasis of the journal, articles will sometimes be followed by reviewers' comments.

Selective Notes on Submissions: Instructions to authors included in each issue of the journal. Authors to prepare manuscripts according to the *Publication Manual of the American Psychological Association* (4th ed.). Submit three (3) copies of the manuscript to the editor.

Journal Frequency: Quarterly

Articles/Pages Published per Year: 20/400

Total Subscribers: 3,100

Book Reviews Accepted: NA

Rejection Rate: NA

Notes From Publisher: Free sample copy available on request.

Journal of Behavioral Medicine

Publisher: Plenum Publishing Corporation
233 Spring Street
New York, NY 10013-1578

Editor: W. Doyle Gentry
Department of Behavioral
Medicine and Psychiatry
University of Virginia Medical
School
P.O. Box 4119
Charlottesville, VA 24502-0119

Editorial Policy: The *Journal of Behavioral Medicine* is a broadly conceived interdisciplinary publication devoted to furthering our understanding of physical health and illness through the knowledge and techniques of behavioral science. Application of this knowledge to prevention, treatment, and rehabilitation is also a major function of the journal, which will include papers from all disciplines engaged in behavioral medicine research: psychology, psychiatry, sociology, epidemiology, anthropology, health economics, and biostatistics. Examples of typical research areas of interest include: the study of appetitive disorders (alcoholism, smoking, obesity) that serve as physical risk factors; adherence to medical regimen and health maintenance behavior; pain; self-regulation therapies and biofeedback for somatic disorders; sociocultural influences on health and illness; and brain–behavior relationships that influence physiological function. Articles considered for publication include: theoretical and review articles, experimental studies, technical and methodological articles, and case studies.

Selective Notes on Submissions: Instructions to authors included in each issue of the journal. Authors to prepare manuscripts according to the *Council of Biology Editors Style Manual.* Submit three (3) copies of the manuscript to the editor at P.O. Box 4119, Lynchburg, VA 24502-0019.

Journal Frequency: Bimonthly

Articles/Pages Published per Year: 42/600

Total Subscribers: NA

Book Reviews Accepted: NA

Rejection Rate: NA

Journal of Biological Rythms

Publisher: Guilford Publications, Inc.
72 Spring Street
New York, NY 10012

Editor: Fred W. Turek
Department of Neurobiology
and Physiology
Northwestern University
2153 North Campus Drive
Evanston, IL 60208-3520

Editorial Policy: This quarterly publishes original, full-length reports of empirical investigations into all aspects of biological rhythmicity. Studies using genetic, biochemical, physiological, behavioral, and modeling approaches to understanding the nature, mechanisms, and functions (including clinical applications) of biological rhythms in all species are welcome.

Selective Notes on Submissions: Instructions to authors included in each issue of the journal. Authors to prepare manuscripts according to the *Council of Biology Editors Style Manual.* Submit four (4) copies of the manuscript to the editor.

Journal Frequency: Bimonthly

Articles/Pages Published per Year: 4/400

Total Subscribers: 600

Book Reviews Accepted: NA

Rejection Rate: NA

Notes From Publisher: Official publication of the Society for Research on Biological Rhythms.

Journal of Black Psychology

Publisher: Sage Publications, Inc.
2455 Teller Road
Thousand Oaks, CA 91320

Editor: Ann Kathleen Burlew, PhD
Editor-in-Chief
The Journal of Black
Psychology
Mail Location #0376
Department of Psychology
University of Cincinnati
Cincinnati, OH 45221

Editorial Policy: The *Journal of Black Psychology* publishes scholarly contributions within the field of psychology toward the understanding of the experience and behavior of Black populations. This includes reports of empirical research, discussions of the status of extant literature and of original theoretical analysis of the various traditional subcategories of psychological functioning. Therefore, the journal publishes work in any of the areas of cognition, personality, social behavior, physiological functioning, child development, education, and clinical application, in addition to empirical research and original theoretical formulations outside traditional boundaries, all integrated by a focus upon the domain of Black populations and the objective of scholarly contribution.

Selective Notes on Submissions: Instructions to authors included in each issue of the journal. Authors to prepare manuscripts according to the *Publication Manual of the Association of Black Psychologists,* 1984. A letter requesting manuscript review and a statement of its purpose and focus should accompany each submission. Include a cover sheet and an abstract of 100–175 words. Omit author's name and affiliation on the first page of the manuscript. Footnotes referring to the identity of the author or institutional affiliation should be on separate pages. Each manuscript will be submitted to a blind reviewer. Submit five (5) double-spaced copies of the manuscript to the editor.

Journal Frequency: Quarterly

Articles/Pages Published per Year: 24/500

Total Subscribers: 1,000

Book Reviews Accepted: Yes

Rejection Rate: NA

Journal of Business and Psychology

Publisher: Human Sciences Press, Inc.
233 Spring Street
New York, NY 10013-1578

Editor: John W. Jones, PhD, ABPP
Business Psychology Research
Institute
c/o McGraw Hill/London House
9701 West Higgins Road
Rosemont, IL 60018-4703

Editorial Policy: The *Journal of Business and Psychology* publishes empirical research, case studies, and literature reviews dealing with psychological programs implemented in business settings and written by psychologists, behavioral scientists, and organizational specialists employed in business, industry, or academia. Articles deal with all aspects of psychology that apply to business settings, including personnel management and loss control; marketing and consumer behavior research; employee assistance, counseling, and health programs; business research methodology and statistics; and computer applications in business settings.

Selective Notes on Submissions: Instructions to authors included in each issue of the journal. Authors to prepare manuscripts according to the *Publication Manual of the American Psychological Association* (4th ed.). Submit four (4) copies of the manuscript to the editor.

Journal Frequency: Quarterly

Articles/Pages Published per Year: 32/440

Total Subscribers: 800

Book Reviews Accepted: 6 per year

Rejection Rate: 75%

Journal of Child Language

Publisher: Cambridge University Press
40 West 20th Street
New York, NY 10011-4211

Editor: Elena Lieven
Department of Psychology
University of Manchester
Manchester M13 9PL
England

Editorial Policy: The journal publishes material on all aspects of the scientific study of language behavior in children and the principles which underlie it. This includes both normal and pathological development, and the study of both monolingual and multilingual children. Articles may report findings from naturalistic observation, experimental techniques, therapy or educational settings; and the subject matter may include sounds, grammar, lexicon, semantics, dialect variation, language use, or any other recognized facet of language study. Articles may be limited to the investigation of one language, or they may be comparative studies; focused on individuals, or presenting statistical treatments of groups. Studies of reading, writing, and the use of sign language are included if they are related to general questions of language development, as are articles with a therapy or remedial education bias. Collections of data are acceptable if they are accompanied by adequate interpretive discussion.

Selective Notes on Submissions: Instructions to authors included in each issue of the journal. Submit two (2) copies of the manuscript to the editor.

Journal Frequency: 3 issue per year

Articles/Pages Published per Year: 45/650

Total Subscribers: 1,850

Book Reviews Accepted: NA

Rejection Rate: NA

Journal of Child Psychology and Psychiatry and Allied Disciplines

Publisher: Cambridge University Press
Publishing Division
The Edinburgh Building
Shaftesbury Road
Cambridge CB2 2RU
England

Editors: Dr. Dorothy Bishop
MRC Applied Psychology Unit
Cambridge

Professor David Skuse
Behavioural Sciences Unit
Institute of Child Health
London

Professor Jim Stevenson
Department of Psychology
University of Southampton

Editorial Policy: This journal aims to enhance theory, research, and clinical practice in child and adolescent psychology and psychiatry and the allied disciplines through the publication of papers concerned with child and adolescent development, especially developmental psychopathology and the developmental disorders. The journal consists of original papers, review articles, brief research reports, annotations, practitioner reviews, book reviews, debate and argument, editorials, and items of information.

Selective Notes on Submissions: Instructions to authors included in each issue of the journal. Authors to prepare manuscripts according to the *Publication Manual of the American Psychological Association* (4th ed.). Submit four (4) copies of the manuscript to the Journal Office, ACP&P, St.

Saviour's House, 39/41 Union Street, London SE1 1SD, England.

Journal Frequency: 8 issues per year

Articles/Pages Published per Year: 96/1076

Total Subscribers: 5,000

Book Reviews Accepted: Yes (by invitation)

Rejection Rate: 75–80%

Notes From Publisher: Free sample copy on request.

Journal of Child Psychotherapy

Publisher: Routledge Journals
11 New Fetter Lane
London EC4P 4EE
England

Editors: Monica Lanyado
British Association of
Psychotherapists
London

Judith Edwards
Tavistock Clinic
London

Editorial Policy: This journal is an essential publication for all those with an interest in the theory and practice of work with children, adolescents and their parents where there are emotional and psychological problems.

The *Journal of Child Psychotherapy* is concerned with a wide spectrum of emotional and behavioral disorders relating to children and adolescents. These range from the more severe conditions of autism, anorexia, depression and the traumas of emotional, physical and sexual abuse to problems such as bed wetting and soiling, eating difficulties and sleep disturbance.

It is unique in its inclusiveness. Unlike other journals in the field, all major theoretical approaches are represented: Freudian, Independent, Jungian, and Kleinian. Occasional special issues focus on topical areas of theory and practice such as autism, adoption and under fives.

Selective Notes on Submissions: Instructions to authors included in each issue of the journal. Authors to prepare manuscripts according to the *Publication Manual of the American Psychological Association* (4th ed.). Submit three (3) copies of the manuscript to the editor. Send manuscripts to the Editors, Journal of Child Psychotherapy, Burgh House, New End Square, London NW3, UK.

Journal Frequency: 3 issue per year

Articles/Pages Published per Year: NA

Total Subscribers: NA

Book Reviews Accepted: NA

Rejection Rate: NA

Journal of Clinical Child Psychology

Publisher: Lawrence Erlbaum Associates, Inc.
365 Broadway
Hillsdale, NJ 07642

Editor: Thomas Ollendick, PhD
Department of Psychology
Virginia Polytechnic Institute
& State University
5088 Derring Hall
Blacksburg, VA 24061-0436

Editorial Policy: The *Journal of Clinical Child Psychology* is the official journal of the Section on Clinical Child Psychology (Section 1), Division of Clinical Psychology (Division 12), American Psychological Association. It publishes original research, reviews, and articles on child advocacy as well as on training and on professional practice in clinical child psychology. Authors need not be members of the Section. Colleagues in other disciplines, students, and consumers are also encouraged to contribute.

Selective Notes on Submissions: Instructions to authors included in each issue of the journal. Authors to prepare manuscripts according to the *Publication Manual of the American Psychological Association* (4th ed.). Submit four (4) copies of the manuscript to the editor.

Journal Frequency: Quarterly

Articles/Pages Published per Year: 52/495

Total Subscribers: 2,000

Book Reviews Accepted: Yes

Rejection Rate: 75%

Journal of Clinical and Experimental Neuropsychology

Publisher: Swets & Zeitlinger
P.O. Box 825
2160 SZ Lisse
The Netherlands

Editor: Byron P. Rourke
Department of Psychology
University of Windsor
Windsor, Ontario
Canada N9B 2X1

Editorial Policy: The *Journal of Clinical and Experimental Neuropsychology* publishes original articles dealing with research and theory in the broad field of behavioral impairment associated with dysfunction at the level of the cerebral hemispheres. The following general topics fall within the areas considered appropriate for inclusion in the journal: (a) the etiology, description, course, and prognosis for the behavioral and psychopathological accompaniments of various types of brain disease; (b) the development, reliability, validity, and utility of techniques of psychological assessment and intervention for persons suffering from brain impairment; and (c) the biological bases of cognitive functions.

Selective Notes on Submissions: Instructions to authors included in each issue of the journal. Authors to prepare manuscripts according to the *Publication Manual of the American Psychological Association* (4th ed.). Submit four (4) copies of the manuscript to the editor.

Journal Frequency: Bimonthly

Articles/Pages Published per Year: 84/1000

Total Subscribers: NA

Book Reviews Accepted: No

Rejection Rate: NA

Journal of Clinical Psychoanalysis

Publisher: International Universities Press, Inc.
59 Boston Post Road
P.O. Box 1524
Madison, CT 06443

Editors: Herbert M. Wyman, MD, and Stephen M. Rittenberg, MD
200 East 89th Street
New York, NY 10128

Editorial Policy: The *Journal of Clinical Psychoanalysis* features contributions from across the spectrum of current psychoanalytic viewpoints. Clinical case material is scrutinized, discussed, and debated. An essential goal of the journal is to convey in clear, jargon-free language what actually happens in an analysis.

Selective Notes on Submissions: Instructions to authors included in each issue of the journal. Only articles submitted solely to the *Journal of Clinical Psychoanalysis* will be considered for publication.

Journal Frequency: Quarterly

Articles/Pages Published per Year: 20/600

Total Subscribers: 1,000

Book Reviews Accepted: Yes

Rejection Rate: 65%

Journal of Clinical Psychology

Publisher: John Wiley & Sons
605 Third Avenue
New York, NY 10158

Editor: Vladimir Pishkin
Journal of Clinical Psychology
3113 NW 62nd Avenue
Oklahoma City, OK 73112

Editorial Policy: NA

Selective Notes on Submissions: Instructions
to authors included in each issue of the
journal. Authors to prepare manuscripts
according to the *Publication Manual of the
American Psychological Association* (4th
ed.). Submit an original and two (2) copies
of the manuscript to the editor. Publication
charges are assessed.

Journal Frequency: Bimonthly

Articles/Pages Published per Year: 120/672

Total Subscribers: 2,600

Book Reviews Accepted: No

Rejection Rate: 69%

Journal of Clinical Psychology in Medical Settings

Publisher: Plenum Publishing Corporation
233 Spring Street
New York, NY 10013

Editor: Ronald H. Rozensky
Department of Psychiatry
Evanston Hospital
2650 Ridge Avenue
Evanston, IL 60201-1789

Editorial Policy: *Journal of Clinical Psychology in Medical Settings* is an international
forum for the publication of peer-reviewed
original papers on both applied and basic
research as related to all areas of endeavor
of psychologists in medical settings and with
all patient groups. Authors of research-
based articles are encouraged to apply their
scientific findings to clinical practice in the
medical setting. Additionally, with a focus
on medical settings, the journal publishes
clinical articles that reflect single-case design
methodology; literature reviews that serve
as a basis for new techniques, heuristic
research challenges, or exemplary clinical
material; papers that address philosophical
issues surrounding training models at the
graduate, internship/residency, or postgraduate level and innovative training
programs or special course materials; articles on licensing, credentialing, and privi-
leging in hospital practice; and discussions
of ethics, the role of psychologists in medical shools, professional practice matters,
practice management, marketing, and the
politics of health care in general.

Selective Notes on Submissions: Instructions
to authors included in each issue of the
journal. Authors to prepare manuscripts
according to the *Publication Manual of the
American Psychological Association* (4th
ed.). Submit four (4) copies of the manuscript to the editor.

Journal Frequency: Quarterly

Articles/Pages Published per Year: 20/400

Total Subscribers: 250

Book Reviews Accepted: NA

Rejection Rate: 68%

Journal of Cognitive Neuroscience

Publisher: MIT Press Journals
                  55 Hayward Street
                  Cambridge, MA 02142

Editor: Dr. Michael S. Gazzaniga
                  Dartmouth Medical School

Editorial Policy: The purpose of the *Journal of Cognitive Neuroscience* is to provide a single forum for research on the biological bases of mental events. The journal publishes papers that bridge the gap between descriptions of information processing and specifications of brain activity. As such, much of the work will be interdisciplinary in character, drawing on developments in computer science, neuropsychology, neuroscience, and cognitive psychology. The journal will not publish research reports that bear solely on descriptions of function without addressing the underlying brain events, or that deal solely with descriptions of neurophysiology or neuroanatomy without regard for function. Papers should be written to be accessible to an interdisciplinary readership. The journal will consider empirical, theoretical, and research reviews within this area. Book reviews and interviews will also be published.

Selective Notes on Submissions: Instructions to authors included in each issue of the journal. Authors to prepare manuscripts according to the *Publication Manual of the American Psychological Association* (4th ed.). Submit four (4) copies of the manuscript to: *Journal of Cognitive Neuroscience*, Program in Cognitive Neuroscience, 6162 Silsby Hall, Dartmouth College, Hanover, NH 03756-3547

Journal Frequency: Bimonthly

Articles/Pages Published per Year: 600 pp.

Total Subscribers: NA

Book Reviews Accepted: Yes

Rejection Rate: NA

Journal of Cognitive Psychotherapy

Publisher: Springer Publishing Company, Inc.
                  536 Broadway
                  New York, NY 10012-3955

Editor: E. Thomas Dowd, PhD
                  Kent State University
                  118 Kent Hall
                  Kent, OH 44242

Editorial Policy: This journal is devoted to the advancement of the clinical practice of cognitive psychotherapy in its broadest sense. It seeks to merge theory, research, and practice and to develop new techniques by an examination of the clinical implications of theoretical development and research findings. The journal publishes case studies, theoretical and research articles of direct practical relevance, literature reviews on clinical topics, and articles describing the clinical implications of topical research.

Selective Notes on Submissions: Instructions to authors included in each issue of the journal. Authors to prepare manuscripts according to the *Publication Manual of the American Psychological Association* (4th ed.). Submit four (4) copies of the manuscript to the editor.

Journal Frequency: Quarterly

Articles/Pages Published per Year: 22/320

Total Subscribers: 850

Book Reviews Accepted: Yes

Rejection Rate: 50%

Journal of College Student Psychotherapy

Publisher: Haworth Press, Inc.
            10 Alice Street
            Binghamton, NY 13904-1580

Editor: Leighton Whitaker, PhD
          220 Turner Road
          Wallingford, PA 19086

Editorial Policy: The *Journal of College Student Psychotherapy* is dedicated to enhancing the lives of college and university students by stimulating high-quality practice, theory, and research in mental and personal development. The journal strives to promote greater care for and knowledge of students.

Selective Notes on Submissions: Instructions to authors included in each issue of the journal. Authors to prepare manuscripts

according to the *Publication Manual of the American Psychological Association* (4th ed.). Submit original and four (4) copies of the manuscript to the editor.

Journal Frequency: Quarterly

Articles/Pages Published per Year: 24/380

Total Subscribers: 500

Book Reviews Accepted: Yes (by invitation only)

Rejection Rate: 50%

Journal of Community and Applied Social Psychology

Publisher: John Wiley & Sons, Ltd.
            Baffins Lane
            Chichester, West Sussex
               P019 IUD
            England

Editors: Jim Orford
           School of Psychology
           University of Birmingham
           Edgbaston, B15 2TT
           England

           Geoffrey Stephenson
           Institute of Social and Applied
               Psychology
           University of Kent at
               Canterbury
           CT2 7LZ
           England

Editorial Policy: This quarterly journal aims to foster international communication among those concerned with the social psychological analysis and critical understanding of community issues and problems and to develop this understanding in the context of proposals for interventions and social policy. The journal will review and report psychological studies of individuals, groups, and professional practice in the broad area of community and applied social psychology. Quantitative research reports and case studies of innovative projects are welcome.

Selective Notes on Submissions: Instructions to authors included in each issue of the journal. Authors to prepare manuscripts according to the *Publication Manual of the American Psychological Association* (4th ed.). Submit three (3) copies of the manuscript to the editor. Submit manuscripts to the editor or associate editor with the closest subject interest (consult a recent journal issue).

Journal Frequency: 5 issues per year

Articles/Pages Published per Year: 30/400

Total Subscribers: NA

Book Reviews Accepted: Yes

Rejection Rate: 66%

Journal of Community Psychology

Publisher: John Wiley & Sons
605 Third Avenue
New York, NY 10158

Editor: Ray Lorion
Department of Psychology

University of Maryland
College Park, MD 20742

Editorial Policy: The *Journal of Community Psychology* is devoted to research, evaluation, assessment, intervention, and review articles that deal with human behavior in community settings. This includes an emphasis on the community as meeting needs and supporting growth and development of its residents. Applied psychology in community settings will need to have clear implications drawn to the community. Descriptive reports on particular groups of persons are considered as appropriate to the journal when the community relevance is made clear. Reviews and articles dealing with theory will be considered. Manuscripts of unusual length will be considered for monograph supplements.

Selective Notes on Submissions: Instructions to authors included in each issue of the journal. Authors to prepare manuscripts according to the *Publication Manual of the American Psychological Association* (4th ed.). Submit three (3) copies of the manuscript to the editor.

Journal Frequency: Quarterly

Articles/Pages Published per Year: 40/384

Total Subscribers: 800

Book Reviews Accepted: No

Rejection Rate: 68%

Journal of Comparative Family Studies

Publisher: Department of Sociology
University of Calgary
2500 University Drive, NW
Calgary, Alberta
Canada T2N 1N4

Editor: G. Kurian
Department of Sociology
University of Calgary
2500 University Drive, NW
Calgary, Alberta
Canada T2N 1N4

Editorial Policy: The *Journal of Comparative Family Studies* deals mainly with comparative family studies, including cross-cultural perspectives, both national and international.

Selective Notes on Submissions: Instructions to authors included in each issue of the journal. Authors to prepare manuscripts according to the style manual of the ASA. Submit three (3) copies of the manuscript to the assistent editor, Carol Cairns.

Journal Frequency: 3 issues per year

Articles/Pages Published per Year: 25–30/ 450

Total Subscribers: 700

Book Reviews Accepted: Yes

Rejection Rate: 75%

Journal of Comparative Psychology

Publisher: American Psychological Association

750 First Street, NE
Washington, DC 20002-4242

Editor: Charles T. Snowden
Department of Psychology
University of Wisconsin
1202 West Johnson Street
Madison, WI 53706

Editorial Policy: The *Journal of Comparative Psychology* publishes original research on the behavior of different species as it relates to evolution, ecology, adaptation, and development. Papers that merely use animals as a means of studying other phenomena (e.g., learning, drug effects, physiological mechanisms) fall outside the scope of this journal. Theoretical papers and review articles will be considered for publication on an occasional basis provided they bear on issues related to psychological research on animals from a comparative perspective.

Selective Notes on Submissions: Instructions to authors included in each issue of the journal. Authors to prepare manuscripts according to the *Publication Manual of the American Psychological Association* (4th ed.). Submit four (4) copies of the manuscript to the editor.

Journal Frequency: Quarterly

Articles/Pages Published per Year: 43/414

Total Subscribers: 1,450

Book Reviews Accepted: No

Rejection Rate: 41%

Journal of Constructivist Psychology

Publisher: Taylor and Francis, Ltd.
1101 Vermont Avenue,
Suite 200
Washington, DC 20005-3521

Editors: Robert A. Neimeyer
Department of Psychology
University of Memphis
Memphis, TN 38152-6400

Greg J. Neimeyer
Department of Psychology
University of Florida
Gainesville, FL 32611

Editorial Policy: The *Journal of Construc–tivist Psychology* provides reports of empirical research, conceptual analyses, critical reviews, and occasional case studies pertaining to constructivist and narrative approaches to psychology and the social sciences. Among the topics suitable for inclusion in the journal are studies of psychotherapy and psychopathology, interpersonal relationships, social–cognitive processes and development, and applications of the theory to educational, organizational, or business settings. Methodological reports of repertory grid technique are also suitable, as are investigations concerning other methods of assessment and research. The journal seeks to foster constructive interchange between constructivism and other relevant approaches in the social sciences.

Selective Notes on Submissions: Instructions to authors included in each issue of the journal. Authors to prepare manuscripts according to the *Publication Manual of the American Psychological Association* (4th

ed.). Submit four (4) copies of the manuscript to the editor.

Journal Frequency: Quarterly

Articles/Pages Published per Year: 16/340

Total Subscribers: NA

Book Reviews Accepted: Yes

Rejection Rate: 70%

Journal of Consulting and Clinical Psychology

Publisher: American Psychological
Association
750 First Street, NE
Washington, DC 20002-4242

Editor: Philip C. Kendall
Department of Psychology
Weiss Hall
Temple University
Philadelphia, PA 19122

Editorial Policy: The *Journal of Consulting and Clinical Psychology* publishes original contributions on the following topics: (a) the development, validity, and use of techniques of diagnosis and treatment in disordered behavior; (b) studies of populations of clinical interest, such as hospital, prison, rehabilitation, geriatric, and similar samples; (c) cross-cultural and demographic studies of interest for the behavior disorders; (d) studies of personality and of its assessment and development where these have a clear bearing on problems of clinical dysfunction;

(e) studies of gender, ethnicity, or sexual orientation that have a clear bearing on diagnosis, assessment and treatment; or (f) case studies pertinent to the preceding topics. The *Journal of Consulting and Clinical Psychology* considers manuscripts dealing with the diagnosis or treatment of abnormal behavior but does not consider manuscripts dealing with the etiology or descriptive pathology of abnormal behavior, which are more appropriate to the *Journal of Abnormal Psychology*. Articles that appear to have a significant contribution to both of these broad areas may be sent to either journal for editorial decision. Papers of a theoretical nature will occasionally be considered within the space limitations of the journal.

Selective Notes on Submissions: Instructions to authors included in each issue of the journal. Authors to prepare manuscripts according to the *Publication Manual of the American Psychological Association* (4th ed.). Submit four (4) copies of the manuscript to the editor.

Journal Frequency: Bimonthly

Articles/Pages Published per Year: 130/ 1025

Total Subscribers: 11,700

Book Reviews Accepted: No

Rejection Rate: 71%

Journal of Consumer Psychology

Publisher: Lawrence Erlbaum Associates, Inc.

10 Industrial Avenue
Mahwah, NJ 07430

Editor: Paul M. Herr
Graduate School of Business Administration
University of Colorado
Campus Box 419
Boulder, CO 80309-0419

Editorial Policy: This journal is devoted to advancing consumer psychology as a dynamic discipline by disseminating knowledge generated and contributed by scholars from a variety of backgrounds, substantive fields, and methodological orientations. To this end, the journal publishes papers providing theoretical analyses, critical reviews, original empirical reports, as well as methodological contributions that shape thought and practice in the discipline of consumer psychology. Topics covered include: the role of advertising, the development and change of consumer attitudes, choice and decision processes, direct brand experience, postpurchase evaluations, leisure activities, consumer socialization, motivational processes, salespersons' influences, and the experiential components of consumption activities.

Selective Notes on Submissions: Instructions to authors included in each issue of the journal. Authors to prepare manuscripts according to the *Publication Manual of the American Psychological Association* (4th ed.). Submit five (5) copies of the manuscript to the editor.

Journal Frequency: Quarterly

Articles/Pages Published per Year: 16/380

Total Subscribers: 732

Book Reviews Accepted: No

Rejection Rate: 85%

Journal of Consumer Research

Publisher: University of Chicago Press
                  Journals Division
                  P.O. Box 37005
                  Chicago, IL 60637

Editor: Brian Sternthal
               Northwestern University
               J. L. Kellogg Graduate School
                  of Management
               2001 Sheridan Road
               Evanston, IL 60208

Editorial Policy: The *Journal of Consumer Research* is an interdisciplinary quarterly that publishes scholarly research aimed at describing and explaining the behavior of consumers in the broadest sense of that term. The primary thrust is academic rather than managerial, with topics ranging from microlevel processes (e.g., brand choice) to more macrolevel issues (e.g., the development of materialistic values). Empirical, theoretical, and methodological articles from fields such as psychology, marketing, economics, and anthropology are featured.

Selective Notes on Submissions: Send five (5) copies of the manuscript to the editor.

Journal Frequency: Quarterly

Articles/Pages Published per Year: NA

Total Subscribers: NA

Book Reviews Accepted: NA

Rejection Rate: NA

Journal of Counseling & Development

Publisher: American Association for
                     Counseling & Development
                  5999 Stevenson Avenue
                  Alexandria, VA 22304

                  Charles D. Claiborn
                  Arizona State University
                  Division of Psychology in
                     Education
                  Tempe, AZ 85287-0611

Editorial Policy: The *Journal of Counseling & Development* is the official journal of the American Association for Counseling & Development. As such, one of its purposes is to publish archival material. The journal also publishes articles that have a broad interest for a readership of counseling and human development specialists.

Selective Notes on Submissions: Instructions to authors included in each issue of the journal. Authors to prepare manuscripts according to the *Publication Manual of the American Psychological Association* (4th ed.). Submit original and two (2) copies of the manuscript to the editor.

Journal Frequency: Bimonthly

Articles/Pages Published per Year: NA

Total Subscribers: NA

Book Reviews Accepted: NA

Rejection Rate: NA

Journal of Counseling Psychology

Publisher: American Psychological
                 Association
                 750 First Street, NE
                 Washington, DC 20002-4242

Editor: Clara E. Hill, PhD
              Department of Psychology
              University of Maryland
              College Park, MD 20742

Editorial Policy: The *Journal of Counseling Psychology* publishes articles on counseling of interest to psychologists and counselors in schools, colleges, universities, private and public counseling agencies, and business, religious, and military settings. The journal gives particular attention to articles reporting the results of empirical studies about counseling processes and interventions, theoretical articles about counseling, and studies dealing with the evaluation of applications of counseling and counseling programs. The journal also considers studies on the selection and training of counselors, the development of counseling materials and methods, and applications of counseling to specific populations and problem areas. Also published occasionally are topical reviews of research and other systematic surveys, as well as research methodology studies directly related to counseling. For further information on content, authors should refer to the July 1988 issue (Vol. 35, No. 3, pp. 219–221) of the journal.

Selective Notes on Submissions: Instructions to authors included in each issue of the journal. Authors to prepare manuscripts according to the *Publication Manual of the American Psychological Association* (4th ed.). Submit five (5) copies of the manuscript to the editor.

Journal Frequency: Quarterly

Articles/Pages Published per Year: 62/509

Total Subscribers: 9,900

Book Reviews Accepted: No

Rejection Rate: 80%

Journal of Cross-Cultural Psychology

Publisher: Sage Publications, Inc.
                 2455 Teller Road
                 Thousand Oaks, CA 91320

Editor: Peter B. Smith
              School of Social Sciences
              University of Sussex
              Falmer, Brighton BN1 9QN
              England

Editorial Policy: The *Journal of Cross-Cultural Psychology* publishes exclusively cross-cultural research reports. Its main emphasis is on empirical research wherein independent variables as influenced by culture may attain different values and the subjects are from at least two different cultural groups. The concern is with individual differences and variation across cultures rather than with societal variation (e.g., sociology). Research exclusively including as subjects members of ethnic minorities within one country must be replicable among or across clearly distinguishable culture groups. Contributions from disciplines other than psychology are encouraged, but all papers should report the results of empirical investigations. A brochure containing general information about *JCCP*, its scope, and editorial policies is available from any member of the Editorial Board or the publisher.

Selective Notes on Submissions: Instructions to authors included in each issue of the journal. Authors to prepare manuscripts according to the *Publication Manual of the American Psychological Association* (4th ed.). Submit four (4) copies of the manuscript to the editor.

Journal Frequency: Bimonthly

Articles/Pages Published per Year: 512 pp.

Total Subscribers: 2,025

Book Reviews Accepted: Yes

Rejection Rate: 78%

Journal of Early Adolescence

Publisher: Sage Publications
2455 Teller Road
Thousand Oaks, CA 91320

Editor: E. Ellen Thornburg, PhD
10030 North Roxbury Drive
Tucson, AZ 85737

Editorial Policy: The *Journal of Early Adolescence* responds to a growing need for a focus on the characteristics of individuals in the age group 10 through 14 years, and is unique in that it provides a well-balanced, interdisciplinary, international perspective on early adolescent development and the factors affecting it. The journal, which is peer reviewed, focuses on research, theoretical, and state-of-the-art papers.

Selective Notes on Submissions: Instructions to authors included in each issue of the journal. Authors to prepare manuscripts according to the *Publication Manual of the American Psychological Association* (4th ed.). Submit five (5) copies of the manuscript to the editor.

Journal Frequency: Quarterly

Articles/Pages Published per Year: 26/512

Total Subscribers: 1,400

Book Reviews Accepted: Yes

Rejection Rate: NA

Journal of Economic Psychology

Publisher: Elsevier Science Publishers B.V.
Molenwerf 1
P.O. Box 211
1000 AE Amsterdam
The Netherlands

Editor: Alan Lewis
University of Bath
School of Social Sciences
Claverton Down
Bath BA2 7AY
England

Editorial Policy: The journal aims to present research that will improve the understanding of behavioral, especially socio-psychological, aspects of economic phenomena and processes. The journal seeks to be a channel for the increased interest in using behavioral science methods for the study of economic behavior, and so to contribute to better solutions of societal problems, by stimulating new approaches and new theorizing about economic affairs. Economic psychology as a discipline studies the psychological mechanisms that underlie consumption and other economic behavior. It deals with preferences, choices, decisions, and factors influencing these, as well as the consequences of decisions and choices with respect to the satisfaction of needs. This includes the impact of external economic phenomena upon human behavior and well-being. Studies in economic psychology may relate to different levels of aggregation, from the household and the individual consumer to the macro level of whole nations. Economic behavior in connection with inflation, unemployment, taxation, economic development, as well as consumer information and economic behavior in the marketplace are thus the major fields of interest. The journal contains (1) reports of empirical research on economic behavior; (2) assessments of the state of the art in various subfields of economic psychology; (3) articles providing a theoretical perspective or a frame of reference for the study of economic behavior; (4) articles explaining the implications of theoretical developments for practical applications; (5) book reviews; and (6) announcements of meetings, conferences, and seminars. Special issues of the journal may be devoted to themes of particular interest. The journal will encourage exchange of information between researchers and practitioners by being a forum for discussion and debate of issues in both theoretical and applied research.

Selective Notes on Submissions: Instructions to authors included in each issue of the journal. Submit four (4) copies of the manuscript to the editor.

Journal Frequency: Quarterly

Articles/Pages Published per Year: 24/736

Total Subscribers: 406

Book Reviews Accepted: Yes

Rejection Rate: NA

Journal of Educational & Behavioral Statistics

Previous Title: Journal of Educational Statistics

Publisher: American Educational Research Association
1230 17th Street, NW
Washington, DC 20036-3078

Editor: Jan de Leeuw
Program in Statistics
Math Science Building, Room 8118
University of California, Los Angeles
Los Angeles, CA 90024-1554

Editorial Policy: The *Journal of Educational & Behavioral Statistics* provides an outlet for papers demonstrating, preferably through concrete example, how the educational statistician can contribute to sound, productive, and creative decision making and practice. The goal of authors seeking to publish in the journal should be to communicate to readers why, when, and how a statistical method should be used. Typically, papers will present new methods of analysis or new applications of better known methods.

Selective Notes on Submissions: Instructions to authors included in each issue of the journal. Authors to prepare manuscripts according to the *Publication Manual of the American Psychological Association* (4th ed.). Submit four (4) copies of the manuscript to the editor. Submit book reviews to Book Review Editor: David M. Rindskopf, City University of New York Graduate Center.

Journal Frequency: Quarterly

Articles/Pages Published per Year: 26/384

Total Subscribers: 3,400

Book Reviews Accepted: Yes

Rejection Rate: 77%

Journal of Educational Measurement

Publisher: National Council on
                 Measurement in Education
                 1230 17th Street, NW
                 Washington, DC 20036-3078

Editor: Rebecca Zwick
              Department of Education
              University of California
              Santa Barbara, CA 93106-9490

Editorial Policy: The *Journal of Educational Measurement (JEM)* publishes measurement research and reports of applications of measurement in an educational context. Solicited reviews of current standardized educational and psychological tests and other important measurement works appear in the Review Section of the journal. For further information on the kinds of articles apropriate for publication in the journal and detailed directions on preparing manuscripts, see *JEM,* Winter 1996.

In addition, comments on technical and substantive issues addressed in articles and reviews previously published in *JEM* are encouraged. Comments will be reviewed, and the authors of the original article will be given the opportunity to respond.

Selective Notes on Submissions: Instructions to authors included in each issue of the journal. Authors to prepare manuscripts according to the *Publication Manual of the American Psychological Association* (4th ed.). Submit three (3) blind copies of the manuscript to the editor. Submit book reviews to Dr. Michael Kolen, American College Testing, 2201 North Dodge Street, Iowa City, IA 52243.

Journal Frequency: Quarterly

Articles/Pages Published per Year: 22/384

Total Subscribers: 3,200

Book Reviews Accepted: Yes

Rejection Rate: NA

Journal of Educational and Psychological Consultation

Publisher: Lawrence Erlbaum Associates
10 Industrial Avenue
Mahwah, NJ 07430-2262

Editor: Joseph E. Zins
339 Teachers College
P.O. Box 210002
University of Cincinnati
Cincinnati, OH 45221-0002

Editorial Policy: The *Journal of Educational and Psychological Consultation (JEPC)* provides a forum for improving the scientific understanding of consultation and organizational change and for describing practical strategies to increase the effectiveness and efficiency of consultation services. To accomplish these goals, *JEPC* publishes articles and special thematic issues that describe formal research, evaluate practice, examine the program implementation process, review relevant literature, investigate systems change, discuss salient issues, and carefully document the translation of theory into practice. In addition, the journal includes reviews of books and other professional materials. Examples of topics of interest include individual, group, and organizational consultation; systems change; teaming; prevention; health promotion; personnel preparation; ethics and professional issues; community–school–family partnerships; school-to-workplace transitions; cultural and ethnic issues; services coordination; program planning, implementation, and evaluation; and educational reform. Authors are requested to include clear statements reflecting the implications of their work for the practice of consultation.

Selective Notes on Submissions: Instructions to authors included in each issue of the journal. Authors to prepare manuscripts according to the *Publication Manual of the American Psychological Association* (4th ed.). Submit five (5) copies of the manuscript to the editor. Include SASE with manuscript submissions for acknowledgment of receipt. Inquiries about manuscript ideas and proposals for theme issues are welcome.

Journal Frequency: Quarterly

Articles/Pages Published per Year: 24/400

Total Subscribers: 750

Book Reviews Accepted: Yes

Rejection Rate: 84%

Journal of Educational Psychology

Publisher: American Psychological Association
750 First Street, NE
Washington, DC 20002-4242

Editor: Michael Pressley
Department of Educational Psychology
SUNY Albany
Albany, NY 12222

Editorial Policy: The *Journal of Educational Psychology* publishes original investigations and theoretical papers dealing with learning and cognition, especially as they relate to problems of instruction, and with the psychological development, relationships, and adjustment of the individual. Journal articles pertain to all levels of education and to all age groups.

Selective Notes on Submissions: Instructions to authors included in each issue of the journal. Authors to prepare manuscripts according to the *Publication Manual of the American Psychological Association* (4th ed.). Submit five (5) copies of the manuscript to the editor.

Journal Frequency: Quarterly

Articles/Pages Published per Year: 51/661

Total Subscribers: 5,200

Book Reviews Accepted: No

Rejection Rate: 77%

Journal of Employment Counseling

Publisher: American Association for Counseling and Development
5999 Stevenson Avenue
Alexandria, VA 22304

Editor: Robert Drummond
University of North Florida
4567 St. Johns Bluff Road, South
Jacksonville, FL 32224

Editorial Policy: The *Journal of Employment Counseling* seks articles illuminating theory or practice in employment counseling, reporting professional experimentation or research, or exploring current client voca-

tional problems, or the professional concerns of counselors.

Selective Notes on Submissions: Instructions to authors included in each issue of the journal. Authors to prepare manuscripts according to the *Publication Manual of the American Psychological Association* (4th ed.). Submit three (3) copies of the manuscript to the editor.

Journal Frequency: Quarterly

Articles/Pages Published per Year: 20/190

Total Subscribers: 2,448

Book Reviews Accepted: Yes

Rejection Rate: NA

Notes From Publisher: Authors are encouraged, but not required, to provide an additional copy of a submission on a 5 1/4" floppy disk in WordPerfect or ASCII.

Journal of Environmental Psychology

Publisher: Academic Press
24-28 Oval Road
London NW1 7DX
England

Editor: David V. Canter
Department of Psychology
University of Liverpool
Eleanor Rathbone Building
Liverpool L69 3BX
England

Editorial Policy: The *Journal of Environmental Psychology* is directed toward individuals in a wide range of disciplines who have an interest in the study of the transactions and interrelationships between people and their sociophysical surroundings (including man-made and natural environments) and the relation of this field to other social and biological sciences and to the environmental professions. The journal publishes internationally contributed empirical studies, reviews of research, and an extensive book review section. Essays discussing challenges in the field are also welcome.

An important forum for the field, the content of the journal reflects the scientifc development and maturation of the study of environmental psychology. Contributions on theoretical, methodological, and practical aspects of human–environment interaction are included, along with innovative and/or interdisciplinary approaches with a psychological emphasis.

Selective Notes on Submissions: Instructions to authors included in each issue of the journal. Authors to prepare manuscripts according to the *Publication Manual of the American Psychological Association* (4th ed.). Submit four (4) copies of the manuscript to the editor. Good quality black and white photographs relevant to the paper are encouraged.

Journal Frequency: Quarterly

Articles/Pages Published per Year: 26/336

Total Subscribers: 600

Book Reviews Accepted: Yes

Rejection Rate: 49%

Journal of the Experimental Analysis of Behavior

Publisher: Society for the Experimental Analysis of Behavior, Inc. Department of Psychology Indiana University Bloomington, IN 47405-1301

Editor: Dr. Richard L. Shull Department of Psychology University of North Carolina-Greensboro Greensboro, NC 27412

Editorial Policy: The *Journal of the Experimental Analysis of Behavior* (ISSN 0022-5002; USPS 867240) is primarily for the original publication of experiments relevant to the behavior of individual organisms. Review articles and theoretical papers will also be considered for publication.

Selective Notes on Submissions: Three (3) copies of the manuscript, prepared according to the format requirements published in the January issue of the current year, should be submitted to the editor.

Journal Frequency: Bimonthly

Articles/Pages Published per Year: 75/1000

Total Subscribers: 2,770

Book Reviews Accepted: Yes

Rejection Rate: 60%

Journal of Experimental Child Psychology

Publisher: Academic Press, Inc.
1250 Sixth Avenue
San Diego, CA 92101

Editor: Lynn S. Liben
Department of Psychology
Penn State University
417B Moore Building
University Park, PA 16802-3104

Editorial Policy: The *Journal of Experimental Child Psychology* is devoted primarily to reports of significant empirical research concerned with expanding our psychological knowledge of the child. Other kinds of manuscripts, including critical reviews, theoretical contributions, and short notes on methodological issues and innovative apparatus, will also be considered but will be reviewed with particular focus upon their value as stimulants to research of substantial importance in the field of psychology. Manuscripts concerning special populations of children should address normal developmental processes as well as providing data on special populations. In all cases, the review of manuscripts is based on methodological adequacy, evidence of replicability of results, theoretical import, and clarity of presentation. Reports of multiple experiments focused on a problem of theoretical interest are encouraged.

Selective Notes on Submissions: Instructions to authors included in each issue of the journal. Authors to prepare manuscripts according to the *Publication Manual of the American Psychological Association* (4th ed.). Submit five (5) copies of the manuscript to the editor.

Journal Frequency: Monthly

Articles/Pages Published per Year: 40/1000

Total Subscribers: NA

Book Reviews Accepted: No

Rejection Rate: NA

Journal of Experimental Education

Publisher: Heldref Publications
1319 18th Street, NW
Washington, DC 20036-1802

Editors: William Asher
Purdue University

Meredith D. Gall
University of Oregon

Bruce Thompson
Texas A&M University

Editorial Policy: The *Journal of Experimental Education* aims to improve educational practice by publishing basic and applied research studies employing the range of quantitative and qualitative methodologies found in the behavioral, cognitive, and social sciences. Published studies address all levels of schooling, from preschool through graduate and professional education, and various educational contexts, including public and private education both in the United States and abroad. The audience for the journal is researchers and practitioners interested in the advancement of educational research and its use to improve the teaching, learning, and schooling process.

Selective Notes on Submissions: Instructions to authors included in each issue of the journal. Authors to prepare manuscripts according to the *Publication Manual of the American Psychological Association* (4th ed.). Submit three (3) copies of the manuscript to the managing editor c/o the publisher.

Journal Frequency: Quarterly

Articles/Pages Published per Year: 28/400

Total Subscribers: NA

Book Reviews Accepted: No

Rejection Rate: 80%

Journal of Experimental Psychology: Animal Behavior Processes

Publisher: American Psychological
                   Association
                   750 First Street, NE
                   Washington, DC 20002-4242

Editor: Mark E. Bouton
                Department of Psychology
                University of Vermont
                Burlington, VT 05405

Editorial Policy: The *Journal of Experimental Psychology: Animal Behavior Processes* publishes experimental studies that contribute significantly to the understanding of learning, memory, perception, motivation, and performance, especially as revealed in the behavior of nonhuman animals. For further information on content, authors

should refer to the editorial in the January 1986 (Vol. 12, No. 1, p. 3) issue of the journal.

Selective Notes on Submissions: Instructions to authors included in each issue of the journal. Authors to prepare manuscripts according to the *Publication Manual of the American Psychological Association* (4th ed.). Submit four (4) copies of the manuscript to the editor.

Journal Frequency: Quarterly

Articles/Pages Published per Year: 26/335

Total Subscribers: 1,900

Book Reviews Accepted: No

Rejection Rate: 71%

Journal of Experimental Psychology: Applied

Publisher: American Psychological
                   Association
                   750 First Street, NE
                   Washington, DC 20002-4242

Editor: Raymond S. Nickerson
                Department of Psychology
                Paige Hall
                Tufts University
                Medford, MA 02155

Editorial Policy: The mission of the *Journal of Experimental Psychology: Applied* is to publish original empirical investigations in experimental psychology that bridge practically oriented problems and psychological theory. The journal also publishes research aimed at developing and testing of models of cognitive processing or behavior in applied situations, including laboratory and field settings. Occasionally, review articles are considered for publication if they contribute significantly to important topics within applied experimental psychology. Areas of interest include applications of perception, attention, decision making, reasoning, information processing, learning, and performance. Settings may be industrial (such as human–computer interface design), academic (such as intelligent computer-aided instruction), or consumer oriented (such as applications of text comprehension theory to the development or evaluation of product instructions).

Selective Notes on Submissions: Instructions to authors included in each issue of the journal. Authors to prepare manuscripts according to the *Publication Manual of the American Psychological Association* (4th ed.). Submit five (5) copies of the manuscript to the editor.

Journal Frequency: Quarterly

Articles/Pages Published per Year: 18/319

Total Subscribers: 1,100

Book Reviews Accepted: No

Rejection Rate: 71%

Journal of Experimental Psychology: General

Publisher: American Psychological Association
750 First Street, NE
Washington, DC 20002-4242

Editor: Nora S. Newcombe
Department of Psychology
Temple University
Philadelphia, PA 19122

Editorial Policy: The *Journal of Experimental Psychology: General* publishes articles in any area of experimental psychology when the articles involve a longer, more integrative report than the usual journal article, leading to an advance in knowledge that is judged to be of interest to the entire community of experimental psychologists. The journal includes but is not limited to articles such as those that have appeared as *Journal of Experimental Psychology* monographs and as chapters in contemporary books of "advances." Republication of a limited number of data may be permitted if necessary to make the article complete and definitive. For further information on content, authors should refer to the March 1983 (Vol. 112, No. 1, pp. 136–137) issue of the journal.

Selective Notes on Submissions: Instructions to authors included in each issue of the journal. Authors to prepare manuscripts according to the *Publication Manual of the American Psychological Association* (4th ed.). Submit four (4) copies of the manuscript to the editor.

Journal Frequency: Quarterly

Articles/Pages Published per Year: 21/444

Total Subscribers: 3,000

Book Reviews Accepted: No

Rejection Rate: 74%

Journal of Experimental Psychology: Human Perception and Performance

Publisher: American Psychological
                   Association
                   750 First Street, NE
                   Washington, DC 20002-4242

Editor: Thomas H. Carr, PhD
                Department of Psychology
                Michigan State University
                129 Psychology Research
                Building
                East Lansing, MI 48824-1117

Editorial Policy: The *Journal of Experimental Psychology: Human Perception and Performance* publishes studies of perception, verbal or motor performance, and related cognitive processes.

Selective Notes on Submissions: Instructions to authors included in each issue of the journal. Authors to prepare manuscripts according to the *Publication Manual of the American Psychological Association* (4th ed.). Submit five (5) copies of the manuscript to the editor.

Journal Frequency: Bimonthly

Articles/Pages Published per Year: 94/1500

Total Subscribers: 2,550

Book Reviews Accepted: No

Rejection Rate: 56%

Journal of Experimental Psychology: Learning, Memory, and Cognition

Publisher: American Psychological
                   Association
                   750 First Street, NE
                   Washington, DC 20002-4242

Editor: James H. Neely
                Department of Psychology
                SUNY Albany
                1400 Washington Avenue
                Albany, NY 12222

Editorial Policy: The *Journal of Experimental Psychology: Learning, Memory, and Cognition* publishes original experimental studies on fundamental encoding, transfer, memory, and cognitive processes in human behavior. For further information on content, authors should refer to the editorial in the January 1985 issue of this journal (Vol. 11, No. 1, pp. 1–2).

Selective Notes on Submissions: Instructions to authors included in each issue of the journal. Authors to prepare manuscripts according to the *Publication Manual of the American Psychological Association* (4th ed.). Submit four (4) copies of the manuscript to the editor.

Journal Frequency: Bimonthly

Articles/Pages Published per Year: 121/ 1694

Total Subscribers: 3,400

Book Reviews Accepted: No

Rejection Rate: 85%

Journal of Experimental Social Psychology

Publisher: Academic Press, Inc.
1250 Sixth Avenue
San Diego, CA 92101

Editor: John M. Levine
Department of Psychology
University of Pittsburgh
822 LRDC Building
Pittsburgh, PA 15260

Editorial Policy: The *Journal of Experimental Social Psychology* is devoted to the publication of research and theory on social interaction and related phenomena, including social cognition and motivation, attitude change, interpersonal relationships, and intragroup and intergroup processes. The journal does not specify appropriate topics for research, but rather seeks to publish significant work reflecting the broad field of social psychology. It is anticipated that most published manuscripts will report results of conceptually based empirical research that advances social psychological theorizing. However, other types of papers, such as theoretical analyses, literature reviews, and methodological comments, are also encour-

aged if they contribute significantly to an understanding of social processes. It is expected that all empirical research submitted for consideration will have been conducted in a manner consistent with the American Psychological Association's *Ethical Principles in the Conduct of Research With Human Participants* (1982).

Selective Notes on Submissions: Instructions to authors included in each issue of the journal. Authors to prepare manuscripts according to the *Publication Manual of the American Psychological Association* (4th ed.). Submit five (5) copies of the manuscript to the editor.

Journal Frequency: Bimonthly

Articles/Pages Published per Year: 28/600

Total Subscribers: NA

Book Reviews Accepted: No

Rejection Rate: 80%

Journal of Family Issues

Publisher: Sage Publications, Inc.
2455 Teller Road
Thousand Oaks, CA 91320

Editor: Constance Shehan
Department of Sociology
University of Florida
Gainesville, FL 32611-2030

Editorial Policy: The *Journal of Family Issues* will devote two issues each year to special topics of current interest. These thematic issues include both articles prepared by invitation and articles submitted for consideration for the special issues. The other two issues each year are devoted wholly to articles, comments, and advocacy pieces on any topic related to family issues. The journal welcomes manuscripts that contribute to the understanding of theory, research, and application pertaining to the family. The journal is devoted to contemporary social issues and social problems related to marriage and family life and to theoretical and professional issues of current interest to those who work with and study families.

Selective Notes on Submissions: Instructions to authors included in each issue of the journal. Authors to prepare manuscripts according to the *Publication Manual of the American Psychological Association* (4th ed.). Submit four (4) copies of the manuscript to the editor.

Journal Frequency: Bimonthly

Articles/Pages Published per Year: 30/570

Total Subscribers: 1,550

Book Reviews Accepted: No

Rejection Rate: 85%

Journal of Family Psychology

Publisher: American Psychological Association
750 First Street, NE
Washington, DC 20002-4242

Editor: Ross D. Parke
Department of Psychology and

Center for Family Studies
0-75
1419 Life Sciences
University of California, Riverside
Riverside, CA 92521-0426

Editorial Policy: The *Journal of Family Psychology* is devoted to the study of the family system from multiple perspectives and to the application of psychological methods of inquiry to that end. The journal publishes original scholarly articles on (a) marital and family processes, life stages and transitions, and marital and family coping; (b) the development and validation of marital and family assessment measures; (c) the outcome and process of marital and family treatment; (d) the development and evaluation of family-focused prevention programs (e.g., preparation for marriage, divorce, teenage pregnancy, transition to parenthood, parenting, and caring for aging relatives); (e) families in transition (separation, divorce, and single parenting; remarriage and the stepfamily; adoption; and death and bereavement); (f) family violence and abuse; (g) employment and the family (e.g., division of household labor, workplace policies, and child care); (h) the family and larger systems (e.g., schools, social agencies, neighborhoods, and governments); (i) ethnicity, social class, gender, and sexual orientation as they relate to the family; and (j) methodological and statistical advances in the study of marriage and the family. The emphasis is on empirical research including, for example, studies involving behavioral, cognitive, emotional, or biological variables. The journal will publish occasional theoretical articles, literature reviews, and meta-analyses, case studies, and brief reports as long as they further the goal of improving scholarship or practice in the field.

Selective Notes on Submissions: Authors to prepare manuscripts according to the *Publication Manual of the American Psychological Association* (4th ed.). Submit three (3) copies of the manuscript to the editor.

Journal Frequency: Quarterly

Articles/Pages Published per Year: 42/462

Total Subscribers: 6,700

Book Reviews Accepted: No

Rejection Rate: 70%

Journal of Family Psychotherapy

Publisher: Haworth Press, Inc.
                    10 Alice Street
                    Binghamton, NY 13904-1580

Editor: Terry Trepper, PhD
                    Family Studies Center
                    Purdue University Calumet
                    Hammond, IN 46323-2094

Editorial Policy: The journal is specifically geared to the needs of psychotherapists interested in helping families. It will publish case studies and reports on treatment programs on different topics relevant to family therapy that are of importance to understanding and effectively helping families, while at the same time presenting new, innovative, state-of-the-art information.

Selective Notes on Submissions: Instructions to authors included in each issue of the journal. Authors to prepare manuscripts

according to the *Publication Manual of the American Psychological Association* (4th ed.). Submit four (4) copies of the manuscript to the editor.

Journal Frequency: Quarterly

Articles/Pages Published per Year: 20 articles

Total Subscribers: 750

Book Reviews Accepted: NA

Rejection Rate: 50%

Journal of Family Therapy

Publisher: Blackwell Publishers
                    108 Cowley Road
                    Oxford, OX4 1JF
                    England

Editors: John Carpenter and
                    Bebe Speed

Editorial Policy: The *Journal* is published on behalf of the Association for Family Therapy and Systemic Practice (UK). The journal seeks to advance the understanding and therapy of human relationships constituted in systems such as couples, families, professional networks and wider groups by publishing articles on theory, research, clinical practice, and training. Articles are selected on the basis of originality, clarity, significance and relevance.

Besides the main body of the journal, there is a short paper section for briefer and less formal papers. The journal also publishes reviews of relevant books and tapes as well as abstracts of original papers in books and other journals relevant to the field.

Selective Notes on Submissions: Instructions to authors included in each issue of the journal. Authors to prepare manuscripts according to the *Publication Manual of the American Psychological Association* (4th ed.). Submit four (4) copies of the manuscript to the editor. Send manuscripts to John Carpenter, JFT Editorial Office, Center for Applied Social Studies, University of Durham, 15 Old Elvet, Durham DH1 3HL, UK.

Journal Frequency: Quarterly

Articles/Pages Published per Year: 25/448

Total Subscribers: 2,400

Book Reviews Accepted: No

Rejection Rate: 50%

Journal of Family Violence

Publisher: Plenum Publishing Corporation
233 Spring Street
New York, NY 10013-1578

Editors: Vincent B. Van Hasselt and
Michel Hersen
Center for Psychological Studies
Nova Southeastern University
3301 College Avenue
Fort Lauderdale, FL 33314

Editorial Policy: The *Journal of Family Violence* is an interdisciplinary forum for the publication of information on clinical and investigative efforts concerning all forms of family violence and its precursors, including spouse battering, child abuse, sexual abuse of children, incest, abuse of the elderly, marital rape, domestic homicide, the alcoholic marriage, and general family conflict. The journal publishes clinical and research reports from a broad range of disciplines including clinical and counseling psychology, sociology, psychiatry, public health, criminology, law, marital counseling, and social work. The primary focus is on investigations using group comparisons and on single-case experimental strategies. Case studies that are of special clinical relevance or that describe innovative evaluation and intervention techniques, reviews, and theoretical discussions that contribute substantially to our understanding of family violence are also published.

Selective Notes on Submissions: Instructions to authors included in each issue of the journal. Submit three (3) copies of the manuscript to one of the editors.

Journal Frequency: Quarterly

Articles/Pages Published per Year: 24/400

Total Subscribers: NA

Book Reviews Accepted: NA

Rejection Rate: NA

Journal of Gay and Lesbian Psychotherapy

Publisher: Haworth Press, Inc.
10 Alice Street
Binghamton, NY 13904-1580

Editor: David L. Scasta, MD
1439 Pineville Road
New Hope, PA 18938

Editorial Policy: A practical, multidisciplinary forum for the exposition and discussion of issues relating to the use of psychotherapy with gay, lesbian, and bisexual clients, the journal is divided into two sections: a clinical section and an experimental section with emphasis on the clinical applications.

Selective Notes on Submissions: Instructions to authors included in each issue of the journal. Submit three (3) copies of the manuscript to the editor.

Journal Frequency: Quarterly

Articles/Pages Published per Year: 30/400

Total Subscribers: 1,000

Book Reviews Accepted: No

Rejection Rate: NA

Journal of General Psychology

Publisher: Heldref Publications
1319 18th Street, NW
Washington, DC 20036-1802

Editor: Garvin Chastain
Boise State University

Editorial Policy: The *Journal of General Psychology* is devoted to experimental, physiological, and comparative psychology. Preference is given to manuscripts that establish functional relationships, involve a series of integrated studies, or contribute to the development of new theoretical insights. Human and animal studies and mathematical and other theoretical investigations are appropriate. Technological reports of significance to these areas, as well as reports of applied research, are welcome. Studies of monograph length would be welcomed by *Genetic, Social, and General Psychology Mongraphs.*

Selective Notes on Submissions: Instructions to authors included in each issue of the journal. Authors to prepare manuscripts according to the *Publication Manual of the American Psychological Association* (4th ed.). Typesetting charge to authors of $50 per table, $20 per figure, and $25 for heavy use of statistics. Submit the original and one (1) copy of the manuscript to the Managing Editor, Journal of General Psychology, 1319 18th Street, NW, Washington, DC 20036-1802.

Journal Frequency: Quarterly

Articles/Pages Published per Year: 30/400

Total Subscribers: 1,250

Book Reviews Accepted: No

Rejection Rate: 17%

Journal of Genetic Psychology

Publisher: Heldref Publications
1319 18th Street, NW
Washington, DC 20036-1802

Editor: John E. Horrocks
Ohio State University
Columbus, OH 43210

Editorial Policy: The *Journal of Genetic Psychology* is devoted to research and theory in developmental and clinical psychology. Although the major thrust of the journal is empirical research and the exposition and criticism of theory, occasional applied and descriptive articles will be accepted, as will briefly reported replications and refinements. Prospective authors are particularly encouraged to make explicit the theoretical contribution of their research. Submissions may deal with the biological as well as the behavioral and social aspects of developmental and clinical psychology. Studies of monograph length in areas appropriate to this journal would be welcomed by *Genetic, Social, and General Psychology Monographs.*

Selective Notes on Submissions: Instructions to authors included in each issue of the journal. Authors to prepare manuscripts according to the *Publication Manual of the American Psychological Association* (4th ed.). Submit the original and one (1) copy of the manuscript to the Managing Editor, Journal of Genetic Psychology, 1319 18th Street, NW, Washington, DC 20036-1802. NOTE: Typesetting charges to author of $50/table, $20/figure, and $25 for heavy use of statistics.

Journal Frequency: Quarterly

Articles/Pages Published per Year: 46/400–544

Total Subscribers: 1,192

Book Reviews Accepted: No

Rejection Rate: 43%

Journal of Geriatric Psychiatry: Official Journal of the Boston Society for Gerontologic Psychiatry

Publisher: International Universities Press, Inc.
59 Boston Post Road
P.O. Box 1524
Madison, CT 06443

Editors: Bennett Gurian, MD, and
Margery Silver, EdD
83 Horace Road
Belmont, MA 02178

Editorial Policy: The *Journal of Geriatric Psychiatry* presents the latest thinking and most recent findings in the field of geriatric psychiatry designed for psychiatrists, psychologists, social workers, social scientists, and other mental health personnel.

Selective Notes on Submissions: Instructions to authors included in each issue of the journal. Authors to prepare manuscripts according to the *Publication Manual of the American Psychological Association* (4th ed.). Submit five (5) copies of the manuscript to the editor.

Journal Frequency: Bimonthly

Articles/Pages Published per Year: 20/320

Total Subscribers: 1,000

Book Reviews Accepted: Yes

Rejection Rate: NA

Journal of the History of the Behavioral Sciences

Publisher: John Wiley & Sons
605 Third Avenue
New York, NY 10158

Editor: John C. Burnham
Department of History
Ohio State University
Columbus, OH 43210

Editorial Policy: NA

Selective Notes on Submissions: Instructions to authors included in each issue of the journal. Authors to prepare manuscripts according to the *Chicago Manual of Style,* University of Chicago Press. Submit two (2) copies of the manuscript to the editor.

Journal Frequency: Quarterly

Articles/Pages Published per Year: 52/384

Total Subscribers: 1,000

Book Reviews Accepted: Yes

Rejection Rate: 67%

Journal of Homosexuality

Publisher: Haworth Press, Inc.
10 Alice Street
Binghamton, NY 13904-1580

Editor: John P. DeCecco
Center for Research and
Education in Sexuality
Psychology Building, Room 502
San Francisco State Univerity
San Francisco, CA 94132

Editorial Policy: The *Journal of Homosexuality* is devoted to theoretical, empirical, and historical research on homosexuality, heterosexuality, sexual identity, social sex roles, and the sexual relationships of both men and women.

Selective Notes on Submissions: Submit four (4) copies of the manuscript to the editor. Instructions to authors included in each issue of the journal. Authors to prepare manuscripts according to the *Publication Manual of the American Psychological Association* (4th ed.).

Journal Frequency: Quarterly

Articles/Pages Published per Year: 50/400

Total Subscribers: 2,000

Book Reviews Accepted: Yes

Rejection Rate: 50%

Journal of Humanistic Psychology

Publisher: Sage Publications, Inc.
2455 Teller Road
Newbury Park, CA 91320

Editor: Thomas C. Greening, PhD
1314 Westwood Boulevard
Los Angeles, CA 90024

Editorial Policy: The *Journal of Humanistic Psychology* began publication in 1961 and is the journal of the Association for Humanistic Psychology. It publishes experiential reports, theoretical papers, personal essays, research studies with an emphasis on human science methods, applications of humanistic psychology, humanistic analyses of contemporary culture, and occasional poems. Topics of special interest are authenticity, encounter, consciousness, self-actualization, self-transcendence, creativity, personal growth, holistic healing, humanistic psychotherapy, confluent education, values, identity, and love. The journal is a forum for diverse statements about humanistic psychology, including criticisms. Each writer speaks for himself or herself. The editor makes no effort to achieve an official AHP consensus.

Selective Notes on Submissions: Instructions to authors included in each issue of the journal. Authors to prepare manuscripts according to the *Publication Manual of the American Psychological Association* (4th ed.). Submit two (2) copies of the manuscript to the editor.

Journal Frequency: Quarterly

Articles/Pages Published per Year: 30/520

Total Subscribers: 3,325

Book Reviews Accepted: No

Rejection Rate: 90%

Journal of Instructional Psychology

Publisher: Journal of Instructional Psychology
P.O. Box 8826
Spring Hill Station
Mobile, AL 36689-0826

Editor: George E. Uhlig, EdD
P.O. Box 8826
Spring Hill Station
Mobile, AL 36689-8826

Editorial Policy: The *Journal of Instructional Psychology* publishes articles dealing with issues related to instruction, instructional design, and educational management and gives preference to manuscripts focusing on bilingual and multicultural issues, at-risk youth, and educational technology. Authors share in the publication costs.

Selective Notes on Submissions: Write for *Guidelines for Authors.* Manuscripts should conform to the *Publication Manual of the American Psychological Association* (4th ed.). Two (2) original clean copies of the manuscript should be submitted.

Journal Frequency: Quarterly

Articles/Pages Published per Year: 50/350

Total Subscribers: 300

Book Reviews Accepted: Yes (also software and hardware reviews)

Rejection Rate: 25%

Journal of Interpersonal Violence

Publisher: Sage Publications, Inc.
2455 Teller Road
Thousand Oaks, CA 91320

Editor: Jon R. Conte
School of Social Work JH-30
University of Washington
4101 15th Avenue, NE
Seattle, WA 98195

Editorial Policy: The *Journal of Interpersonal Violence* is devoted to the study and treatment of victims and perpetrators of interpersonal violence. It provides a forum for discussion of the concerns and activities of professionals and researchers working with domestic violence, child sexual abuse, rape and sexual assault, physical child abuse, and violent crime. With its dual focus on victims and victimizers, the journal will publish material that addresses the causes, effects, treatment, and prevention of all types of violence.

Selective Notes on Submissions: Instructions to authors included in each issue of the journal. Authors to prepare manuscripts according to the *Publication Manual of the American Psychological Association* (4th ed.). Submit three (3) copies of the manuscript to the editor.

Journal Frequency: Bimonthly

Articles/Pages Published per Year: 52/864

Total Subscribers: 4,575

Book Reviews Accepted: No

Rejection Rate: 60%

Journal of Language and Social Psychology

Publisher: Sage Publications, Inc.
2455 Teller Road
Thousand Oaks, CA 91320

Editors: Howard Giles and James Bradac
Department of Communications
University of California
Santa Barbara, CA 93106

Editorial Policy: NA

Selective Notes on Submissions: Instructions to authors included in each issue of the journal. Authors to prepare manuscripts according to the *Publication Manual of the American Psychological Association* (4th ed.). Submit four (4) copies of the manuscript to the editors.

Journal Frequency: Quarterly

Articles/Pages Published per Year: 16/280

Total Subscribers: 370

Book Reviews Accepted: Yes

Rejection Rate: 75–80%

Journal of Marital and Family Therapy

Publisher: American Association for
Marriage and Family
Therapy
1133 Fifteenth Street, NW
Suite 300
Washington, DC 20005-2710

Editor: Douglas H. Sprenkle
Purdue University
Marriage and Family Therapy
Program
1269 Fowler House
West Lafayette, IN 47907-1269

Editorial Policy: The *Journal of Marital and Family Therapy* is published in accordance with the purposes of the sponsoring organization, the American Association for Marriage and Family Therapy, to advance the professional understanding of marital and family behavior and to improve the psychotherapeutic treatment of marital and family disharmony. Toward that end, the journal publishes articles on research, theory, clinical practice and training in marital and family therapy.

Articles are selected on the basis of appropriateness, clarity, significance, timeliness, and contribution to the field of marital and family therapy. Papers published in the journal are selected from materials presented at the AAMFT conferences and from papers submitted directly to the Editor. Authors need not be members of the AAMFT. No remuneration is paid for accepted manuscripts.

Selective Notes on Submissions: Instructions to authors included in each issue of the journal. Authors to prepare manuscripts according to the *Publication Manual of the American Psychological Association* (4th ed.). Submit four (4) copies of the manuscript to the editor.

Journal Frequency: Quarterly

Articles/Pages Published per Year: 36/640

Total Subscribers: NA

Book Reviews Accepted: NA

Rejection Rate: NA

Journal of Marriage and the Family

Publisher: National Council on Family
Relations
3989 Central Avenue, NE
Suite 550
Minneapolis, MN 55421

Editor: Robert M. Milardo
Department of Human
Development and Family
Studies
Unoversity of Maine
Orono, ME 04469

Editorial Policy: The *Journal of Marriage and the Family* is a prestigious and scientific forum for the publication of original theory, research interpretation, and critical discussion of materials related to marriage and the family.

Selective Notes on Submissions: Authors to prepare manuscripts according to the *Publication Manual of the American Psychologi-*

cal Association (4th ed.). Five (5) copies of manuscripts for possible publication should be submitted directly to the editor, and should be prepared according to manuscript specifications obtainable from the editor and/or described in the February issue of the journal.

Journal Frequency: Quarterly

Articles/Pages Published per Year: 80/1200

Total Subscribers: 7,000

Book Reviews Accepted: Contact editor for directions

Rejection Rate: 80–85%

Notes From Publisher: Average turn-around time on new submissions is seven weeks. $15 submission fee.

Journal of Mathematical Psychology

Publisher: Academic Press, Inc.
              1250 Sixth Avenue
              San Diego, CA 92101

Editor: Hans Colonius
              Fachbereich 5
              Institut fur Kognitionsforschung
              Universitat Oldenburg
              26111 Oldenburg
              Germany

Editorial Policy: The *Journal of Mathematical Psychology* publishes research articles, monographs and reviews, notes and comments, and book reviews in all areas of mathematical and theoretical psychology.

Empirical research is welcomed when it is directly relevant to theoretical questions within psychology. The submission of papers concerned with the development or experimental testing of psychological process models is especially encouraged. Work in the area of fundamental measurement continues to be of interest to the journal. Some example target areas for this journal are (1) perception and/or psychophysics, (2) work in fundamental measurement or scaling, (3) psychometric research if tied to explication of psychological concepts or process models, (4) artificial intelligence and computer simulation (e.g., computational vision as applied to human vision) of psychological processes, (5) learning and memory, (6) motivational dynamics, (7) neuropsychological theories, (8) psycholinguistics, (9) problem solving, and (10) human factors and human–computer interaction.

Selective Notes on Submissions: Instructions to authors included in each issue of the journal. Authors to prepare manuscripts according to the *Publication Manual of the American Psychological Association* (4th ed.). Submit four (4) copies of the manuscript to the Editorial Office, 525 B Street, Suite 1900, San Diego, CA 92101-4495

Journal Frequency: Quarterly

Articles/Pages Published per Year: 33/650

Total Subscribers: NA

Book Reviews Accepted: Yes

Rejection Rate: NA

Journal of Memory and Language

Publisher: Academic Press, Inc.
1250 Sixth Avenue
San Diego, CA 92101

Editor: Rebecca Treiman
c/o Academic Press, Inc.
525 B Street, Suite 1900
San Diego, CA 92101-4495

Editorial Policy: The *Journal of Memory and Language* publishes original research in the areas of human memory and language processing. Although most of the articles published make both an empirical and theoretical contribution, purely theoretical articles are also welcome. The overriding criterion for acceptance of an article for publication is that it must make a significant scientific contribution. The evaluation of an article's quality takes into consideration the significance of the issue that it addresses and the precision with which the problem is specified. The design of experiments must bear a clear and credible relation to the theoretical issues they address, and similarly, the results of experiments must have clear theoretical implications. The research methodology and data analysis must be sound.

Selective Notes on Submissions: Instructions to authors included in each issue of the journal. Authors to prepare manuscripts according to the *Publication Manual of the American Psychological Association* (4th ed.). Submit five (5) copies of the manuscript to the editor.

Journal Frequency: 8 issues per year

Articles/Pages Published per Year: 60/1208

Total Subscribers: NA

Book Reviews Accepted: No

Rejection Rate: NA

Journal of Mental Health Counseling

Publisher: Sage Periodicals Press
2455 Teller Road
Thousand Oaks, CA 91320

Editor: Earl J. Ginter
University of Georgia
Division of Developmental
Studies
106 Clark Howell
Athens, GA 30602-3334

Editorial Policy: *Journal of Mental Health Counseling* publishes articles on all aspects of practice, theory, and research related to mental health counseling. The journal is divided into four sections: *Practice* includes manuscripts relating first person (and other) accounts of counseling experiences, ethical dilemmas, innovative techniques, credentialing, and trends in marketing, financing, managing, and evaluating mental health practices. *Theory* focuses on the bridge between mental health practice and research. This section includes papers on the expansion, refinement, and development of counseling, prevention, and consultation theories. *Research* encourages traditional empirical articles as well as papers on the application of research methodology and statistics to the practice of mental health counseling. *Professional Exchange* includes brief reports (750 words or less) written in a literary or scholarly style that addresses experiences, observations, hypotheses, concerns, challenges, and pilot research projects related to all aspects of mental health counseling.

Selective Notes on Submissions: Submit three (3) copies of the manuscript to the editor.

Journal Frequency: Quarterly

Articles/Pages Published per Year: 44/440

Total Subscribers: NA

Book Reviews Accepted: NA

Rejection Rate: NA

Journal of Mental Imagery

Publisher: Brandon House, Inc.
P.O. Box 240
Bronx, NY 10471

Editor: Akhter Ahsen, PhD
Brandon House, Inc.
P.O. Box 240
Bronx, NY 10471

Editorial Policy: Mental imagery enjoys a central position among mental phenomena. Currently, the use of imagery is growing in a variety of disciplines, including experimental and clinical psychology and psychiatry, neuropsychology, education, creative arts, sociology and literature. The *Journal of Mental Imagery* is dedicated solely to the study and application of imagery. Each issue

will include original articles devoted to these various dimensions of the imagery phenomenon.

Selective Notes on Submissions: Instructions to authors included in each issue of the journal. Authors to prepare manuscripts according to the *Publication Manual of the American Psychological Association* (4th ed.). Submit three (3) copies of the manuscript to the editor. Author charges for tabular materials.

Journal Frequency: Quarterly

Articles/Pages Published per Year: 34/412

Total Subscribers: 5,375

Book Reviews Accepted: Yes

Rejection Rate: NA

Journal of Mind and Behavior

Publisher: The Institute of Mind and
Behavior, Inc.
P.O. Box 522
Village Station
New York, NY 10014

Editor: Raymond C. Russ, PhD
Department of Psychology
5742 Little Hall
University of Maine
Orono, ME 04469-5742

Editorial Policy: The *Journal of Mind and Behavior (JMB)* is dedicated to the interdisciplinary approach within psychology and related fields, building on the assumption of a unified science. Mind and behavior juxtapose, interact, and causally relate to each other in multidirectional ways; *JMB* urges the exploration of these interrelationships. The editors are particularly interested in scholarly work in the following areas: the psychology, philosophy, and sociology of experimentation and the scientific method; the relationship between methodology, operationism, and theory construction; the mind/body problem in the social sciences, medicine, literature, and art; philosophical impact of a mind/body epistemology upon psychology; phenomenological, teleological, existential, and introspective reports relevant to psychology, psychosocial methodology, and social philosophy; issues pertaining to the ethical study of cognition, self-awareness, and higher functions of conciousness in animals; historical perspectives on the course and nature of science. *JMB* is based on the premise that all meaningful statements about human behavior rest ultimately upon observation, with no one scientific method possessing, a priori, greater credence than another. Emphasis on experimental control should not preclude the experiment as a measure of behavior outside the scientific laboratory. The editors recognize the need to propagate ideas and speculations as well as the need to form empirical situations for testing them. However, the editors believe in a working reciprocity between theory and method, and in a unity among the sciences. Manuscripts should accentuate this interdisciplinary approach, either explicitly in their content or implicitly within their point of view.

Selective Notes on Submissions: Instructions to authors included in each issue of the journal. Authors to prepare manuscripts according to the *Publication Manual of the American Psychological Association* (4th

ed.). Submit four (4) copies of the manuscript to the editor. Manuscript handling fee for nonsubscribers.

Journal Frequency: Quarterly

Articles/Pages Published per Year: 24/700

Total Subscribers: 1,089

Book Reviews Accepted: Yes

Rejection Rate: 83%

Notes From Publisher: The *Journal of Mind and Behavior* also publishes commentaries, book reviews, letters to the editor, and special issues.

Journal of Multicultural Counseling and Development

Publisher: American Counseling
                           Association
                           5999 Stevenson Avenue
                           Alexandria, VA 22304

Editor: Frederick D. Harper
                      Howard University

Editorial Policy: The *Journal of Multicultural Counseling and Development* is concerned with research, theory, or program applications pertinent to multicultural and ethnic minority interests in all areas of counseling and human development.

Selective Notes on Submissions: Instructions to authors included in each issue of the

journal. Authors to prepare manuscripts according to the *Publication Manual of the American Psychological Association* (4th ed.). Submit three (3) copies of the manuscript to the editor, c/o the publisher.

Journal Frequency: Quarterly

Articles/Pages Published per Year: 20/200

Total Subscribers: NA

Book Reviews Accepted: NA

Rejection Rate: NA

Journal of Music Therapy

Publisher: National Association for Music Therapy, Inc.
8455 Colesville Road, Suite 930
Silver Spring, MD 20910-3392

Editor: Jayne M. Standley
Journal of Music Therapy
Center for Music Research
School of Music
Florida State University
Tallahassee, FL 32306-2098

Editorial Policy: The *Journal of Music Therapy* publishes only the very best of articles submitted concerning the psychology of music, applied music therapy techniques of all types (psychoanalytical to empirical), perception of music, and effects of music on human behavior. Papers are selected on the basis of their quality and contribution to existing knowledge according to peer review.

Selective Notes on Submissions: Instructions to authors included in each issue of the journal. Authors to prepare manuscripts according to the *Publication Manual of the American Psychological Association* (4th ed.). Submit five (5) copies of the manuscript to the editor.

Journal Frequency: Quarterly

Articles/Pages Published per Year: NA

Total Subscribers: NA

Book Reviews Accepted: Yes

Rejection Rate: 50%

Suggested Index Terms: Music therapy, medicine, special education, mental health, geriatrics

Journal of Nonverbal Behavior

Publisher: Human Sciences Press
233 Spring Street
New York, NY 10013-1578

Editor: Ronald E. Riggio
Department of Psychology
Claremont McKenna College
Claremont, CA 91711

Editorial Policy: The *Journal of Nonverbal Behavior* publishes original theoretical, empirical, and methodological research in the areas of nonverbal behavior, including proxemics, kinesics, paralanguage, facial expression, eye contact, face-to-face interaction, nonverbal emotional expression, and other areas which add significantly to our understanding of nonverbal processes, communication, and behavior. While primarily psychological, the journal welcomes manuscripts from such related fields as anthropology, linguistics, and sociology. "Notes in Brief" is a section of each issue devoted to short and/or informal reports, notes, reviews, etc.

Selective Notes on Submissions: Instructions to authors included in each issue of the journal. Authors to prepare manuscripts according to the *Publication Manual of the American Psychological Association* (4th ed.). Submit the original and four (4) copies of the manuscript to the editor.

Journal Frequency: Quarterly

Articles/Pages Published per Year: 16/240

Total Subscribers: NA

Book Reviews Accepted: No

Rejection Rate: NA

Journal of Occupational Health Psychology

Publisher: Educational Publishing Foundation
750 First Street, NE
Washington, DC 20002-4242

Editor: James Campbell Quick
College of Business Administration
University of Texas at Arlington
P.O. Box 19313
Arlington, TX 76019-0313

Editorial Policy: The *Journal of Occupational Health Psychology* publishes research, theory, and public policy articles in occupational health psychology, an interdisciplinary field representing a broad range of backgrounds, interests, and specializations. Occupational health psychology concerns the application of psychology to improving the quality of worklife and to protecting and promoting the safety, health, and well-being of workers. The journal has a threefold focus on the work environment, the individual, and the work-family interface. The journal seeks scholarly articles, from both researchers and practitioners, concerning psychological factors in relationship to all aspects of occupational health. Included in this broad domain of interest are articles in which work-related psychological factors play a role in the etiology of health problems, articles examining the psychological and associated health consequences of work, and articles concerned with the use of psychological approaches to prevent or mitigate occupational health problems. Special attention is given to articles with a prevention emphasis. Manuscripts dealing with issues of contemporary relevance to the workplace, especially with regard to minority, cultural, or occupationally under–represented groups, or topics at the interface of the family and the workplace are encouraged.

Selective Notes on Submissions: Instructions to authors included in each issue of the journal. Authors to prepare manuscripts according to the *Publication Manual of the American Psychological Association* (4th ed.). Submit four (4) copies of the manuscript to the editor.

Journal Frequency: Quarterly

Articles/Pages Published per Year: 30/420

Total Subscribers: 220

Book Reviews Accepted: No

Rejection Rate: NA

Journal of Occupational and Organizational Psychology

Publisher: British Psychological Society
             13A Church Street
             East Finchley
             London N2 8DX
             England

Editor: Professor Anthony Keenan
             Department of Business
                 Organization
             Herriot-Watt University
             Edinburgh, Scotland

Editorial Policy: The *Journal of Occupational and Organizational Psychology* publishes empirical and conceptual papers which aim to increase understanding of people and organizations at work. Its domain is broad, covering industrial, organizational, engineering, vocational and personnel psychology as well as behavioral aspects of industrial relations, ergonomics, human factors, and industrial sociology. Innovative or interdisciplinary approaches with a psychological emphasis are particularly welcome. Articles are likely to be of the following kinds: (a) empirical research papers containing new quantitative or qualitative factual material, (b) critical surveys of a field, (c) theoretical contributions, (d) prescriptive articles containing methodological, statistical or procedural suggestions, and (e) assessments of the applications of work and organizational

psychology. Papers using student populations as a substitute for work-based populations are not normally accepted.

Selective Notes on Submissions: Instructions to authors included in each issue of the journal. Authors to prepare manuscripts according to the BPS style guide. Authors may also use the *Publication Manual of the American Psychological Association* (4th ed.). Submit four (4) copies of the manuscript to the BPS Journals Office.

Journal Frequency: Quarterly

Articles/Pages Published per Year: 31/352

Total Subscribers: 2,270

Book Reviews Accepted: Yes

Rejection Rate: 79%

Journal of Organizational Behavior

Publisher: John Wiley & Sons Ltd.
             Baffins Lane
             Chichester
             West Sussex PO19 1UD
             England

Editor: Cary L. Cooper
             Manchester School of
                 Management
             University of Manchester
             P.O. Box 88, Sackville Street
             Manchester M60 1QD
             England

Editorial Policy: The *Journal of Organizational Behavior* aims to report and review the growing research in the industrial/

organizational psychology and organizational behavior fields throughout the world. The journal will focus on research and theory in all the topics associated with occupational/organizational behavior including motivation, work performance, equal opportunities at work, job design, career processes, occupational stress, quality of work life, job satisfaction, personnel selection, training, organizational change, research methodology in occupational/organizational behavior, employment, job analysis, behavioral aspects of industrial relations, managerial behavior, organizational structure and climate, leadership and power.

Book reviews are a feature of the *Journal of Organizational Behavior*. The Book Review Editor is Dr. Carolyn R. Dexter, Penn State University, School of Business Administration, 777 West Harrisburg Pike, Middletown, PA 10757. Books consistent with the aims and scope of the journal should be sent to the journal editor at the Manchester School of Management, University of Manchester Institute of Science and Technology, P.O. Box 88, Manchester M60 1QD, England.

Selective Notes on Submissions: Instructions to authors included in each issue of the journal. Authors to prepare manuscripts according to the Harvard system. Submit five (5) copies of the manuscript to the editor.

Journal Frequency: 6 issues per year plus 1 supplement

Articles/Pages Published per Year: 49/800

Total Subscribers: 800

Book Reviews Accepted: Yes

Rejection Rate: 80%

Journal of Parapsychology

Publisher: Parapsychology Press
402 North Buchanan Boulevard
Durham, NC 27701-1728

Editor: John A. Palmer

Editorial Policy: The journal is devoted mainly to original reports of experimental research in parapsychology. It also publishes research reviews, theoretical and methodological articles that are closely linked to the empirical findings in the field, book reviews, news, comments, letters, and abstracts.

Selective Notes on Submissions: Instructions to authors included in each issue of the journal. Authors to prepare manuscripts according to the *Publication Manual of the American Psychological Association* (4th ed.). Submit one (1) unstapled (original) and three (3) stapled copies of the manuscript to the editor in care of the publisher.

Journal Frequency: Quarterly

Articles/Pages Published per Year: 16/400

Total Subscribers: 1,000

Book Reviews Accepted: Yes

Rejection Rate: 25%

Notes From Publisher: Experimental reports should include full description of experimental procedures, and the data and computations should be double-checked.

Journal of Pediatric Psychology

Publisher: Plenum Publishing Corporation
                  233 Spring Street
                  New York, NY 10013-1578

Editor: Anne Kazak, PhD
                  Division of Oncology
                  Children's Hospital
                  34th Street/Civic Center Plaza
                  Philadelphia, PA 19104

Editorial Policy: The *Journal of Pediatric Psychology* publishes articles relating to theory, research, and professional practice in pediatric psychology. Pediatric psychology is an interdisciplinary field addressing the full range of physical and mental development, health, and illness issues affecting children, adolescents, and families. The journal publishes papers on a wide variety of topics exploring the relationship between the psychological and physical well-being of children and adolescents, including understanding, assessment, and intervention with developmental disorders; evaluation and treatment of behavioral and emotional problems and concomitants of disease and illness; the role of psychology in pediatric medicine; the promotion of health and development; and the prevention of illness and injury among children and youth. Articles are welcome from authors in psychology and related disciplines serving children and families.

Selective Notes on Submissions: Instructions to authors included in each issue of the journal. Authors to prepare manuscripts according to the *Publication Manual of the American Psychological Association* (4th ed.). Submit four (4) copies of the manuscript to the editor.

Journal Frequency: Bimonthly

Articles/Pages Published per Year: 60/900

Total Subscribers: 1,531

Book Reviews Accepted: NA

Rejection Rate: 84%

Journal of Personality

Publisher: Duke University Press
                  Box 6697
                  College Station
                  Durham, NC 27708

Editor: Howard Tennen
                  Department of Psychiatry
                  University of Connecticut Health
                  Center
                  Farmington, CT 06030

Editorial Policy: The journal is devoted to scientific investigations in the field of personality. Current stress is on experimental studies of personality and behavior dynamics, personality development, and individual differences in the cognitive, affective, and interpersonal domains. The scope of the journal is not fixed, however, and it is intended to reflect all areas of significant current research. Papers ought to make a substantial empirical or theoretical contribution; short reports will be judged accordingly. Papers concerned exclusively with test construction or validation will ordinarily not be considered.

Selective Notes on Submissions: Instructions to authors included in each issue of the

journal. Authors to prepare manuscripts according to the *Publication Manual of the American Psychological Association* (4th ed.). Submit four (4) copies of the manuscript to the editor.

Journal Frequency: Quarterly

Articles/Pages Published per Year: 32/894

Total Subscribers: 2,000

Book Reviews Accepted: No

Rejection Rate: 75–80%

Journal of Personality Assessment

Publisher: Lawrence Erlbaum Associates, Inc.
365 Broadway
Hillsdale, NJ 07642

Editor: Bill N. Kinder
Department of Psychology
University of South Florida
Tampa, FL 33620

Editorial Policy: The *Journal of Personality Assessment* publishes commentaries, case reports, and research studies dealing with the evaluation and application of methods of personality assessment. Articles submitted for publication should address theoretical, empirical, pedagogical, or professional aspects of using psychological tests or interview data to measure or describe personality processes and their behavioral implications. The journal is broadly concerned with the development and utilization of personality assesssment methods in clinical, counseling, community, cross-cultural, forensic, and health psychology settings; with the assessment of persons of all ages; and with both normal and abnormal personality functioning. Manuscripts pertaining to personality processes but not specifically to their assessment will ordinarily not be considered for publication.

Selective Notes on Submissions: Instructions to authors included in each issue of the journal. Authors to prepare manuscripts according to the *Publication Manual of the American Psychological Association* (4th ed.). Submit three (3) copies of the manuscript to the editor.

Journal Frequency: Quarterly

Articles/Pages Published per Year: 101/1347

Total Subscribers: 3,400

Book Reviews Accepted: Yes

Rejection Rate: 76%

Journal of Personality Disorders

Publisher: Guilford Publications, Inc.
72 Spring Street
New York, NY 10012

Editor: John Livesley, PhD, MD
Department of Psychiatry
University of British Columbia
2255 Wesbrook Mall
Vancouver
Canada BC V6T 2A1

Editorial Policy: The *Journal of Personality Disorders* is a forum devoted to the coverage of all issues pertaining to the diagnosis and treatment of clinically significant personality disorders. This multidisciplinary quarterly presents research on normal and pathological personality and development, new methodologies for assessing personality, clinical nosologies for personality disorders, epidemiological research, treatment innovations, and outcome research. The journal encourages dialogues among proponents of the major schools of thought. Including regular departments and special features on current topics, the journal endeavors to keep the reader abreast of new assessment tools, treatment planning and techniques, controversial issues, and the contemporary journal and book literature.

Selective Notes on Submissions: Instructions to authors included in each issue of the journal. Authors to prepare manuscripts according to the *Publication Manual of the American Psychological Association* (4th ed.). Submit four (4) copies of the manuscript to the editor.

Journal Frequency: Quarterly

Articles/Pages Published per Year: 45/384

Total Subscribers: 1,500

Book Reviews Accepted: No

Rejection Rate: NA

Journal of Personality and Social Psychology

Publisher: American Psychological Association

750 First Street, NE
Washington, DC 20002-4242

Editors: Arie Kruglanski, Chester A. Insko, and Ed Diener

Editorial Policy: The *Journal of Personality and Social Psychology* publishes original papers in all areas of personality and social psychology. It emphasizes empirical reports but may include specialized theoretical, methodological, and review papers. The journal is divided into three independently edited sections: Attitudes and Social Cognition includes papers on attitudes dealing with such topics as the formation or change of beliefs and attitudes, measurement of attitudes, and the relation between attitudes and behavior. Papers on social cognition deal with the formation and utilization of knowledge about the social world and embrace such topics as social and person perception, attributional processes, and information processing. Interpersonal Relations and Group Processes focuses on psychological and structual features of interaction in dyads and groups. Appropriate to this section are papers on the nature and dynamics of interactions and social relationships, including interpersonal attraction, communication, emotion, and relationship development, and on group and organizational processes such as social influence, group decision making and task performance, intergroup relations, and aggression and prosocial behavior. Personality Processes and Individual Differences encourages papers on all aspects of personality psychology as traditionally defined. This includes personality assessment, measurement, structure, and dynamics. All methodological approaches will be considered.

Selective Notes on Submissions: Instructions to authors included in each issue of the journal. Authors to prepare manuscripts according to the *Publication Manual of the American Psychological Association* (4th ed.). Submit six (6) copies of the manuscript as follows:

Attitudes and Social Cognition: Arie Kruglanski, editor, Department of Psychology, University of Maryland, College Park, MD 20742;

Interpersonal Relations and Group Processes: Chester A. Insko, editor, Department of Psychology, University of North Carolina, Chapel Hill, NC 27599-3270; and

Personality Processes and Interpersonal Differences: Ed Diener, editor, Department of Psychology, University of Illinois, 603 East Daniel, Champaign, IL 61820.

Journal Frequency: Monthly

Articles/Pages Published per Year: 182/ 2370

Total Subscribers: 5,600

Book Reviews Accepted: No

Rejection Rate: 83%

Journal of Phenomenological Psychology

Publisher: Humanities Press International, Inc.
165 First Avenue
Atlantic Highlands, NJ 07716

Editor: Frederick J. Wertz
Department of Psychology
FCLC
Fordham University
Lincoln Center
New York, NY 10023

Editorial Policy: The *Journal of Phenomenological Psychology* publishes articles that advance the discipline of psychology from a phenomenological perspective as understood by scholars who work within the continental sense of phenomenology. Within that tradition, however, phenomenology is understood in the broadest possible sense and is not meant to convey the thought of any one individual. Indeed, our hope is that by means of articles appearing in this journal, radical breakthroughs in phenomenological thought will be possible. Therefore, the journal especially seeks "breakthrough" articles and the reporting of research findings that contain the broadest possible significance for the field of phenomenological psychology. Otherwise, however, articles may be theoretical or empirical, individual or social. Any legitimate psychological phenomenon may be researched, reflected on, or theorized about. The overall aim is to capture a psychological understanding of the human person in relation to himself or herself, the world, or others. The assumption is that this field is still in the process of developing, and thus articles depicting creative, innovative applications or phenomenological approaches to concrete psychological problems are the type being sought.

Selective Notes on Submissions: Instructions to authors included in each issue of the journal. Authors to prepare manuscripts according to the *Publication Manual of the American Psychological Association* (4th ed.). Submit four (4) copies of the manuscript to the editor.

Journal Frequency: Bimonthly

Articles/Pages Published per Year: 10/220

Total Subscribers: NA

Book Reviews Accepted: Yes

Rejection Rate: NA

Journal of Polymorphous Perversity

Publisher: Wry-Bred Press, Inc.
P.O. Box 1454
Madison Square Station
New York, NY 10159-1454

Editor: Glenn C. Ellenbogen

Editorial Policy: The *Wall Street Journal* called our journal "a social scientist's answer to *Mad* magazine." We seek to publish well-written spoofs of psychology, generally written to closely parallel real scientific research articles both in content and style. While we publish primarily humorous and satirical lampoons of psychology, we also actively seek to publish real research studies that have a zany slant and are written in a humorous, or amusing, wry, dry, quasi-scientific style. Example of a previously published real research study: academic status as a function of the size (in cm.) of employment advertisements appearing in *The Cronicle of Higher Education*.

Selective Notes on Submissions: No style sheet included. Authors may (but are not required to) prepare manuscripts according to the *Publication Manual of the American*

Psychological Associaton (4th ed.). Submit three (3) copies of the manuscript to the editor.

Journal Frequency: Biannually

Articles/Pages Published per Year: 19/48

Total Subscribers: 3,213

Book Reviews Accepted: No

Rejection Rate: 97%

Notes From Publisher: Manuscripts are reviewed by the Editor and 1 or more of 17 associate editors. We accept 1 out of every 33 manuscripts submitted. We generally do not publish manuscripts written in the first person, unless the material involves a clinical vignette. Publication Guidelines are available (send an SASE).

Journal of Psychoeducational Assessment

Publisher: The Psychoeducational
Corporation
505 22nd Street
Knoxville, TN 37916

Editor: Bruce A. Bracken
Department of Psychology
University of Memphis
Memphis, TN 38152

Editorial Policy: The *Journal of Psychoeducational Assessment* publishes manuscripts relevant for practicing psychologists, educational diagnosticians, special educators, academic trainers, and others interested in psychoeducational assessment. Mainly interested in articles that describe innovative assessment strategies, relationships among existing instruments, diagnostic procedures, and the relationship between assessment and instruction. Review articles of assessment techniques, strategies, and instrumentation are particularly welcome. Implications for the practitioner should be clearly emphasized.

Selective Notes on Submissions: Instructions to authors included in each issue of the journal. Authors to prepare manuscripts according to the *Publication Manual of the American Psychological Association* (4th ed.). Submit four (4) copies of the manuscript to the editor.

Journal Frequency: Quarterly

Articles/Pages Published per Year: 60/384

Total Subscribers: 940

Book Reviews Accepted: Yes

Rejection Rate: 70%

Journal of Psychohistory

Publisher: The Association of
             Psychohistory, Inc.
             140 Riverside Drive
             Suite 1414
             New York, NY 10024

Editor: Lloyd de Mause

Editorial Policy: The journal welcomes contributions of articles on childhood and the family, past and present; psychohistory in its broadest terms, individual or group; applied psychoanalysis, except for purely literary studies; political psychology and the psychology of historical movements; and psychoanalytic anthropology.

Selective Notes on Submissions: Instructions to authors included in each issue of the journal. Authors to prepare manuscripts according to the *Chicago Manual of Style*, the University of Chicago Press.

Journal Frequency: Quarterly

Articles/Pages Published per Year: 30/500

Total Subscribers: 3,500

Book Reviews Accepted: Yes

Rejection Rate: 50%

Notes From Publisher: All schools of psychology welcome. Very fast approval process.

Journal of Psycholinguistic Research

Publisher: Plenum Publishing Corporation
             233 Spring Street
             New York, NY 10013-1578

Editor: R. W. Rieber
             John Jay College of Criminal
               Justice
             City University of New York
             445 West 59th Street
             New York, NY 10019

Editorial Policy: This international journal publishes carefully selected papers from the several disciplines engaged in psycho-linguistic research. It hopes to provide a single, recognized medium for communications among linguists, psychologists, biologists, sociologists, and others. It welcomes original theoretical and experimental papers, critical surveys, and book reviews covering a broad range of approaches to the study of the communicative process, including: the social and anthropological bases of communication; development of speech and language; semantics (problems in linguistic meaning); biological foundations; psycho-pathological aspects; and educational psycholinguistics.

Selective Notes on Submissions: Instructions to authors included in each issue of the journal. Authors to prepare manuscripts according to the *Publication Manual of the American Psychological Association* (4th ed.). Submit three (3) copies of the manuscript to the editor.

Journal Frequency: Bimonthly

Articles/Pages Published per Year: 30/600

Total Subscribers: NA

Book Reviews Accepted: NA

Rejection Rate: NA

Journal of Psychological Type

Publisher: Association for Psychological Type

Editor: Thomas G. Carskadon
Mississippi State University
Department of Psychology
Box 6161
Mississippi State, MS 39762

Editorial Policy: The *Journal of Psychological Type* publishes original articles relating to the Myers-Briggs Type Indicator and theories of psychological types as described by Carl Jung, Isabel Myers, and others, including various contemporary approaches which use the MBTI or similar instuments. Single research studies, integrative research reviews, thoeretical papers, "action research," and descriptions of practical applications of type are welcome in all areas. All articles and data must be original—i.e., not having been published previously and not in press or under editorial review elsewhere.

Selective Notes on Submissions: Instructions to authors included in each issue of the journal. Authors to prepare manuscripts according to the *Publication Manual of the American Psychological Association* (4th ed.). Submit three (3) copies of the manuscript to the editor.

Journal Frequency: Quarterly

Articles/Pages Published per Year: NA

Total Subscribers: 5,000

Book Reviews Accepted: NA

Rejection Rate: NA

Journal of Psychology: Interdisciplinary and Applied

Publisher: Heldref Publications
1319 18th Street, NW
Washington, DC 20036-1802

Editors: Garvin Chastain
Boise State University

Leonard W. Doob
Yale University

John E. Horrocks
Ohio State University

Editorial Policy: The *Journal of Psychology* is an interdisciplinary journal that publishes research and theoretical articles in the general field of psychology. Emphasis is placed on the following: (1) integration of divergent data, fields, and theories of psychology and related disciplines; (2) decidedly new avenues for thinking and research, particularly with reference to public interest, community, education, industry, management, and measurement; (3) outrageous critcism of the present status of the behavioral disciplines; and (4) analysis of the interrelations of novel populations or those of unusual scale. Studies of monograph length in areas appropriate to this journal would be welcomed by *Genetic, Social, and General Psychology Monographs.*

Selective Notes on Submissions: Instructions to authors included in each issue of the journal. Authors to prepare manuscripts according to the *Publication Manual of the American Psychological Association* (4th ed.). Note: Typesetting charges to authors of $50/table; $20/ figure; and $25 for heavy

use of statistics. Submit one (1) copy of the manuscript to the Managing Editor, The Journal of Psychology, Heldref Publications, 1319 18th Street, NW, Washington, DC 20036-1802.

Journal Frequency: Bimonthly

Articles/Pages Published per Year: 56/600

Total Subscribers: 1,462

Book Reviews Accepted: No

Rejection Rate: 40%

Journal of Psychology and Judaism

Publisher: Human Sciences Press
233 Spring Street
New York, NY 10013-1578

Editor: Reuven P. Bulka
1747 Featherston Drive
Ottawa, Ontario
Canada K1H 6P4

Editorial Policy: The *Journal of Psychology and Judaism* is dedicated to exploring the relationship between psychology and Judaism and examines this relationship on both a clinical and philosophical level. The journal publishes articles that are related to the spheres of psychology and Judaism and have implications concerning the synthesis of the two areas. The journal serves as a forum for discussion and development of integrated approaches to uniquely Jewish problems in the clinical and meta-clinical realms.

Selective Notes on Submissions: Instructions to authors included in each issue of the

journal. Authors to prepare manuscripts according to the *Publication Manual of the American Psychological Association* (4th ed.). Submit three (3) copies of the manuscript to the editor.

Journal Frequency: Quarterly

Articles/Pages Published per Year: 20/256

Total Subscribers: 1,000

Book Reviews Accepted: Yes

Rejection Rate: 60%

Journal of Psychology and Theology

Publisher: Rosemead School of Psychology
Biola University
13800 Biola Avenue
La Mirada, CA 90639-0001

Editor: Patricia L. Pike
13800 Biola Avenue
La Mirada, CA 90639

Editorial Policy: The purpose of the *Journal of Psychology and Theology* is to communicate recent scholarly thinking on the interrelationships of psychological and theological concepts and to consider the application of these concepts to a variety of professional settings. All articles should be consistent with an evangelical theological position. Material in the following categories will be considered for publication: (1) Theoretical or applied articles dealing with the integration of psychology and theology. (2) Research articles which have relevance to theology, the psychology of religion, the ministry of the church or the integration of psychology and theology. (3) Articles dealing with pastoral counseling or the theory and application of psychological data to the work of the church. (4) Theoretical, applied, or research articles bearing on the relationship of psychology to the intercultural context of Christian world mission(s). (5) Theoretical, research, and applied articles dealing with the family and relationships within the Christian community. (6) Reviews of articles in other journals relevant to the integration of psychology and theology. (7) Reactions to current or past journal articles. (8) Reviews of relevant books from the field of psychology and theology.

Selective Notes on Submissions: Instructions to authors included in each issue of the journal. Authors to prepare manuscripts according to the *Publication Manual of the American Psychological Association* (4th ed.). Submit three (3) copies of the manuscript to the editor.

Journal Frequency: Quarterly

Articles/Pages Published per Year: 30/380

Total Subscribers: 1,500

Book Reviews Accepted: Yes

Rejection Rate: 60%

Journal of Psychopathology and Behavioral Assessment

Publisher: Plenum Publishing Corporation
233 Spring Street
New York, NY 10013-1578

Editor: Henry E. Adams, PhD
Department of Psychology
University of Georgia
Athens, GA 30602

Editorial Policy: Formerly the *Journal of Behavioral Assessment*. The *Journal of Psychopathology and Behavioral Assessment* publishes articles on basic research, theory, and clinical investigation in psychopathology and behavioral assessment. The journal seeks to foster scientific understanding of psychopathology by focusing on objective measurement and classification of normal and abnormal behavior; predisposing, precipitating, and maintaining factors (psychological and/or biological) of abnormal behavior; data-based theories of psychopathology; and scholarly reviews of major topics in psychopathology and objective assessment. Case studies are considered if they contribute significantly to developing knowledge in the journal's area of interest. Articles on therapeutic intervention are considered only if they provide substantial advancement of knowledge in these areas. The journal publishes technical notes on instrumentation, commentaries on controversial issues, and book reviews in the aforementioned areas.

Selective Notes on Submissions: Instructions to authors included in each issue of the journal. Authors to prepare manuscripts according to the *Publication Manual of the American Psychological Association* (4th ed.). Submit three (3) copies of the manuscript to the editor.

Journal Frequency: Quarterly

Articles/Pages Published per Year: 35/400

Total Subscribers: NA

Book Reviews Accepted: Yes

Rejection Rate: 40%

Journal of Psychotherapy Integration

Publisher: Plenum Press
233 Spring Street
New York, NY 10013

Editor: Hal Arkowitz
Department of Psychology
University of Arizona
Tucson, AZ 85721

Editorial Policy: *Journal of Psychotherapy Integration* is the official journal of SEPI, the Society for the Exploration of Psychotherapy Integration. The journal is devoted to publishing original peer-reviewed papers that move beyond the confines of single-school or single-theory approaches to psychotherapy and behavior change, and that significantly advance our knowledge of psychotherapy integration. The journal publishes papers presenting new data, theory, or clinical techniques relevant to psychotherapy integration, as well as papers that review existing work in the area. Of particular relevance to the goals of the journal are papers that integrate our knowledge of psychotherapy and behavior change with developments in the broader fields of psychology and psychiatry (e.g., cognitive sciences, psychobiology, health psychology, and social psychology). Only articles relating to the integration of different therapies will be considered. Articles may emphasize theory, research, or practice.

Selective Notes on Submissions: Instructions to authors included in each issue of the journal. Authors to prepare manuscripts according to the *Publication Manual of the American Psychological Association* (4th ed.). Submit four (4) copies of the manuscript to the editor.

Journal Frequency: Quarterly

Articles/Pages Published per Year: 20/360

Total Subscribers: 800

Book Reviews Accepted: Yes

Rejection Rate: 80%

Journal of Rational–Emotive and Cognitive Behavior Therapy

Publisher: Human Sciences Press
                  233 Spring Street
                  New York, NY 10013-1578

Editor: Michael E. Bernard, PhD
               Department of Educational
                   Psychology and
                   Administration
               California State University
               1250 Bellflower Boulevard
               Long Beach, CA 90840-2201

Editorial Policy: The *Journal of Rational–Emotive and Cognitive Behavior Therapy* seeks to provide a forum to stimulate research and discussion into the development and promulgation of rational–emotive therapy (RET) and other forms of cognitive-behavioral therapy. It particularly welcomes manuscripts related to the following: (a) research into the theory and practice of RET; (b) theoretical discussions and literature reviews into the cognitive bases of the development and alleviation of emotional, behavioral, and interpersonal disorders; (c) applications of RET into new arenas and populations; (d) descriptions of innovative techniques and procedures; and (e) case studies.

Selective Notes on Submissions: Instructions to authors included in each issue of the journal. Authors to prepare manuscripts according to the *Publication Manual of the American Psychological Association* (4th ed.). Submit the original and two (2) copies of the manuscript to the editor.

Journal Frequency: Quarterly

Articles/Pages Published per Year: NA

Total Subscribers: 1,900

Book Reviews Accepted: NA

Rejection Rate: NA

Journal of Reality Therapy

Publisher: Institute for Reality Therapy
                  Northeastern University
                  203 Lake Hall
                  Boston, MA 02115

Editor: Lawrence Litwack

Editorial Policy: The *Journal of Reality Therapy* is directed to the publication of manuscripts concerning research, theory development, or specific descriptions of the successful application of reality therapy principles in field settings. This journal is the official publication of the Institute for Reality Therapy.

Selective Notes on Submissions: Instructions to authors included in each issue of the journal. Authors to prepare manuscripts according to the *Publication Manual of the American Psychological Association* (4th ed.). Submit three (3) copies of the manuscript to the editor at the editorial office: Journal of Reality Therapy, Boston-Bouve College, Northeastern University, 203 Lake Hall, 360 Huntington Avenue, Boston, MA 02115.

Journal Frequency: Semiannually

Articles/Pages Published per Year: 20–30/ 100–150

Total Subscribers: 1,500

Book Reviews Accepted: Yes

Rejection Rate: 50%

Journal of Research in Personality

Publisher: Academic Press, Inc.
1250 Sixth Avenue
San Diego, CA 92101

Editors: William Griffit and
David C. Funder
Department of Psychology
University of California,
Riverside
Riverside, CA 92521

Editorial Policy: The *Journal of Research in Personality* will publish studies in the field of personality and in related fields basic to the understanding of personality. Subject matter will include treatments of genetic, physiological, motivational, learning, peceptual, cognitive, and social processes of both normal and abnormal kinds in both human and animal subjects. Equal emphasis will be placed on experimental and descriptive research, with preference given to presentations of an integrated series of independent studies concerned with significant theoretical issues relating to personality. The journal will also publish theoretical articles and critical reviews of current experimental and methodological interest, as well as brief notes and critiques.

Selective Notes on Submissions: Instructions to authors included in each issue of the journal. Authors to prepare manuscripts according to the *Publication Manual of the American Psychological Association* (4th ed.). Submit three (3) copies of the manuscript to the editor.

Journal Frequency: Quarterly

Articles/Pages Published per Year: 28/550

Total Subscribers: NA

Book Reviews Accepted: No

Rejection Rate: 70%

Journal of School Psychology

Publisher: Elsevier Science
660 White Plains Road
Tarrytown, NY 10591-5153

Editor: Joel Myers
              Department of Counseling and
                 Psychological Services
              Georgia State University
              University Plaza
              Atlanta, GA 30303-3083

Editorial Policy: The *Journal of School Psychology (JSP)* publishes original articles on research and practice relevant to the development of school psychology as both a scientific and an applied specialty. The journal also reviews tests, books, and other professional materials of interest to school psychologists. Most manuscripts published by *JSP* are unsolicited. However, *JSP* occasionally addresses a timely topic for which manuscripts are invited. *JSP* is particularly interested in assisting able school psychologists who have not published regularly. Brief reports and commentaries of no more than two printed pages will be considered for publication. At the discretion of the editor, rebuttals to published commentaries may be invited. They must be willing to make an extended report of the manuscript available to readers upon request. Authors must agree not to publish a full-length report with another journal and these brief reports should be carefully designed and well executed studies that, because they represent a replication or specialized topic, would not be accepted as a regular article.

Selective Notes on Submissions: Instructions to authors included in each issue of the journal. Authors to prepare manuscripts according to the *Publication Manual of the American Psychological Association* (4th ed.). Submit four (4) copies of the manuscript to the editor.

Journal Frequency: Quarterly

Articles/Pages Published per Year: 43/435

Total Subscribers: 2,300

Book Reviews Accepted: NA

Rejection Rate: NA

Notes From Publisher: Free sample copy available upon request.

Journal of Sex Education and Therapy

Publisher: Guilford Publications, Inc.
                72 Spring Street
                New York, NY 10012

Editor: R. Taylor Segraves, MD
                School of Medicine
                Department of Psychiatry
                Metro Health Medical Center
                Case Western Reserve
                   University,
                3395 Scranton Road
                Cleveland, OH 44109

Editorial Policy: Official journal of the American Association of Sex Educators, Counselors and Therapists (AASECT).

Selective Notes on Submissions: Instructions to authors included in each issue of the journal. Authors to prepare manuscripts according to the *Publication Manual of the American Psychological Association* (4th ed.). Submit three (3) copies of the manuscript to the editor.

Journal Frequency: Quarterly

Articles/Pages Published per Year: 28/320

Total Subscribers: 3,000

Book Reviews Accepted: Yes

Rejection Rate: 50%

Notes From Publisher: Manuscripts will be considered in the following categories: research reports, articles, field reports, guest editorials, and letters to the editor.

Journal of Sex and Marital Therapy

Publisher: Brunner/Mazel, Inc.
19 Union Square West
New York, NY 10003

Editors: Clifford J. Sager and
R. Taylor Segraves

Editorial Policy: The *Journal of Sex and Marital Therapy* provides an active and contemporary forum for the new clinical techniques and conceptualizations that are emerging from the practice of sex and marital therapy. As a clinical and therapeutically oriented journal, it will emphasize information on new therapeutic techniques, research on outcome, special clinical problems, as well as the theoretical parameters of sexual functioning and marital relationships.

Selective Notes on Submissions: Authors to prepare manuscripts according to the *Publication Manual of the American Psychological Association* (4th ed.). Submit three (3) copies of the manuscript to R. T. Segraves,

MD, MHMC-Psychiatry, 2500 Metro Health Drive, Cleveland, OH 44109-1998

Journal Frequency: Quarterly

Articles/Pages Published per Year: 28/290

Total Subscribers: 2,000

Book Reviews Accepted: NA

Rejection Rate: NA

Journal of Sex Research

Publisher: Society for the Scientific Study of Sex, Inc.
P.O. Box 208
Mt. Vernon, IA 52314

Editor: John DeLamater
Department of Sociology
University of Wisconsin
Madison, WI 53706-1393

Editorial Policy: The *Journal of Sex Research* serves as a forum for the interdisciplinary exchange of knowledge among professionals concerned with the scientific study of sexuality. The journal intends to inform its readers, to provoke the exchange of ideas, to stimulate research, and to promote the integration of the diversity that exists in contemporary scientific sexology. Articles reporting original empirical research, theoretical essays, methodological articles, historical articles, clinical reports, and teaching papers are publishable. Book reviews are also included. The primary criterion for acceptable manuscripts is that an important problem or issue be delineated and that a clear, specific answer (or potential answer) be presented.

Selective Notes on Submissions: Instructions to authors included in each issue of the journal. Authors to prepare manuscripts according to the *Publication Manual of the American Psychological Association* (4th ed.). Submit four (4) copies of the manuscript to the editor.

Journal Frequency: Quarterly

Articles/Pages Published per Year: 28/400

Total Subscribers: 1,700

Book Reviews Accepted: Yes

Rejection Rate: 90%

Journal of Social Behavior and Personality

Publisher: Select Press
P.O. Box 37
Corte Madera, CA 94976

Editor: Rick Crandall, PhD

Editorial Policy: The *Journal of Social Behavior and Personality* tries to do things differently. We are truly interdisciplinary. We are looking for articles that are not just more of the same. We are crusading to improve editorial and review procedures. Our speed is one indication of that. We use page costs for partial funding. In return, we are free of artificially imposed rejection

rates. We try to treat authors as valued customers. Even when rejecting papers, we usually provide specific suggestions for improvement.

Selective Notes on Submissions: Instructions to authors included in each issue of the journal. Authors to prepare manuscripts according to the *Publication Manual of the American Psychological Association* (4th ed.). Submit four (4) copies of the manuscript to Journal of Social Behavior and Personality, P.O. Box 37, Corte Madera, CA 94976. *Note*: Journal requires submitter to include stamped envelopes (see instructions in each issue) or $10.00 with each manuscript submitted. Accepted papers billed to authors at $25.00 per typeset page.

Journal Frequency: Quarterly

Articles/Pages Published per Year: 80/800

Total Subscribers: NA

Book Reviews Accepted: NA

Rejection Rate: 50%

Journal of Social and Clinical Psychology

Publisher: Guilford Publications, Inc.
72 Spring Street
New York, NY 10012

Editor: C. R. Snyder, PhD
Department of Psychology
Fraser Hall
University of Kansas
Lawrence, KA 66045

Editorial Policy: The *Journal of Social and Clinical Psychology* incorporates reports of clinical and experimental social research, invited reviews, short "point-counterpoint" exchanges on controversial issues, book reviews, and, occasionally, autobiographical reflections regarding the seeds of important research, theory, or approaches to clinical practice. Among the topic areas typifying the social–clinical interface addressed in the journal are close relationships; attributions, beliefs, labels, and interactional patterns in mental health and illness; helplessness and perceived control; emotions, nonverbal behavior, and psychopathology; social skills; stress and coping; behavioral medicine and health psychology; development of social relationships; social psychophysiology and neuropsychology; client–therapist interactions; and bias and stereotyping in social interaction and clinical practice.

Selective Notes on Submissions: Instructions to authors included in each issue of the journal. Authors to prepare manuscripts according to the *Publication Manual of the American Psychological Association* (4th ed.). Submit five (5) copies of the manuscript to the editor. There is a $15.00 submission fee made payable to Guilford Press, but this can be waived in instances of financial hardship (e.g., graduate students).

Journal Frequency: Quarterly

Articles/Pages Published per Year: 30/512

Total Subscribers: NA

Book Reviews Accepted: Yes

Rejection Rate: 80%

Journal of Social Issues

Publisher: Blackwell Publishers
                  238 Main Street
                  Cambridge, MA 02142

Editor: Phyllis Katz, PhD
                  Institute for Research on Social
                     Problems
                  520 Pearl Street
                  Boulder, CO 80302

Editorial Policy: The *Journal of Social Issues* is sponsored by The Society for the Psychological Study of Social Issues (SPSSI), a group of over 3,000 psychologists and allied social scientists who share a concern with research on the psychological aspects of important social issues. SPSSI is governed by Kurt Lewin's dictum that "there is nothing so practical as a good theory." In various ways, the society seeks to bring theory and practice into focus on human problems of the group, the community, and the nation, as well as the increasingly important ones that have no national boundaries. This journal has as its goal the communication of scientific findings and interpretations in a nontechnical manner but without sacrifice of professional standards. (This is a publication of APA's Division 9.)

Selective Notes on Submissions: The journal does not accept unsolicited manuscripts or book reviews. Issues are organized around an integral theme. Ideas and questions regarding issue proposals should be addressed to the editor.

Journal Frequency: Quarterly

Articles/Pages Published per Year: 45/740

Total Subscribers: 5,000

Book Reviews Accepted: No

Rejection Rate: NA

Journal of Social and Personal Relationships

Publisher: Sage Publications, Ltd.
                   6 Bonhill Street
                   London EC2A 4PU
                   England

Editor: Steve Duck
                   Department of Communication
                       Studies
                   University of Iowa
                   Iowa City, IA 52242

Editorial Policy: The *Journal of Social and Personal Relationships* welcomes the submission of articles on all aspects of social and personal relationships from any academic discipline on the understanding that these are original articles not under consideration by other journals. Empirical, review, and theoretical articles as well as overviews of research programs are invited.

Selective Notes on Submissions: Instructions to authors included in each issue of the journal. Submit three (3) copies of the manuscript to the editor.

Journal Frequency: Bimonthly

Articles/Pages Published per Year: 40/800

Total Subscribers: NA

Book Reviews Accepted: Yes

Rejection Rate: NA

Suggested Index Terms: Sociology

Journal of Social Psychology

Publisher: Heldref Publications
                   1318 18th Street, NW
                   Washington, DC 20036-1802

Editor: Leonard W. Doob
                   Yale University

Editorial Policy: The *Journal of Social Psychology* is devoted to experimental, empirical, and especially field studies of groups, cultural effects, cross-national problems, language, and ethnicity. The journal places a higher priority in acceptance and publication of cross-cultural and field research than on laboratory research employing college or university students. But this policy does not mean a commitment in advance to accept all cross-cultural and field studies or to reject all laboratory studies. Longer papers may be evaluated in *Genetic, Social, and General Psychology Monographs.*

Selective Notes on Submissions: Instructions to authors included in each issue of the journal. Authors to prepare manuscripts according to the *Publication Manual of the American Psychological Association* (4th ed.). Typesetting charges to authors of $50/table, $20/figure, and $25 for heavy use of statistics. Submit the original and one (1) copy of the manuscript to the Managing

Editor, Journal of Social Psychology, 1319 18th Street, NW, Washington, DC 20036-1802.

Journal Frequency: Bimonthly

Articles/Pages Published per Year: 101/860

Total Subscribers: 2,065

Book Reviews Accepted: No

Rejection Rate: 30%

Journal of Sport and Exercise Psychology

Publisher:	Human Kinetics Publishers, Inc. 1607 North Market Street Champaign, IL 61820-2200
Editor:	Thelma Horn Department of PEHSS Phillips Hall Miami University Oxford, OH 45056

Editorial Policy: The *Journal of Sport and Exercise Psychology* is designed to stimulate and communicate research theory in all areas of sport and exercise psychology. The journal emphasizes original research reports that advance our understanding of human behavior as it relates to sport and exercise. Comprehensive reviews employing both qualitative and quantitative methods are also encouraged, as well as brief reports of soundly designed research studies that are of special interest or limited importance. Areas of interest include research in social, clinical, developmental, and experimental psychology as well as psychobiology and personality. Moreover, the terms *sport* and *exercise* may pertain to either the independent or dependent variables. Generally speaking, work on motor control processes, studies of sport as a social institution, or broader social issues are beyond the scope of the journal. A wide variety of methods are acceptable for studying sport and exercise psychology topics.

Selective Notes on Submissions: Instructions to authors included in each issue of the journal. Authors to prepare manuscripts according to the *Publication Manual of the American Psychological Association* (4th ed.). Submit four (4) copies of the manuscript to the editor.

Journal Frequency: Quarterly

Articles/Pages Published per Year: 28/432

Total Subscribers: 1,797

Book Reviews Accepted: Yes

Rejection Rate: 86%

Journal of Theoretical and Philosophical Psychology

Publisher:	American Psychological Association Division 24 c/o 750 First Street, NE Washington, DC 20002-4242
Editor:	Brent Slife Department of Psychology

Brigham Young University
1072 SWKT
Provo, UT 84602-5378

Editorial Policy: The *Journal of Theoretical and Philosophical Psychology* is the journal of Division 24 of the American Psychological Association, the Division of Theoretical and Philosophical Psychology. Its aim is to inform division members of the current thinking, issues, and events relevant to their theoretical and philosophical interests in psychology. The journal is a forum for the full range of orientations and psychological subject matters.

Theoretical contributions of all kinds are welcomed, especially articles, position pieces, reviews, and commentaries. The term "theoretical contribution" is not intended to exclude empirical studies, particularly when they have significant theoretical import.

Selective Notes on Submissions: Instructions to authors included in each issue of the journal. Authors to prepare manuscripts according to the *Publication Manual of the American Psychological Association* (4th ed.). Submit four (4) copies of the manuscript to the editor.

Journal Frequency: 2 issues per year

Articles/Pages Published per Year: 9/208

Total Subscribers: 1,000

Book Reviews Accepted: Yes

Rejection Rate: 68%

Journal for the Theory of Social Behaviour

Publisher: Basil Blackwell Publishers, Ltd.
108 Cowley Road
Oxford OX4 1JF
England

Editor: Charles W. Smith
Department of Sociology
Queens College, CUNY
Flushing, NY

Editorial Policy: The *Journal for the Theory of Social Behaviour* seeks to publish original theoretical/methodological manuscripts of good quality bearing on social behavior. As an interdisciplinary journal, wide latitude is given to the manner in which this may be done, including (a) critiques of existing concepts and theories, (b) proposals for innovative research methods, (c) analysis of philosophic assumptions of the social sciences, (d) presentation of new models of man, and (e) discussions dealing with the relationship of everyday life behaviors with those situated within an experimental setting. Though the primary focus of the journal is theoretical, manuscripts should have potential applicability to the research process. The journal is not interested in publishing articles which focus solely upon nonsocial behavior, which ignore individual agency, which are purely technical in orientation, or which lack interdisciplinary relevance.

Selective Notes on Submissions: Instructions to authors included in each issue of the journal. Submit five (5) copies of the manuscript to the editor.

Journal Frequency: Quarterly

Articles/Pages Published per Year: 22/500

Total Subscribers: 1,000

Book Reviews Accepted: No

Rejection Rate: 80%

Journal of Transpersonal Psychology

Publisher: Transpersonal Institute
                   P.O. Box 4437
                   Stanford, CA 94309

Editor: Miles A. Vich
                   345 California Avenue,
                       Suite No. 1
                   Palo Alto, CA 94306

Editorial Policy: The founding and authoritative journal in this field, publishing original papers, reports, research studies, and reviews. Concerned with theory, practice, and research of transpersonal experience, concepts, and practices. Focuses on full human awareness, the integration of psychological and spiritual experience, and the transcendence of self. This orientation is eclectic, cross-cultural, and interdisciplinary, with strong connections to Western psychology and Eastern and Western spiritual traditions. Audience is international and national, professional and academic, and includes graduate-level lay readers. Referenced articles of all lengths are peer-reviewed by leading authorities.

Selective Notes on Submissions: All manuscripts, and an abstract of not more than 150 words, should be submitted in triplicate, double-spaced to the editor.

Journal Frequency: Semiannual

Articles/Pages Published per Year: 12/220

Total Subscribers: 3,800

Book Reviews Accepted: invited submissions

Rejection Rate: NA

Journal of Traumatic Stress

Publisher: Plenum Press
                   233 Spring Street
                   New York, NY 10013

Editor: Dean G. Kilpatrick
                   MUSC-National Crime Victims
                       Center
                   Department of Psychiatry and
                       Behavioral Sciences
                   171 Ashley Avenue
                   Charleston, SC 29425-0742

Editorial Policy: Published for the International Society for Public Stress Studies. *Journal of Traumatic Stress* is an interdisciplinary forum for the publication of peer-reviewed original papers (reviewed blind to authorship) on biopsychosocial aspects of trauma. Papers focus on theoretical formulations, research, treatment, prevention, education/training, and legal and policy concerns. *Journal of Traumatic Stress* serves as a primary reference for professionals who study and treat people exposed to highly stressful and traumatic events (directly or through their occupational roles), such as war, disaster, accident, violence or abuse (criminal or familial), hostage-taking, or life-threatening illness. The journal publishes original articles, brief reports, review papers, commentaries, and, from time to time, special issues devoted to a single topic.

Selective Notes on Submissions: Instructions to authors included in each issue of the journal. Authors to prepare manuscripts according to the *Publication Manual of the American Psychological Association* (4th ed.). Submit four (4) copies of the manuscript to the editor.

Journal Frequency: Quarterly

Articles/Pages Published per Year: 40/650

Total Subscribers: 2,500

Book Reviews Accepted: No

Rejection Rate: 85%

Journal of Vocational Behavior

Publisher: Academic Press, Inc.
1250 Sixth Avenue
San Diego, CA 92101-4495

Editor: Howard E. A. Tinsley
Department of Psychology
Southern Illinois University
Carbondale, IL 62901-6502

Editorial Policy: The *Journal of Vocational Behavior* publishes empirical, methodological, and theoretical articles related to such issues as the validation of theoretical constructs, developments in instrumentation, program comparisons, and research method-ology as related to vocational development, preference, choice and selection, implementation, satisfaction, and effectiveness throughout the life span and across cultural, national, sex, and other demographic boundaries. Brief notes of a methodological, instrumental, or replicative nature will also be considered for publication. Because of limitations in available journal space, authors are encouraged to integrate two or more short papers based on a series of related studies into one longer manuscript rather than to submit the shorter manuscripts separately.

Selective Notes on Submissions: Instructions to authors included in each issue of the journal. Authors to prepare manuscripts according to the *Publication Manual of the American Psychological Association* (4th ed.). Submit on computer disk with five (5) copies of the manuscript to the Journal of Vocational Behavior, Editorial Office, 525 B Street, Suite 1900, San Diego, CA 92101-4495.

Journal Frequency: Bimonthly

Articles/Pages Published per Year: 50/850

Total Subscribers: NA

Book Reviews Accepted: No

Rejection Rate: 76%

Journal of Youth and Adolescence

Publisher: Plenum Publishing Corporation
233 Spring Street
New York, NY 10013-1578

Editor: Daniel Offer, MD
Department of Psychiatry and
Behavioral Sciences
Northwestern University
Medical School
303 East Superior Street,
#P 554
Chicago, IL 60611-3053

Editorial Policy: This multidisciplinary research publication provides a single, high-level medium of communication for psychiatrists, psychologists, biologists, sociologists, educators, and professionals in many other disciplines who address themselves to the subject of youth and adolescence. The journal publishes papers based on experimental evidence and data, theoretical papers, comprehensive review articles, and clinical reports of relevance to research.

Selective Notes on Submissions: Instructions to authors included in each issue of the journal. Authors to prepare manuscripts according to the *CBE Style Manual*. Submit three (3) copies of the manuscript to the editor.

Journal Frequency: Bimonthly

Articles/Pages Published per Year: 40/600

Total Subscribers: 3,000

Book Reviews Accepted: NA

Rejection Rate: 65%

Language and Cognitive Processes

Publisher: Psychology Press
27 Church Road
Hove, East Sussex BN3 2FA
England

Editor: Lorraine Tyler
Department of Psychology
Birbeck College
Malet Street
London WC1E 7HX
England

Editorial Policy: *Language and Cognitive Processes* has been established to provide an international forum for the publication of theoretical and experimental research into the mental processes and representations involved in language use. Although the psychological study of language has attracted increasing research interest over the past three decades, no single journal has emerged as the common focus of this research. Instead, significant papers related to the psychological issues in language processing and representation are scattered among many different specialized journals. *Language and Cognitive Processes* provides such papers with the broad readership they deserve. Research relevant to the psychological theory of language stems from a wide variety of disciplines, and the content of *Language and Cognitive Processes* reflects this interdisciplinary perspective. Apart from research in experimental and developmental psychology, *Language and Cognitive Processes* publishes work derived from linguistics, computer science, and AI. Contributions are accepted in the form of experimental and observational studies, theoretical discussions, short notes and replies, and review articles.

Selective Notes on Submissions: Instructions to authors included in each issue of the journal. Authors to prepare manuscripts according to the *Publication Manual of the American Psychological Association* (4th ed.). Submit four (4) copies of the manuscript to the editor.

Journal Frequency: Quarterly

Articles/Pages Published per Year: 24/450

Total Subscribers: 400

Book Reviews Accepted: NA

Rejection Rate: NA

Law and Human Behavior

Publisher: Plenum Publishing Corporation
233 Spring Street
New York, NY 10013-1578

Editor: Richard L. Wiener, PhD
Department of Psychology
Saint Louis University
221 North Grand Boulevard
Saint Louis, MO 63103

Editorial Policy: *Law and Human Behavior* is a multidisciplinary forum for the publication of articles and discussions of issues arising out of the relationship between human behavior and the law, legal system, and legal process. The journal encourages submission of articles, notes/discussions, and book review essays from people in the fields of law and psychology, and the related disciplines of sociology, criminology, psychiatry,

political science, anthropology, philosophy, history, economics, communication, and other appropriate disciplines. (This is a publication of APA's Division 41.)

Selective Notes on Submissions: Instructions to authors included in each issue of the journal. Authors to prepare manuscripts according to either the Uniform System of Citation, distributed by the Harvard Law Review Association, Cambridge, MA, or the *Publication Manual of the American Psychological Association* (4th ed.). Submit the original and two (2) copies of the manuscript to the editor.

Journal Frequency: Bimonthly

Articles/Pages Published per Year: 35/661

Total Subscribers: 1,980

Book Reviews Accepted: Yes

Rejection Rate: 85%

Learning and Individual Differences

Publisher: JAI Press, Inc.
55 Old Post Road
No. 2, P.O. Box 1678
Greenwich, CT 06836-1678

Editor: Frank N. Dempster
College of Education
University of Nevada
Las Vegas, NV 89154

Editorial Policy: *Learning and Individual Differences* is a multidisciplinary journal that publishes articles reporting research that makes a substantial contribution to an understanding of individual differences within an educational context. Various theoretical approaches that contribute to an understanding of the learning process will be considered. Such comparisons may include quantitative models and computer simulations where appropriate. Topics of interest might include, but not be limited to, memory and cognition, intelligence, reading, motivation, neuropsychology, psychopharmacology, computer models, and life-span development. Single-experiment, theoretical and review articles will be considered, but preference will be given to integrative articles containing multiple experiments that focus on theory and/or methodological development. Alternative contributions may include open commentaries of particular articles. Studies concerned with classroom or clinical application will be considered if the work makes an important contribution to basic knowledge. Comparative findings yielding *both* differences and/or non-differences between predefined ability and/or diagnostic groups are welcome.

Selective Notes on Submissions: Instructions to authors included in each issue of the journal. Authors to prepare manuscripts according to the *Publication Manual of the American Psychological Association* (4th ed.). Submit four (4) copies of the manuscript to the editor.

Journal Frequency: Quarterly

Articles/Pages Published per Year: 20/320

Total Subscribers: 500

Book Reviews Accepted: No

Rejection Rate: 70%

Learning and Memory

Publisher: Cold Spring Harbor Laboratory
                            Press
                            10 Skyline Drive
                            Plainview, NY 11803

Editors: Ronald Davis
                            Erick Kandel
                            Richard Morris
                            Carla Shatz
                            Larry Squire
                            Charles Stevens

Editorial Policy: The current literature of learning and memory is large but fragmented. Until now, there has been no single journal devoted to this area of study and no dominant journal that demands attention by serious workers in the area, regardless of specialty. *Learning and Memory* publishes experimental studies in humans and animals on cognition, behavior, development, neuropsychology, neurophysiology, biochemistry, cell biology, and genetics, in the form of peer-reviewed research pepers, commissioned reviews and commentaries, theories and models, and short communications and letters.

Selective Notes on Submissions: Page Charges: $25/page. Instructions to authors included in each issue of the journal. Submit five (5) copies of the manuscript to the editor. Manuscripts should be sent to the Managing Editor, Leaning and Memory, Cold Spring Harbor Laboratory, 1 Bungtown Road, Cold Spring Harbor, NY 11724.

Journal Frequency: 6 issues per year

Articles/Pages Published per Year: 30/440

Total Subscribers: NA

Book Reviews Accepted: No

Rejection Rate: NA

Learning and Motivation

Publisher: Academic Press, Inc.
1250 Sixth Avenue
San Diego, CA 92101

Editor: Steven F. Maier
Department of Psychology
University of Colorado
Campus Box 345
Boulder, CO 80309

Editorial Policy: *Learning and Motivation*
publishes original experimental papers
addressed to the analysis of basic phenomena and mechanisms of learning and motivation, including papers on biological and
evolutionary influences upon the learning
and motivation processes. Studies involving
either animal or human subjects are invited.
Publication in *Learning and Motivation* is
subject to the editor's judgment that inclusion will make a substantial contribution to
our understanding of basic principles of
learning and motivation and to general
behavioral theory. Monographic reports of
an integrated series of experiments, as well
as papers reporting a single experiment will
be published. Preference is given to longer,
more substantive papers.

Selective Notes on Submissions: Instructions
to authors included in each issue of the
journal. Authors to prepare manuscripts

according to the *Publication Manual of the
American Psychological Association* (4th
ed.). Submit four (4) copies of the manuscript to the editor.

Journal Frequency: Quarterly

Articles/Pages Published per Year: 23/450

Total Subscribers: NA

Book Reviews Accepted: No

Rejection Rate: NA

Legal and Criminological Psychology

Publisher: British Psychological Society

Editor: Mary McMurran
Sally Lloyd-Bostock

Editorial Policy: *Legal and Criminological
Psychology* publishes original papers which
advance professional and scientific knowledge in the field of legal and criminal psychology broadly defined. Theoretical, review
and empirical studies in any of the following
areas are welcomed:

• New legislation

• Management of offenders

• Crime prevention

• Victimology

• Mental health and the law

• Impact of law on behavior

- Public attitudes to crime and the law

- Policing and crime detection

- Child and family issues

- Legal decision making

- Civil law procedures

- Interviewing, interrogation, and testimony

- Court processes

- Disputes and litigation

- Legal development and policy

- Role of the expert witness

- Sentencing and penology

- Ethical issues

- Assessment and treatment of criminal behavior

- Professional training

Selective Notes on Submissions: Instructions to authors included in each issue of the journal. Authors to prepare manuscripts according to the British Psychological Society, but *Publication Manual of the American Psychological Association* (4th ed.) accepted. Submit four (4) copies of the manuscript to the editor. Send manuscripts to: Legal and Criminological Psychology Journals Office, 13a Church Lane, London N2 8DX, England.

Journal Frequency: 2 issues per year

Articles/Pages Published per Year: 22/300

Total Subscribers: NA

Book Reviews Accepted: Yes

Rejection Rate: 68%

literature and psychology

Publisher: literature and psychology
Department of English
Rhode Island College
Providence, RI 02908

Editor: Morton Kaplan and
Richard Feldstein
Department of English
Rhode Island College
Providence, RI 02908

Editorial Policy: *literature and psychology* is a quarterly journal of literary criticism informed by psychoanalysis. Contributions that apply depth psychology (psychoanalysis) to literature should be sent to Morton Kaplan for issues No. 1 and No. 2. Contributions that apply post-structuralist forms of psychoanalysis to theory, literature, or film, as well as those that feature interdisciplinary approaches (psychoanalysis and feminism, deconstruction, semiotics, or Marxism) should be sent to Richard Feldstein for issues No. 3 and No. 4.

Selective Notes on Submissions: Instructions to authors included in each issue of the journal. Authors to prepare manuscripts according to the *MLA Style Sheet*. Submit two (2) copies of the manuscript to the appropriate editor.

Journal Frequency: Quarterly

Articles/Pages Published per Year: 16/280

Total Subscribers: 1,000

Book Reviews Accepted: NA

Rejection Rate: NA

Memory and Cognition

Publisher: Psychonomic Society, Inc.
1710 Fortview Road
Austin, TX 78704

Editor: Morton Ann Gernsbacher, PhD
Department of Psychology
University of Wisconsin
1202 West Johnson Street
Madison, WI 53706-1611

Editorial Policy: *Memory and Cognition* publishes articles concerned with the broad range of topics in human experimental psychology that its title encompasses. It may also contain papers devoted primarily to the development of theory and papers representing scholarly reviews of the existing literature.

Selective Notes on Submissions: Instructions to authors included in each issue of the journal. Authors to prepare manuscripts according to the *Publication Manual of the American Psychological Association* (4th ed.). Submit five (5) copies of the manuscript to the editor.

Journal Frequency: Bimonthly

Articles/Pages Published per Year: 70/800

Total Subscribers: 2,320

Book Reviews Accepted: NA

Rejection Rate: NA

Merrill-Palmer Quarterly: Journal of Developmental Psychology

Previous Title: Merrill-Palmer Quarterly

Publisher: Wayne State University Press
4809 Woodward Avenue
Detroit, MI 48202

Editor: Carolyn U. Shantz
Department of Psychology
Wayne State University
Detroit, MI 48202

Editorial Policy: Experimental, theoretical, and review papers that are original and concerned with issues in human development are published in the *Merrill-Palmer Quarterly*. The primary focus of the journal is on infant, child, and adolescent development, and contexts of development, such as the family and school. There is a special interest in integrative papers that summarize an area of research or a topic in terms that are meaningful to professionals with a wide range of specializations. Occasional issues are devoted entirely or in large part to a single theme. Persons interested in organizing a thematic collection of papers are asked to make preliminary inquiry to the editor. Commentaries on papers published in the quarterly are also invited.

Selective Notes on Submissions: Instructions to authors included in each issue of the journal. Authors to prepare manuscripts according to the *Publication Manual of the American Psychological Association* (4th ed.).

Journal Frequency: Quarterly

Articles/Pages Published per Year: 40/600

Total Subscribers: 1,290

Book Reviews Accepted: Yes

Rejection Rate: 80%

Military Psychology

Publisher: Lawrence Erlbaum Associates, Inc.
365 Broadway
Hillsdale, NJ 07642

Editor: Martin F. Wiskof
BDM International, Inc.
Suite 230
2600 Garden Road
Monterey, CA 93940

Editorial Policy: Focusing on psychological research and practice within a military environment, this new journal facilitates communication between researchers and practitioners. It provides for a timely publication of original empirical research that furthers scientific knowledge in the field. *Military Psychology* fills the gap between the Department of Defense and civilian researchers by providing a forum that both

military and nonmilitary psychologists need to keep current in their research.

Selective Notes on Submissions: Instructions to authors included in each issue of the journal. Authors to prepare manuscripts according to the *Publication Manual of the American Psychological Association* (4th ed.). Submit five (5) copies of the manuscript to the editor.

Journal Frequency: Quarterly

Articles/Pages Published per Year: 19/278

Total Subscribers: NA

Book Reviews Accepted: No

Rejection Rate: 56%

Monographs of the Society for Research in Child Development

Publisher: University of Chicago Press
Journals Division
P.O. Box 37005
Chicago, IL 60637

Editor: Rachel K. Clifton
University of Massachusetts—Amherst
Department of Psychology
Amherst, MA 01003

Editorial Policy: What gets published in the *Monographs*? In essence, any research that generates authoritative new findings and uses these to foster a fresh and better-integrated perspective on some conceptually significant issue or controversy. The aim of *Monographs* is not only to advance specialized knowledge on particular topics but also to enhance cross-fertilization among the disciplines and subfields. Ideally, therefore, the links between the specific issues under study and questions relating to developmental processes in general should be as clearly apparent to the general reader as they are to the specialist. Traditionally, the most typical submissions have been individually or group-authored reports originating from programmatic research projects whose findings would fail to achieve their full potential if they were fragmented into separate journal articles. (Reprinted from the SRCD Newsletter, 1988, Autumn.)

Selective Notes on Submissions: Authors to prepare manuscripts according to the *Publication Manual of the American Psychological Association* (4th ed.). Submit manuscripts to the editor.

Journal Frequency: Irregular

Articles/Pages Published per Year: NA

Total Subscribers: 5,600

Book Reviews Accepted: NA

Rejection Rate: NA

Notes From Publisher: Potential authors may wish to consult the editor directly about matters of appropriate length, topic, and style. A more detailed "Guidelines to Authors and Typists" is available on request from the editor and should be obtained before final typing of the manuscript.

Motivation and Emotion

Publisher: Plenum Publishing Corporation
                233 Spring Street
                New York, NY 10013-1578

Editor: Alice M. Isen
                510 Malott Hall
                Cornell University
                Ithaca, NY 14853

Editorial Policy: *Motivation and Emotion* publishes theoretical papers, state-of-the-art and synoptic reviews, position papers, and original research reports of either a basic or applied nature from any areas of psychology and behavioral science, provided that the focus is on motivation and/or emotion. Articles in which motivational or emotional variables are only incidental will not be considered for publication. The editors are particularly interested in receiving manuscripts which attempt to integrate research findings in the field(s) and which advance general theory (or theories). While the primary focus of the journal will be on human motivation, studies involving animals are acceptable provided that they have relevance to general motivation and/or emotion theory. The journal includes articles on physiological, behavioral, and social levels, and also specifically invites articles dealing with stress research and theory, personality organization, and environmental psychology, to the extent that they are interpretable within the framework of general theories of motivation and emotion.

Selective Notes on Submissions: Instructions to authors included in each issue of the journal. Authors to prepare manuscripts according to the *Publication Manual of the*

American Psychological Association (4th ed.). Submit the original and four (4) copies of the manuscript to the editor.

Journal Frequency: Quarterly

Articles/Pages Published per Year: 16/320

Total Subscribers: 491

Book Reviews Accepted: NA

Rejection Rate: NA

Multivariate Behavioral Research

Publisher: Lawrence Erlbaum Associates, Inc.
10 Industrial Avenue
Mahwah, NJ 07430-2262

Editor: Roger E. Milsap
Psychology Department
Baruch College CUNY
17 Lexington Avenue
New York, NY 10010-5526

Editorial Policy: This journal invites submissions of substantive, methodological, or theoretical articles in all areas of the behavioral and social sciences. Substantive articles report on applications of multivariate research methods in these sciences. Methodological articles present new developments in statistical methods, or address methodological issues in current research. Methodological articles may also serve didactic purposes, illustrating the use of multivariate research methods for a wide research audience. Theoretical articles provide research syntheses by integrating the findings of different studies within a specific area. Alternatively, theoretical articles may present multivariate solutions to current research problems in the behavioral or social sciences. Finally, shorter papers suitable for the notes and commentary section of the journal will be considered. The Editor should be consulted concerning the appropriateness, for this journal, of papers that may not clearly fit any of the preceding descriptions.

Selective Notes on Submissions: Instructions to authors included in each issue of the journal. Authors to prepare manuscripts according to the *Publication Manual of the American Psychological Association* (4th ed.). Submit four (4) copies of the manuscript to the editor.

Journal Frequency: Quarterly

Articles/Pages Published per Year: 32/512

Total Subscribers: 1,000

Book Reviews Accepted: No

Rejection Rate: NA

Multivariate Experimental Clinical Research

Publisher: Psychology Press
Department of Psychology
Box 34
Wichita State University
Wichita, KS 67260-0034

Editor: Charles Burdsal, Jr.
Box 34
Department of Psychology
Wichita State University
Wichita, KS 67260-0034

Editorial Policy: The primary aim of *Multivariate Experimental Clinical Research* is to provide a publication outlet for research in the areas covered and indicated currently by the terms of personality study, clinical diagnosis and therapy, extending into the learning, social, physiological, applied, and developmental aspects of these. Although due representation is given to theoretical articles which may have a methodological basis, the journal is not one of multivariate statistical methods. Although multivariate in outlook, both manipulative and non-manipulative research is accepted. In fact, preference is given to dynamic, manipulative and time-sequential studies. Particular encouragement is provided for pioneer experimental attacks on what is designated personality dynamics and motivation, as well as the natural expansion thereof into structured learning theory.

Selective Notes on Submissions: Instructions to authors included in each issue of the journal. Authors to prepare manuscripts according to the *Publication Manual of the American Psychological Association* (4th ed.). Submit three (3) copies of the manuscript to the John E. Cornell, PhD, Review Editor, GRECC/ALMMVH (182), 7400 Merton Minter Boulevard, San Antonio, TX 78284.

Journal Frequency: Triannually

Articles/Pages Published per Year: 12/105

Total Subscribers: 400

Book Reviews Accepted: Yes

Rejection Rate: 25%

Music Perception

Publisher: University of California Press
Periodicals Department
2120 Berkeley Way
Berkeley, CA 94720

Editor: Jamshed J. Bharucha
Department of Psychology
Dartmouth College
Hanover, NH 03755

Editorial Policy: *Music Perception* publishes original theoretical and empirical papers, methodological articles, and critical reviews concerning the study of music. Articles addressed to musical issues are welcome from a broad range of disciplines, including music theory, psychology, linguistics, neurology, neurophysiology, ethology, artificial intelligence, computer technology, and physical and architectural acoustics.

Selective Notes on Submissions: Instructions to authors included in each issue of the journal. Authors to prepare manuscripts according to the *Publication Manual of the American Psychological Association* (4th ed.). Submit four (4) copies of the manuscript to the editor.

Journal Frequency: Quarterly

Articles/Pages Published per Year: 28/512

Total Subscribers: 750

Book Reviews Accepted: Yes

Rejection Rate: NA

Suggested Index Terms: Music, sound, perception, cognition, performance

Neurobiology of Learning and Memory

Publisher: Academic Press
             6277 Sea Harbor Drive
             Orlando, FL 32887-4900

Editors: James L. McGaugh
             Department of Psychology
             University of California
             Irvine, CA 92697

             William T. Greenough
             Beckman Institute
             Department of Psychology
             University of Illinois
             405 N. Mathews Avenue
             Urbana, IL 61801

Editorial Policy: *Neurobiology of Learning and Memory* publishes articles concerned with neural and behavioral plasticity, including learning and memory and related aspects of neural adaptation, at all levels of analysis from molecular biology through behavior.

Selective Notes on Submissions: Instructions to authors included in each issue of the journal. Submit four (4) copies of the manuscript to the editor. Rapid communications: three (3) copies to one of the editors and one to the Editorial Office. Other manuscripts: four (4) copies to the Editorial

Office, 525B Street, Suite 1900, San Diego, CA 92101-4495

Journal Frequency: 6 issues per year

Articles/Pages Published per Year: 60/540

Total Subscribers: NA

Book Reviews Accepted: No

Rejection Rate: 50%

Neuropsychiatry, Neuropsychology, and Behavioral Neurology

Publisher: Raven Press
             1185 Avenue of the Americas
             New York, NY 10036

Editor: Michael Alan Taylor, MD
             Department of Psychiatry and
             Behavioral Sciences
             University of Health Sciences
             Chicago Medical School
             3333 Green Bay Road
             North Chicago, IL 60064

Editorial Policy: The journal welcomes contributions from all sources on any subject pertinent to the fields incorporated in its title. Each contribution will be reviewed by at least two members of the editorial board and will be judged on the basis of its scientific merit, timeliness, and readability. We will give priority to papers of multidisciplinary interest and to articles that provide original data on theoretical concepts, basic brain processes, or major clinical issues. Brief Reports focusing on preliminary studies, instructive case reports, and interesting but circumscribed clinical topics will be a regular feature, as well as Editorials, Guest Editorials, Book Reviews, and a News section.

Selective Notes on Submissions: Instructions to authors included in each issue of the journal. Submit three (3) copies of the manuscript to the editor.

Journal Frequency: Quarterly

Articles/Pages Published per Year: 44/250

Total Subscribers: NA

Book Reviews Accepted: NA

Rejection Rate: NA

Neuropsychologia

Publisher: Elsevier Science, Ltd.
The Boulevard
Langford Lane
Kidlington, Oxford OX5 1GB
England

Editor: Professor G. Berlucchi
Dipartimento di Scienze
Neurologiche e della Visione
Sezione di Fisiologia Umana
Strada Le Grazie 8
I-37134 Verona
Italy

Editorial Policy: *Neuropsychologia* considers for publication empirical rather than purely theoretical papers, using experimental methods and dealing with the relationship between brain functions and behavior. This

includes research in the various fields of behavioral neurosciences in both humans (normal and brain lesioned) and animals.

Selective Notes on Submissions: Instructions to authors included in each issue of the journal. Submit three (3) copies of the manuscript to the editor.

Journal Frequency: Monthly

Articles/Pages Published per Year: 140/1373

Total Subscribers: 2,000

Book Reviews Accepted: Yes

Rejection Rate: 55%

Neuropsychology

Publisher: American Psychological
Association
750 First Street, NE
Washington, DC 20002-4242

Editor: Laird S. Cermak
Department of Veterans Affairs
Medical Center (151A)
150 South Huntington Avenue
Boston, MA 02130

Editorial Policy: The mission of *Neuropsychology* is to foster (a) basic research, (b) the integration of basic and applied research, (c) improved practice in the field of neuropsychology, broadly conceived. The primary function of *Neuropsychology* is to publish original, empirical research in the field.

Occasionally, scholarly reviews and theoretical papers also will be published, all with the goal of promoting empirical research on the relation between brain and human cognitive, emotional, and behavioral function. Sought are submissions of human experimental, cognitive, and behavioral research with implications for neuropsychological theory and practice. Articles that increase understanding of neuropsychological functions in both normal and disordered states and across the life span are encouraged. Applied clinical research that will stimulate systematic experimental, cognitive, and behavioral investigations as well as improve the effectiveness, range, and depth of application is germane. *Neuropsychology* seeks to be the vehicle for the best research and ideas in the field.

Selective Notes on Submissions: Instructions to authors included in each issue of the journal. Authors to prepare manuscripts according to the *Publication Manual of the American Psychological Association* (4th ed.). Submit four (4) copies of the manuscript to the editor.

Journal Frequency: Quarterly

Articles/Pages Published per Year: 63/604

Total Subscribers: 5,750

Book Reviews Accepted: No

Rejection Rate: 76%

Neuropsychology Review

Publisher: Plenum Press
233 Spring Street
New York, NY 10013

Editor: Antonio Puente
Department of Psychology
University of North Carolina at Wilmington
Wilmington, NC 28403-3297

Editorial Policy: *Neuropsychology Review* publishes original scholarly review articles in the areas of neuropsychology and behavioral neurology. Articles in the areas of clinical psychology and psychiatry are considered if the topic is of particular interest to clinical neuropsychologists or behavioral neurologists. The journal is an international forum for the publication of peer-reviewed comprehensive integrative evaluative reviews of significant topics in neuropsychological assessment, neurobehavioral aspects of disorders of the central nervous system, treatment and rehabilitation of neurological disorders, and theoretical analyses of human brain function. Animal-model research is considered if there are apparent implications for human brain funtion.

Selective Notes on Submissions: Instructions to authors included in each issue of the journal. Authors to prepare manuscripts according to the *Publication Manual of the American Psychological Association* (4th ed.). Submit four (4) copies of the manuscript to the editor.

Journal Frequency: Quarterly

Articles/Pages Published per Year: 16/250

Total Subscribers: 500

Book Reviews Accepted: No

Rejection Rate: 60%

New Ideas in Psychology

Publisher: Elsevier Science
                   660 White Plains Road
                   Tarrytown, NY 10591-5153

Editor: Richard F. Kitchener, PhD
                   Department of Philosophy
                   Colorado State University
                   Fort Collins, CO 80523

Editorial Policy: *New Ideas in Psychology* is devoted to innovative theory in psychology. It does this in several ways, by dealing with (1) how new ideas develop (conceptual issues in theory construction, scientific creativity, and growth of knowledge); (2) exploratory theorizing (broad problems in any field of psychology, focusing on new and plausible hypotheses); (3) ideas in progress (heuristic insights, suggestive or intriguing speculations). *New Ideas in Psychology* provides a forum for theorizers. It is open to letters, comments, or debate, and puts a special emphasis on seminal and controversial ideas. Empirical papers are welcome, but only as long as they focus on conceptual issues and are theoretically creative.

Selective Notes on Submissions: Instructions to authors included in each issue of the journal. Authors to prepare manuscripts according to the *Publication Manual of the American Psychological Association* (4th ed.). Submit three (3) copies of the manuscript to the editor.

Journal Frequency: 3 issues per year

Articles/Pages Published per Year: 15/300

Total Subscribers: NA

Book Reviews Accepted: NA

Rejection Rate: NA

Notes From Publisher: Free sample copy available upon request.

New Zealand Journal of Psychology

Publisher: New Zealand Psychological
                   Society
                   P.O. Box 4092
                   Wellington
                   New Zealand

Editor: Associate Professor Nigel R.
                   Long
                   Psychology Department
                   Massey University
                   Private Bag 11222
                   Palmerston North
                   New Zealand

Editorial Policy: The *New Zealand Journal of Psychology* publishes articles from both New Zealand and overseas authors which report empirical research or make theoretical contributions to any area of psychology. Articles that review previous research and comment on general or specific issues in research and practice in psychology are also included. The journal also publishes brief reports and book reviews.

Selective Notes on Submissions: Instructions to authors included in each issue of the journal. Authors to prepare manuscripts according to the *Publication Manual of the American Psychological Association* (4th ed.). Submit three (3) copies of the manuscript to the editor.

Journal Frequency: Biannually

Articles/Pages Published per Year: 15/100

Total Subscribers: 700

Book Reviews Accepted: Yes

Rejection Rate: NA

Omega: Journal of Death and Dying

Publisher: Baywood Publishing Company, Inc.
26 Austin Avenue
P.O. Box 337
Amityville, NY 11701

Editor: Robert J. Kastenbaum, PhD
Department of Communication
Arizona State University
Tempe, AZ 85284

Editorial Policy: Drawing significant contributions from the fields of psychology, sociology, medicine, anthropology, law, education, history and literature, *Omega* has emerged as an internationally recognized forum on the subject of death and dying. It will serve as a reliable guide for clinicians, social workers, and health professionals who must deal with problems in crisis management.

Selective Notes on Submissions: Authors to prepare manuscripts according to the *Publication Manual of the American Psychological Association* (4th ed.). Submit three (3) copies of the manuscript to the editor.

Journal Frequency: 8 issues per year

Articles/Pages Published per Year: 48/720

Total Subscribers: 1,300

Book Reviews Accepted: Yes (contact editor)

Rejection Rate: 70%

Organizational Behavior and Human Decision Processes

Publisher: Academic Press, Inc.
1250 Sixth Avenue
San Diego, CA 92101

Editor: James C. Naylor
Department of Psychology
Ohio State University
142 Townshend Hall
1885 Neil Avenue Mall
Columbus, OH 43210

Editorial Policy: The journal *Organizational Behavior and Human Decision Processes* will publish papers describing original empirical research and theoretical developments in all areas of human performance theory and organizational psychology. Preference will be given to those articles which contribute to the development of principles or theories relevant to human performance or organizational behavior.

Selective Notes on Submissions: Instructions to authors included in each issue of the journal. Authors to prepare manuscripts according to the *Publication Manual of the*

American Psychological Association (4th ed.). Submit at least four (4) copies of the manuscript to the editor.

Journal Frequency: 12 issues per year

Articles/Pages Published per Year: 84/1440

Total Subscribers: 1,500

Book Reviews Accepted: No

Rejection Rate: 75%

Pastoral Psychology

Publisher: Plenum Publishing Corporation
233 Spring Street
New York, NY 10013-1578

Editor: Lewis R. Rambo
San Francisco Theological
Seminary
San Anselmo, CA 94960

Editorial Policy: *Pastoral Psychology* provides a forum for discussion of the work of ministry as this work is illuminated by comments from other professionals, by behavioral science research and theory, and by theological awareness and critique.

Selective Notes on Submissions: Information concerning the preparation of manuscripts can be obtained from the editor. Submit three (3) copies of the manuscript to the editor.

Journal Frequency: Bimonthly

Articles/Pages Published per Year: 20/300

Total Subscribers: NA

Book Reviews Accepted: NA

Rejection Rate: NA

Peace and Conflict: Journal of Peace Psychology

Publisher: Lawrence Erlbaum Associates, Inc.
10 Industrial Avenue
Mahwah, NJ 07430-2262

Editor: Milton Schwebel, PhD
Graduate Study of Applied and
Professional Psychology
Rutgers University
Piscataway, NJ 08855-0819

Editorial Policy: *Peace and Conflict: Journal of Peace Psychology* welcomes scholarly manuscripts from authors all over the world on a wide array of subjects concerning peace; nonviolent conflict resolution; reconciliation; and the causes, consequences, and prevention of war and other forms of destructive conflict. These other forms of conflict may be within nations, communities, or families. Possible topics are reflected by the titles of the task forces of the American Psychological Association's Division of Peace Psychology: Children, Families, and War; Militarism, Conversion, and Disarmament; Internation Liaison; Conflict Resolution; Student Involvement; Ethnicity and Peace; Feminism and Peace; Peace and Education; Peace and Sustainable Development; Public Policy and Action. The journal publishes a mixture of empirical, theoretical, clinical, and historical work, as well as policy analyses, case studies, interpretive essays, interviews, and book reviews. Integrative, interdisciplinary work that makes a connection between different areas and issues concerning peace is also welcome. Finally, the journal invites papers that reflect diverse cultural perspectives. (Journal of Division 48, Peace Psychology, of the American Psychological Association)

Selective Notes on Submissions: Instructions to authors included in each issue of the journal. Authors to prepare manuscripts according to the *Publication Manual of the American Psychological Association* (4th ed.). Submit four (4) copies of the manuscript to the editor.

Journal Frequency: Quarterly

Articles/Pages Published per Year: 24/450

Total Subscribers: 700

Book Reviews Accepted: Yes (for consideration)

Rejection Rate: 75%

Perception

Publisher: Pion, Ltd.
207 Brondesbury Park
London NW2 5JN
England

Editor: Richard L. Gregory

Editorial Policy: *Perception* is a scholarly journal reporting experimental results and theoretical ideas ranging over the fields of animal, human, and machine perception. Topics covered include physiological mechanisms and clinical neurological disturbances; psychological data on pattern and object perception in animals and humans; the role of experience in developing perception skills such as driving and flying; effects of culture on perception and aesthetics; errors, illusions, and perceptual phenomena occurring in controlled conditions, with emphasis on their theoretical significance; cognitive experiments and theories relating knowledge to perception; development of categories and generalizations; strategies for interpreting sensory patterns in terms of objects by organisms and machines; special problems associated with perception of pictures and symbols; verbal and nonverbal skills; reading; and philosophical implications of experiments and theories of perception for epistemology, aesthetics, and art.

Papers may be full experimental reports or preliminary results, accounts of new phenomena or effects, or theoretical discussions or comments. Descriptions of novel apparatus and techniques are also acceptable.

Selective Notes on Submissions: Instructions to authors included in each issue of the journal. Submit four (4) copies of the manuscript to the editor or the associate editor for America: Suzanne McKee, Smith-Kettlewell Eye Research Institute, 2232 Webster Street, San Francisco, CA 94115.

Journal Frequency: Monthly

Articles/Pages Published per Year: 80/800

Total Subscribers: NA

Book Reviews Accepted: NA

Rejection Rate: NA

Perception and Psychophysics

Publisher: Psychonomic Society, Inc.
1710 Fortview Road
Austin, TX 78704

Editor: Myron L. Braunstein
Department of Cognitive
Sciences
School of Social Sciences
University of California
Irvine, CA 92717-5100

Editorial Policy: *Perception and Psychophysics* publishes articles that deal with sensory processes, perception, and psychophysics. While the majority of published articles are reports of experimental investigations in these content areas, articles that are primarily theoretical or that present integrative and evaluative reviews are accepted. Studies employing either human or animal subjects are welcome.

Selective Notes on Submissions: Instructions to authors included in each issue of the journal. Authors to prepare manuscripts according to the *Publication Manual of the American Psychological Association* (4th ed.). Submit five (5) copies of the manuscript to the editor.

Journal Frequency: Monthly

Articles/Pages Published per Year: 150/ 1300

Total Subscribers: 1,840

Book Reviews Accepted: NA

Rejection Rate: NA

Perceptual and Motor Skills

Publisher: Perceptual and Motor Skills
Box 9229
Missoula, MT 59807

Editor: R. B. Ammons and
C. H. Ammons
P.O. Box 9229
Missoula, MT 59807

Editorial Policy: The purpose of this refereed journal is to encourage scientific originality and creativity. Material of the following kinds is carried: experimental or theoretical articles dealing with perception and/or motor skills, especially as affected by experience; articles on general methodology; and new material listings and reviews. All material of scientific merit will be taken in some form. An attempt is made to balance critical editing by specific suggestions from multiple referees of each paper as to changes and to make the approach interdisciplinary, including such fields as anthropology, physical education, physical therapy, orthopedics, time and motion study, and sports psychology.

Selective Notes on Submissions: Instructions to authors included in each issue of the journal. Authors to prepare manuscripts according to the *Publication Manual of the American Psychological Association* (4th ed.). Submit four (4) copies of the manuscript to the editor.

Journal Frequency: Bimonthly

Articles/Pages Published per Year: 380/ 2500

Total Subscribers: 2,000

Book Reviews Accepted: No

Rejection Rate: 65%

Notes From Publisher: Thorough, prompt refereeing, constructive evaluation, efficiency, and high quality of printing may be expected.

Personality and Individual Differences

Publisher: Elsevier Science, Ltd.
Bampfylde Street
Exeter EX1 2AH
England

Editors: H. J. Eysenck and
S. B. G. Eysenck
Department of Psychology
Institute of Psychiatry
De Crespigny Park
Denmark Hill
London SE5 8AF
England

Editorial Policy: *Personality and Individual Differences* publishes research papers on individual differences in temperament, intelligence, attitudes, and abilities. The journal investigates the major dimensions of individual differences in the context of experimental, physiological, pharmacological, clinical, medical, genetic, statistical, and social psychology and determines the causes and concomitants of individual differences using the concepts derived from these disciplines.

Selective Notes on Submissions: Instructions to authors included in each issue of the journal. Authors to prepare manuscripts according to the *Publication Manual of the American Psychological Association* (4th ed.). Submit three (3) copies of the manuscript to the editor.

Journal Frequency: Monthly

Articles/Pages Published per Year: 190/1200

Total Subscribers: 800

Book Reviews Accepted: Yes

Rejection Rate: 80%

Notes From Publisher: Free sample copy available upon request.

Personality and Social Psychology Bulletin

Publisher: Sage Publications, Inc.
2455 Teller Road
Thousand Oaks, CA 91320

Editor: John Dovidio, PhD
Department of Psychology
Colgate University
Colgate, NY 13346

Editorial Policy: The *Personality and Social Psychology Bulletin (PSPB)* publishes a variety of articles dealing with all areas of personality and social psychology. Integrative theoretical, methodological, and metatheoretical pieces relevant to the interface of personality and social psychology are especially welcome. In addition, *PSPB* serves as an outlet for publication of relatively brief empirical reports, including, but not necessarily limited to, single experiments, case reports, observational studies, simulations, content analyses, surveys, and replications. *PSPB* also publishes special pieces of particular interest to members of the Society for Personality and Social Psychology, such as selected book reviews, symposia, and invited addresses. Submissions in all of these categories are welcome at any time. (*PSPB* is a publication of APA's Division 8.)

Selective Notes on Submissions: Instructions to authors included in each issue of the journal. Authors to prepare manuscripts according to the *Publication Manual of the American Psychological Association* (4th ed.). Submit five (5) copies of the manuscript to the editor. *PSPB* uses a blind reviewing system. Authors' names, institutions, and other identifying information should appear on only two of the five submitted copies. Three copies should have the authors' names and affiliations removed from the title page and author notes and/or footnotes that contain identifying information deleted.

Journal Frequency: Monthly

Articles/Pages Published per Year: 96/1200

Total Subscribers: 4,250

Book Reviews Accepted: No

Rejection Rate: 70%

Notes From Publisher: Submission fee of $20 for members of the Society and $30 for nonmembers.

Personality and Social Psychology Review

Publisher: Lawrence Erlbaum Associates, Inc.
10 Industrial Avenue
Mahwah, NJ 07430-2262

Editor: Dr. Marilynn Brewer
Department of Psychology
The Ohio State University
1885 Neil Avenue Mall
Columbus, OH 43221

Editorial Policy: An official publication of the Society for Personality and Social Psychology: *PSPR* will seek to publish the best available *theoretical, conceptual, and review* articles in the fields of personality and social psychology. *PSPR's* articles will be theory-based reviews of empirical contributions to a substantive area of research and offer integrative theoretical formulations concerning work in a given area of personality and/or social psychology. Thus, articles published in *PSPR* would be similar in quality and type to those published in such journals as *Psychological Bulletin, Psychological Review,* and the *American Psychologist.*

Selective Notes on Submissions: Instructions to authors included in each issue of the journal. Authors to prepare manuscripts according to the *Publication Manual of the American Psychological Association* (4th ed.). Submit five (5) copies of the manuscript to the editor. *PSPR* uses a blind reviewing system. Authors' names, institutions, and other identifying information should appear on only two of the five submitted copies. Three copies should have the authors' names and affiliations removed from the title page and other author notes and/or footnotes that contain identifying information deleted.

Journal Frequency: Quarterly

Articles/Pages Published per Year: NA

Total Subscribers: NA

Book Reviews Accepted: NA

Rejection Rate: NA

Personnel Psychology

Publisher: Personnel Psychology, Inc.
745 Haskins Road, Suite A
Bowling Green, OH 43402

Editor: John R. Hollenbeck
Graduate School of Business
Management Department
Michigan State University
East Lansing, MI 48824

Editorial Policy: *Personnel Psychology* publishes empirical applied research dealing with a wide range of personnel problems facing public and private sector organizations. Articles deal with all aspects of personnel psychology, including employee selection, training and development, job analysis, productivity improvement programs, work attitudes, labor–management relations, and compensation and reward systems. Critical state-of-the-art reviews of the research literature in these areas are also published regularly.

Selective Notes on Submissions: Instructions to authors included in each issue of the journal. Authors to prepare manuscripts according to the *Publication Manual of the American Psychological Association* (4th ed.). Submit four(4) copies of the manuscript to the editor.

Journal Frequency: Quarterly

Articles/Pages Published per Year: 25/1062

Total Subscribers: 3,100

Book Reviews Accepted: Yes

Rejection Rate: 85%

Philosophical Psychology

Publisher: Carfax Publishing Company
P.O. Box 25
Abingdon OX14 3UE
England

Editors: John Rust
Department of Psychology
Goldsmiths' College
University of London
New Cross, London SE14 6NW
England

William Bechtel
Department of Philosophy
Campus Box 1073
Washington University
St. Louis, MO 63130-4899

Editorial Policy: *Philosophical Psychology* is an international journal launched to develop and strengthen the links between philosophy and psychology in both pure and applied settings by publishing original, independently refereed contributions to this growing field of study and research.

The editorial board is especially keen to encourage publication of articles that deal with the application of philosophical psychology to the cognitive and brain sciences and to areas of applied psychology, with particular emphasis on articles concerned with research into discourse analysis, connectionism, and knowledge systems that originate in the expanding common ground between logic as a philosophical area and information processing as a psychological area.

The journal also publishes theoretical articles concerned with the nature and history of psychology, the philosophy of science as applied to psychology, and explorations of the underlying issues (theoretical and ethical) in educational, clinical, occupational, and health psychology.

Selective Notes on Submissions: Instructions to authors included in each issue of the journal. Authors to prepare manuscripts according to the *Publication Manual of the American Psychological Association* (4th ed.). Submit three (3) copies of the manuscript to the editor.

Journal Frequency: Quarterly

Articles/Pages Published per Year: 24/380

Total Subscribers: NA

Book Reviews Accepted: NA

Rejection Rate: NA

Physiology and Behavior

Publisher: Elsevier Science
660 White Plains Road
Tarrytown, NY 10591-5153

Editor: Matthew J. Wayner
Division of Life Sciences
University of Texas at San
Antonio
San Antonio, TX 78285

Editorial Policy: *Physiology and Behavior* will publish original reports of systematic studies in the areas of psychology and behavior, in which at least one variable is physiological and the primary emphasis and theoretical context are behavioral; brief communications that describe a new method, technique, or apparatus; and results of experiments that can be reported briefly, with limited figures and tables.

Selective Notes on Submissions: Instructions to authors included in each issue of the journal. Submit three (3) copies of the manuscript to the editor.

Journal Frequency: Monthly

Articles/Pages Published per Year: 350/ 2100

Total Subscribers: 1,800

Book Reviews Accepted: NA

Rejection Rate: NA

Notes From Publisher: Free sample copy available upon request.

Political Psychology

Publisher: Blackwell Publishers
238 Main Street
Cambridge, MA 02142

Editor: Stanley A. Renshon
The Graduate School and
University Center of The
City University of
New York
33 West 42nd Street
New York, NY 10036-8099

Editorial Policy: *Political Psychology* is an interdisciplinary journal dedicated to examining the relationships between psychological and political phenomena. Articles are from such disciplines as political science, psychology, history, sociology, psychiatry, anthropology, economics, philosophy and religion, government and public administration, psychobiology, and international relations. In addition to scholarly articles that report ongoing research, discuss theory and methodology, and review the relevant literature, *Political Psychology* publishes a forum section of papers that assert a particular position regarding a specific relationship between political and psychological phenomena, bibliographic essays, book reviews, and a news and notes section.

Selective Notes on Submissions: Instructions to authors included in each issue of the journal. Submit four (4) copies of the manuscript to the editor.

Journal Frequency: Quarterly

Articles/Pages Published per Year: 38/800

Total Subscribers: 905

Book Reviews Accepted: Solicited only

Rejection Rate: 78%

Professional Psychology: Research and Practice

Publisher: American Psychological
Association
750 First Street, NE
Washington, DC 20002-4242

Editor: Patrick H. DeLeon
Editor, Professional Psychology
American Psychological
Association
750 First Street, NE
Washington, DC 20002-4242

Editorial Policy: *Professional Psychology: Research and Practice* publishes articles on the application of psychology, including the scientific underpinnings of the profession of psychology. Both data-based and theoretical articles on techniques and practices used in the application of psychology are acceptable. Specifically, this journal is an appropriate outlet for articles on (a) research and theory on public policy as it affects the practice of psychology; (b) current advances in applications from such fields as health psychology, community psychology, psychology of women, clinical neuropsychology, family psychology, psychology of ethnicity and culture, forensic psychology, and other areas; (c) standards of professional practice and delivery of services in a variety of contexts—industries, institutions, and other organizations; (d) education and training of professional psychologists at the graduate level and in continuing education; and (e) research and theory as they concern the interests of those in the practice of psychology. The journal also publishes brief reports on research or practice in professional psychology.

Selective Notes on Submissions: Instructions to authors included in each issue of the journal. Authors to prepare manuscripts according to the *Publication Manual of the American Psychological Association* (4th ed.). Submit three (3) copies of the manuscript to the editor.

Journal Frequency: Quarterly

Articles/Pages Published per Year: 102/603

Total Subscribers: 7,300

Book Reviews Accepted: No

Rejection Rate: 61%

Psychoanalysis and Psychotherapy

Publisher: International Universities Press, Inc.
59 Boston Post Road
Madison, CT 06443

Editors: Bernard F. Riess and
Edith Gould

Editorial Policy: This broad-based journal is written for psychoanalysts and other professionals who are interested in psychoanalysis and the application of psychodynamic principles to diverse fields of study. The papers reflect classical and contemporary theory and technique in psychoanalysis, dynamic psychotherapy, and supervision of the psychoanalytic process. Psychoanalytic perspectives on other clinical modalities, such as group therapy, child and family therapy, and the dynamics and treatment of special populations are an integral part of the journal. Book reviews, discussions of international and community mental health issues and papers on culture are also included.

Selective Notes on Submissions: Instructions to authors included in each issue of the journal. Submit three (3) copies of the manuscript to the editor. Submit manuscripts to Managing Editor: Marci Wood, Postgraduate Center for Mental Health, 124 East 28th Street, New York, NY 10016.

Journal Frequency: 2 issues per year

Articles/Pages Published per Year: 20/200

Total Subscribers: NA

Book Reviews Accepted: NA

Rejection Rate: NA

Psychoanalytic Psychology

Publisher: Lawrence Erlbaum Associates, Inc.
365 Broadway
Hillsdale, NJ 07642

Editor: Bertram J. Cohler
Committee on Human Development
University of Chicago
5730 South Woodlawn Avenue
Chicago, IL 60637

Editorial Policy: *Psychoanalytic Psychology* is designed to serve as a focal point for the publication of original contributions that broaden and enhance the interaction between psychoanalysis and psychology. Manuscripts are solicited that involve issues in psychology raised by psychoanalysis and issues in psychoanalysis raised by psychology. The journal, a quarterly, will publish clinical papers, experimental research papers, and literature reviews. (This is a publication of APA's Division 39.)

Selective Notes on Submissions: Instructions to authors included in each issue of the journal. Authors to prepare manuscripts according to the *Publication Manual of the American Psychological Association* (4th ed.). Submit four (4) copies of the manuscript to the editor.

Journal Frequency: Quarterly

Articles/Pages Published per Year: 30/576

Total Subscribers: 4,430

Book Reviews Accepted: Yes

Rejection Rate: NA

Psychoanalytic Review

Publisher:	Guilford Publications, Inc. 72 Spring Street New York, NY 10012
Editor:	Martin Schulman/NPAP 150 West 13th Street New York, NY 10011

Editorial Policy: The *Psychoanalytic Review* is a publication of the National Psychological Association for Psychoanalysis, Inc. devoted to psychoanalysis and culture.

Selective Notes on Submissions: Authors to prepare manuscripts according to the *Publication Manual of the American Psychological Association* (4th ed.). Submit four (4) copies of the manuscript to the editor.

Journal Frequency: Bimonthly

Articles/Pages Published per Year: 60/960

Total Subscribers: 2,200

Book Reviews Accepted: Yes

Rejection Rate: NA

Psychobiology

Publisher:	Psychonomic Society, Inc. 1710 Fortview Road Austin, TX 78704
Editor:	Dr. Raymond Kesner Department of Psychology University of Utah Salt Lake City, UT 84112

Editorial Policy: *Psychobiology* publishes articles concerned with the biological substrates of behavior and cognitive function. Experimental and theoretical contributions in a wide range of disciplines—anatomy, biology, clinical neuropsychology, computational neuroscience, electrophysiology, endocrinology, pharmacology, physiology, psychology—are welcome, as are studies with a developmental perspective. Short communications are also published, with minimal delay.

Selective Notes on Submissions: Instructions to authors included in each issue of the journal. Authors to prepare manuscripts according to the *Publication Manual of the American Psychological Association* (4th ed.), except that in the abbreviation of physical units, the style of the American Institute of Physics is to be followed. Submit four (4) copies of the manuscript to the editor.

Journal Frequency: Quarterly

Articles/Pages Published per Year: 420 pp.

Total Subscribers: 1,180

Book Reviews Accepted: NA

Rejection Rate: NA

Psychological Assessment

Publisher: American Psychological
                  Association
                  750 First Street, NE
                  Washington, DC 20002-4242

Editor: Stephen N. Haynes
               Department of Psychology
               University of Hawaii
               2430 Campus Road
               Honolulu, HI 96822

Editorial Policy: *Psychological Assessment* publishes mainly empirical articles concern-

ing clinical assessment and evaluation. Papers that fall within the publication domain include investigations related to the development, validation, and evaluation of assessment techniques. Diverse modalities (e.g., cognitive and motoric) and methods of assessment (e.g., inventories, interviews, direct observations, and psychophysiological measures) are within the domain of the journal, especially as they are evaluated in clinical research or practice. Also included are assessment topics that emerge in the context of such issues as cross-cultural studies, ethnicity, minority status, gender, and sexual orientation. Case studies occasionally will be considered if they identify novel assessment techniques that permit evaluation of the nature, course, or treatment of clinical dysfunction. Nonempirical papers, including highly focused reviews and methodological papers, are considered if they facilitate interpretation and evaluation of specific assessment techniques.

Selective Notes on Submissions: Instructions to authors included in each issue of the journal. Authors to prepare manuscripts according to the *Publication Manual of the American Psychological Association* (4th ed.). Submit three (3) copies of the manuscript to the editor.

Journal Frequency: Quarterly

Articles/Pages Published per Year: 65/540

Total Subscribers: 6,550

Book Reviews Accepted: No

Rejection Rate: 90%

Psychological Bulletin

Publisher: American Psychological Association
750 First Street, NE
Washington, DC 20002-4242

Editor: Nancy Eisenberg
Department of Psychology
Arizona State University
Tempe, AZ 85287

Editorial Policy: *Psychological Bulletin* publishes evaluative and integrative reviews and interpretations of substantive and methodological issues in scientific psychology. Original research is reported only for illustrative purposes. Integrative reviews that summarize a literature may set forth major developments within a particular research area or provide a bridge between related specialized fields within psychology or between psychology and related fields. In all cases, reviews that develop connections between areas of research are particularly valuable. Expository articles may be published if they are deemed accurate, broad, clear, and pertinent. The target audience is a broad range of psychologists and allied behavioral scientists. Manuscripts dealing with issues of contemporary social relevance; minority, cultural, or underrepresented groups; or other topics at the interface of psychological science and society are welcomed. Original theoretical articles should be submitted to the *Psychological Review*, even when they include reviews of research literature. Literature reviews should be submitted to the *Bulletin*, even when they develop an integrated theoretical statement.

Selective Notes on Submissions: Instructions to authors included in each issue of the journal. Authors to prepare manuscripts according to the *Publication Manual of the American Psychological Association* (4th ed.). Submit five (5) copies of the manuscript to the editor.

Journal Frequency: Bimonthly

Articles/Pages Published per Year: 58/998

Total Subscribers: 7,300

Book Reviews Accepted: No

Rejection Rate: 75%

Psychological Inquiry

Publisher: Lawrence Erlbaum Associates, Inc.
365 Broadway
Hillsdale, NJ 07642

Editor: Roy Baumeister
Department of Psychology
Case Western University
Cleveland, OH 44106

Editorial Policy: An international forum for inquiry, criticism, and review, *Psychological Inquiry* publishes theoretical and issue-oriented articles in the areas of personality, social development, health, and clinical psychology. Each target article (either on theoretical development or analytical review) is followed by peer commentaries and a response from the author. This highly respected journal also presents multiple, in-depth reviews of significant books.

Selective Notes on Submissions: Instructions to authors included in each issue of the journal. Authors to prepare manuscripts according to the *Publication Manual of the American Psychological Association* (4th ed.). Submit three (3) copies of the manuscript to the editor.

Journal Frequency: Quarterly

Articles/Pages Published per Year: 4/300 (each issue contains one target article with commentaries)

Total Subscribers: NA

Book Reviews Accepted: Yes

Rejection Rate: NA

Psychological Medicine

Publisher: Cambridge University Press
40 West 20th Street
New York, NY 10011-4211

Editor: Eugene Paykel
Department of Psychiatry
University of Cambridge
Addenbrooke's Hospital
Cambridge CB2 2QQ
England

Editorial Policy: *Psychological Medicine* publishes original research in clinical psychiatry and the basic sciences related to it. Each issue contains several guest editorials by respected scholars and researchers from a wide range of fields. These authoritative pieces not only provide up-to-date surveys of recent findings and issues, but offer a historical and interdisciplinary perspective

not often found in more traditional journals. There is a large and comprehensive book review section. Monograph supplements are published periodically and are included in the subscription price. Future supplements are "Eating disorders in a general practice population" and "The natural history of schizophrenia."

Selective Notes on Submissions: Instructions to authors included in each issue of the journal. Authors to prepare manuscripts according to the *Publication Manual of the American Psychological Association* (4th ed.). Submit three (3) copies of the manuscript to the editor.

Journal Frequency: Bimonthly

Articles/Pages Published per Year: 80/3500

Total Subscribers: 1,700

Book Reviews Accepted: NA

Rejection Rate: NA

Psychological Methods

Publisher: American Psychological Association
750 First Street, NE
Washington, DC 20002-4242

Editor: Mark I. Appelbaum
Department of Psychology - Department 0109
University of California at San Diego
9500 Gilman Drive
La Jolla, CA 92093-0109

Editorial Policy: *Psychological Methods* is devoted to the development and dissemination of methods for collecting, understanding, and interpreting psychological data. Its purpose is the dissemination of innovations in research design, measurement, methodology, and statistical analysis to the psychological community; its further purpose is to promote effective communication about related substantive and methodological issues. The audience is diverse and includes those who develop new procedures, those who are responsible for undergraduate and graduate training in design, measurement, and statistics, as well as those who employ those procedures in research. The journal solicits original theoretical, quantitative, empirical, and methodological articles; reviews of important methodological issues; tutorials; articles illustrating innovative applications of new procedures to psychological problems; articles on the teaching of quantitative methods; and reviews of statistical software. Submissions should illustrate through concrete example how the procedures described or developed can enhance the quality of psychological research. The journal welcomes submissions that show the relevance to psychology of procedures developed in other fields. Empirical and theoretical articles on specific tests or test construction should have a broad thrust; otherwise, they may be more appropriate for *Psychological Assessment.*

Selective Notes on Submissions: Instructions to authors included in each issue of the journal. Authors to prepare manuscripts according to the *Publication Manual of the American Psychological Association* (4th ed.). Submit five (5) copies of the manuscript to the editor. New in 1996.

Journal Frequency: Quarterly

Articles/Pages Published per Year: 32/440

Total Subscribers: NA

Book Reviews Accepted: No

Rejection Rate: 89%

Psychological Record

Publisher: Kenyon College
Gambier, OH 43022

Editor: Charles E. Rice
Kenyon College
Gambier, OH 43022

Editorial Policy: The *Psychological Record* is a journal of general psychology. Since 1937 it has published psychological theory, research, and commentary concerned with a broad range of topics in the discipline. Rapid publication of accepted manuscripts assures that each issue contains very recent work.

Selective Notes on Submissions: Authors to prepare manuscripts according to the *Publication Manual of the American Psychological Association* (4th ed.). Submit three (3) copies of the manuscript to the editor.

Journal Frequency: Quarterly

Articles/Pages Published per Year: 48/600

Total Subscribers: 1,399

Book Reviews Accepted: Yes

Rejection Rate: 40%

Psychological Reports

Publisher: Psychological Reports
                  Box 9229
                  Missoula, MT 59807

Editor: R. B. Ammons and
                  C. H. Ammons
                  Box 9229
                  Missoula, MT 59807

Editorial Policy: The purpose of this refereed journal is to encourage scientific originality and creativity in the field of general psychology, for the person who is first a psychologist, then a specialist. It carries experimental, theoretical, and speculative articles; comments; special reviews; and a listing of new books and other material received. Controversial material of scientific merit is welcomed. An attempt is made to balance critical editing with specific suggestions by multiple referees as to changes to meet standards. Publication is prompt (i.e., within 4–6 weeks of acceptance).

Selective Notes on Submissions: Instructions to authors included in each issue of the journal. Authors to prepare manuscripts according to the *Publication Manual of the American Psychological Association* (4th ed.). Submit four (4) copies of the manuscript to the editors.

Journal Frequency: Quarterly

Articles/Pages Published per Year: 352/2800

Total Subscribers: 1,800

Book Reviews Accepted: No

Rejection Rate: 67%

Notes From Publisher: Thorough, prompt refereeing, constructive evaluation, and high quality of printing may be expected.

Psychological Research

Publisher: Springer Verlag
                  Heidelberger Platz 3
                  D-1000 Berlin 33
                  Germany

Editor: J. Eugelkamp
                  Universitat des Saarlandes
                  Fachrichtung 6.4-Psychologie
                  Postfach 66
                  D-66041 Saarbruden
                  Germany

Editorial Policy: An international journal of perception, learning, and communication. The editors welcome original reports of experimental investigations concerned with problems in the field of cognitive psychology. The journal may also contain papers of a theoretical or historical nature provided that they are relevant to cognitive psychology.

Selective Notes on Submissions: Instructions to authors included in each issue of the journal. Authors to prepare manuscripts according to the *Publication Manual of the American Psychological Association* (4th ed.). Submit four (4) copies of the manuscript to the editor.

Journal Frequency: Quarterly

Articles/Pages Published per Year: 40/264

Total Subscribers: NA

Book Reviews Accepted: No

Rejection Rate: NA

Psychological Review

Publisher: American Psychological
Association
750 First Street, NE
Washington, DC 20002-4242

Editor: Robert A. Bjork
Department of Psychology
University of California,
Los Angeles
1282A Franz Hall
405 Hilgard Avenue
Los Angeles, CA 90024-1563

Editorial Policy: *Psychological Review* publishes articles that make important theoretical contributions to any area of scientific psychology. Preference is given to papers that advance theory rather than review it and to statements that are specifically theoretical rather than programmatic. Papers that point out critical flaws in existing theory or demonstrate the superiority of one theory over another will also be considered. Papers devoted primarily to surveys of the literature, problems of methods and design, or reports of empirical findings are ordinarily not appropriate. Discussions of previously published articles will be considered for publication as theoretical notes on the basis of the scientific contribution represented.

Selective Notes on Submissions: Instructions to authors included in each issue of the journal. Authors to prepare manuscripts according to the *Publication Manual of the American Psychological Association* (4th ed.). Submit four (4) copies of the manuscript to the editor.

Journal Frequency: Quarterly

Articles/Pages Published per Year: 33/751

Total Subscribers: 6,600

Book Reviews Accepted: No

Rejection Rate: 65%

Psychological Science

Publisher: Cambridge University Press
40 West 20th Street
New York, NY 10011-4211

Editor: John Kihlstom
Yale University
Department of Psychology
P.O. Box 208205
New Haven, CT 06520-8205

Editorial Policy: *Psychological Science* encourages submission of papers covering not only psychology in the traditional sense but topics in related fields (including cognitive science, neuroscience, linguistics, and social sciences) that are relevant to psychological research, theory, or application. Preference will be given to articles that are deemed to be of general theoretical significance or of broader interest across specialties of psychology and related fields and that are written to be intelligible to a wide range of readers.

Selective Notes on Submissions: Instructions to authors included in each issue of the journal. Authors to prepare manuscripts according to the *Publication Manual of the American Psychological Association* (4th ed.). Submit four (4) copies of the manuscript to the editor.

Journal Frequency: Bimonthly

Articles/Pages Published per Year: 70/360

Total Subscribers: NA

Book Reviews Accepted: NA

Rejection Rate: NA

Psychology: A Journal of Human Behavior

Publisher: Psychology: A Journal of
              Human Behavior
              Dr. Cash Kowalski, Managing
              Editor
              Ohio State University
              College of Business
              Columbus, OH 43210

Editor: Joseph P. Cangemi
              P.O. Box U-121
              College Heights Post Office
              Bowling Green, KY 42101

Editorial Policy: *Psychology* is a quality journal devoted to basic research, theory,

and techniques and arts of practice in the general field of psychology. For the purpose of clarifying the philosophy of this journal, psychology is defined as the study of human behavior. There are numerous papers on important aspects of psychology which can find no place in the professional literature. This journal is dedicated to filling this void.

Selective Notes on Submissions: Instructions to authors included in each issue of the journal. Authors to prepare manuscripts according to the *Publication Manual of the American Psychological Association* (4th ed.). Submit three (3) copies of the manuscript to the editor.

Journal Frequency: 3 issues per year

Articles/Pages Published per Year: 65/250

Total Subscribers: 1,200

Book Reviews Accepted: Yes

Rejection Rate: 60%

Notes From Publisher: This journal is totally self-suporting. Authors pay a page fee of $30/ms page.

Psychology of Addictive Behaviors

Publisher: Educational Publishing
              Foundation
              750 First Street, NE
              Washington, DC 20002-4242

Editor: Susan J. Curry, PhD
              Center for Health Studies
              1730 Minor Avenue, Suite 1600
              Seattle, WA 98101

Editorial Policy: *Psychology of Addictive Behaviors* publishes peer-reviewed original articles related to the psychological aspects of addictive behaviors. Articles on the following topics are included: (a) alcohol and alcoholism, (b) drug use and abuse, (c) eating disorders, (d) smoking and nicotine addiction, and (e) other compulsive behaviors (e.g., gambling). Full-length research reports, literature reviews, essays, brief reports, comments, and innovative case studies are published, as well as book and media reviews.

Selective Notes on Submissions: Instructions to authors included in each issue of the journal. Authors to prepare manuscripts according to the *Publication Manual of the American Psychological Association* (4th ed.). Submit four (4) copies of the manuscript to the editor.

Journal Frequency: Quarterly

Articles/Pages Published per Year: 24/258

Total Subscribers: 1,490

Book Reviews Accepted: No

Rejection Rate: 60%

Psychology and Aging

Publisher: American Psychological
                 Association
                 750 First Street, NE
                 Washington, DC 20002-4242

Editor: Leah L. Light
              Pitzer College

1050 North Mills Avenue
Claremont, CA 91711-6110

Editorial Policy: *Psychology and Aging* publishes original articles on adult development and aging. Such original articles include reports of research, which may be applied, biobehavioral, clinical, educational, experimental (laboratory, field, or naturalistic studies), methodological, or psychosocial. Although the emphasis is on original research investigations, occasional theoretical analyses of research issues, practical clinical problems, or policy may appear, as well as critical reviews of a content area in adult development and aging. Clinical case studies that have theoretical significance are also appropriate. Brief reports are acceptable with the author's agreement not to submit a full report to another journal; a 75–100 word abstract plus 185 48-space lines of text and references constitute absolute limitations on space for such brief reports.

Selective Notes on Submissions: Instructions to authors included in each issue of the journal. Authors to prepare manuscripts according to the *Publication Manual of the American Psychological Association* (4th ed.). Submit four (4) copies of the manuscript to the editor.

Journal Frequency: Quarterly

Articles/Pages Published per Year: 63/679

Total Subscribers: 3,325

Book Reviews Accepted: No

Rejection Rate: 66%

Psychology and Marketing

Publisher: John Wiley & Sons, Inc.
605 Third Avenue
New York, NY 10158

Editor: Ronald J. Cohen, PhD
Department of Psychology
St. John's University
Grand Central and Utopia
Parkways
Jamaica, NY 11439

Executive Editor:
Rajan Nataraajan
Department of Marketing and
Transportation
College of Business
235 Business Building
Auburn University
Auburn, AL 36849-5246

Editorial Policy: *Psychology and Marketing* publishes original research and review articles dealing with the application of psychological theories and techniques to marketing. As an interdisciplinary journal, it serves practitioners and academicians in the fields of psychology and marketing and is an appropriate outlet for articles designed to be of interest, concern, and applied value to its audience of professionals and scholars. Specifically, some of the types of articles published in this journal are as follows: (1) descriptions of the development, validity, and/or use of psychological knowledge or techniques that can be brought to bear on marketing problems; (2) descriptions of the development, validity, and/or use of marketing knowledge or techniques derived from the psychological literature; (3) psychological studies or profiles of individuals or groups who might potentially benefit from the marketing of a particular product or service; (4) studies of personality and behavior change where these studies have a direct bearing on questions concerning consumer behavior and marketing strategies; (5) exploration of issues of law, ethics, and values in psychology and marketing; (6) psychological investigation of interpersonal and interagency (e.g., research supplier–client) relationships in marketing; and (7) case studies and cross-cultural reports pertinent to all of the preceding topics. This journal is designed to provide a unique forum for the presentation and discussion of innovative perspectives on marketing and psychology.

Selective Notes on Submissions: Instructions to authors included in each issue of the journal. Authors to prepare manuscripts according to the *Publication Manual of the American Psychological Association* (4th ed.). Submit five (5) copies of the manuscript to the executive editor.

Journal Frequency: 8 issues per year

Articles/Pages Published per Year: 40/800

Total Subscribers: 700

Book Reviews Accepted: Yes

Rejection Rate: 85%

Psychology of Music

Publisher: Society for Research in
Psychology of Music and
Music Education
Membership Secretary,
Ms. Nicola Dibben

Department of Music
The University
Sheffield S10 2TN
England

Editor:　David J. Hargreaves
Department of Psychology
The University
Leicester LE1 7RH
England

Editorial Policy: The editor welcomes contributions directed at increasing scientific understanding of any psychological aspect of music. This includes studies of listening, performing, creating, memorizing, analyzing, describing, learning, and teaching, as well as applied, social, developmental, and attitudinal studies. Submissions may be either (a) reports of original empirical investigations containing systematic analysis of relevant data, or (b) reviews, critiques, and other contributions of a theoretical nature. Special encouragement will be given to studies carried out in naturalistic contexts, and to those which address the interface between music psychology and music education.

Selective Notes on Submissions: Instructions to authors included in each issue of the journal. Authors to prepare manuscripts according to the *Publication Manual of the American Psychological Association* (4th ed.). Submit three (3) copies of the manuscript to the editor.

Journal Frequency: 2 issues per year

Pages Published per Year: 12/200

Total Subscribers: NA

Book Reviews Accepted: NA

Rejection Rate: NA

Psychology, Public Policy, and Law

Publisher:　American Psychological
Association
750 First Street, NE
Washington, DC 20002-4242

Editor:　Bruce D. Sales
Department of Psychology
University of Arizona
Tucson, AZ 85721

Editorial Policy: *Psychology, Public Policy, and Law* focuses on the links between psychology as a science and public policy and law. It publishes articles that (a) critically evaluate the contributions and potential contributions of psychology and relevant information derived from related disciplines (hereinafter psychology) to public policy and legal issues (e.g., linking knowledge on risk assessment to global climate change and energy policy and law; analyzing the fit between FDA policies on food labeling and research on comprehension); (b) assess the desirability of different public policy and legal alternatives in light of the scientific knowledge base in psychology (e.g., family leave policies and law considered against a background of knowledge about socialization in dual-career families; retirement policies and law in light of health, life cycle, and aging); (c) articulate research needs that address public policy and legal issues for which there is currently insufficient theoretical and empirical knowledge or publish the results of large-scale empirical work addressed to such concerns; and (d) examine public policy and legal issues relating to the conduct of psychology and related disciplines (e.g., human subjects, protection policies, informed consent procedures). This journal does not routinely serve as an outlet for primary reports of empirical research. Empirical research that is published must make a significant contribution to public policy or the law. Such empirical work is typically multistudy, multijurisdictional, longitudinal, or in some other way extremely broad in scope, of major national significance, or both.

Selective Notes on Submissions: Instructions to authors included in each issue of the journal. Authors to prepare manuscripts according to the *Publication Manual of the American Psychological Association* (4th ed.) or Bluebook (15th ed.). Submit four (4) copies of the manuscript to the editor.

Journal Frequency: Quarterly

Articles/Pages Published per Year: 37/972

Total Subscribers: 2,300

Book Reviews Accepted: No

Rejection Rate: NA

Psychology in the Schools

Publisher: John Wiley & Sons, Inc.
                   605 Third Avenue
                   New York, NY 10158

Editor: Gerald B. Fuller
                   P.O. Box 4150
                   Traverse City, MI 49685

Editorial Policy: *Psychology in the Schools* is a quarterly journal devoted to research,

opinion, and practice. Manuscripts are invited that range in appeal from those that deal with theoretical and other problems of the school psychologist to those directed to the teacher, the counselor, the administrator and other personnel workers in schools and colleges, public and private organizations. Preference will be given to manuscripts that clearly describe implications for the practitioner in the schools.

Selective Notes on Submissions: Instructions to authors included in each issue of the journal. Authors to prepare manuscripts according to the *Publication Manual of the American Psychological Association* (4th ed.). Submit three (3) copies of the manuscript to the editor.

Journal Frequency: Quarterly

Articles/Pages Published per Year: 80/384

Total Subscribers: 1,600

Book Reviews Accepted: Yes

Rejection Rate: 65%

Psychology of Women Quarterly

Publisher: Cambridge University Press
                   40 West 20th Street
                   New York, NY 10011-4211

Editor: Nancy Felipe Russo, PhD
                   Psychology Department
                   Arizona State University
                   Tempe, AZ 85287-1104

Editorial Policy: *Psychology of Women Quarterly* is the journal publication of Division 35 of the American Psychological Association. Empirical studies, critical reviews, theoretical articles, and invited book reviews are published in the quarterly. Unusual findings in studies otherwise not warranting a full report may be written as brief reports. Only articles germane to the psychological study of women will be considered, and these may include the study of sex-related differences, psychobiological factors, role development and change, career choice and training, management variables, education, discrimination, therapeutic processes, social processes, and sexuality. These suggestions are not meant to be exhaustive, but rather to guide investigations in the psychology of women. The quarterly aims to encourage and develop a body of feminist research. The use of sexist language in articles is not acceptable.

Selective Notes on Submissions: Instructions to authors included in each issue of the journal. Authors to prepare manuscripts according to the *Publication Manual of the American Psychological Association* (4th ed.). Submit five (5) copies of the manuscript to the editor with a $10 processing fee.

Journal Frequency: Quarterly

Articles/Pages Published per Year: 53/535

Total Subscribers: 3,800

Book Reviews Accepted: NA

Rejection Rate: 90%

Psychometrika

Publisher: Psychometric Society
c/o Dr. Ralph DeAyala
Benjamin Building
University of Maryland
College Park, MD 20742

Editor: Dr. Willem J. Heiser
Department of Data Theory
Faculty of Social Sciences
Leiden University
P.O. Box 9555
2300 RB Leiden
The Netherlands

Editorial Policy: *Psychometrika* contains articles on the development of quantitative models for psychological phenomena, and on quantitative methodology in the social and behavioral sciences, including new mathematical and statistical techniques for the evaluation of psychological data, and the application of such techniques. Empirical studies will be considered only if they involve new or particularly interesting uses of quantitative techniques.

Selective Notes on Submissions: Prospective authors are referred to the "Rules for Preparation of Manuscript for *Psychometrika*," contained in the March 1984 issue. Reprints of these "Rules" are available from the managing editor upon request. A manuscript which fails to comply with these requirements will be returned to the author for revision. Authors will receive 100 reprints without covers, free of charge. Submit to the editor.

Journal Frequency: Quarterly

Articles/Pages Published per Year: 44/600

Total Subscribers: 2,000

Book Reviews Accepted: Yes

Rejection Rate: NA

Psychopharmacology

Publisher: Springer International
Springer Verlag
Heidelberger Platz 3
D-100 Berlin 33
Germany

Editorial Policy: *Psychopharmacology* is intended to provide a medium for the prompt publication of scientific contributions concerned with the analysis and synthesis of the effects of drugs on behavior, in the broadest sense of the term. Such contributions may be of a clinical nature, or they may deal with specialized investigations in the fields of experimental psychology, neurophysiology, neurochemistry, general pharmacology, and cognate disciplines. Areas covered include clinical psychopharmacology; human experimental psychopharmacology; biochemical neuropharmacology, drug metabolism, and pharmacokinetics; behavioral pharmacology in laboratory animals; and preclinical psychopharmacology.

Selective Notes on Submissions: Instructions to authors included in each issue of the journal. Submit four (4) copies of the manuscript to the editor. Submit to the managing editor of the appropriate area: see recent issue for names and addresses.

Journal Frequency: Bimonthly

Articles/Pages Published per Year: 300/ 2496

Total Subscribers: NA

Book Reviews Accepted: No

Rejection Rate: 60%

Psychophysiology

Publisher: Cambridge University Press
Management Office
40 West 20th Street
New York, NY 10011-4211

Editor: John T. Cacioppo
Ohio State University
Department of Psychology
1885 Neil Avenue
Columbus, OH 43210-1222

Editorial Policy: *Psychophysiology* publishes original articles in any area of psychophysiological research: experimental studies, theoretical papers, evaluative reviews of literature, methodological developments (e.g., experimental procedures, instrumentation, and computer techniques). Archival documents of the Society for Psychophysiological Research are published in *Psychophysiology*. Book reviews, letters to the editor, and interchanges among readers will also be considered, subject to space availability. Papers are published in order of receipt of the finally accepted manuscript. Consult recent editorials in the journal for further information about editorial policies and reviewing procedures.

Selective Notes on Submissions: Instructions to authors included in each issue of the journal. Authors to prepare manuscripts according to the *Publication Manual of the*

American Psychological Association (4th ed.). Submit the original and four (4) copies of the manuscript to the editor.

Journal Frequency: Bimonthly + supplement

Articles/Pages Published per Year: 78/750

Total Subscribers: 2,200

Book Reviews Accepted: Yes

Rejection Rate: 75%

Psychotherapy

Publisher: Division of Psychotherapy (29)
American Psychological
   Association
3875 North 44th Street
Phoenix, Arizona 85018

Editor: Wade H. Silverman, PhD
1514 San Ignacio
Suite 100
Coral Gables, FL 33146

Editorial Policy: The journal welcomes theoretical contributions, research studies, case reports, discussions of actual practice, and papers about issues in training. The journal endeavors to foster their interaction, since ultimately training, practice, theory, and research must all combine to make each other fruitful. Authors are asked to submit only new ideas, the controversial, the good examples of practice-relevant detail that would stimulate another theorist, researcher, or practitioner, and to omit the well-known, the obvious, the lengthy introduction, and the generalities of the traditional article

format. In electing to sponsor the widest scope of orientations rather than one point of view, the journal hopes to maximally inform its readers.

Selective Notes on Submissions: Instructions to authors included in each issue of the journal. Authors to prepare manuscripts according to the *Publication Manual of the American Psychological Association* (4th ed.). Submit four (4) copies of the manuscript to the editor.

Journal Frequency: Quarterly

Articles/Pages Published per Year: 88/700

Total Subscribers: 7,000

Book Reviews Accepted: No

Rejection Rate: 78%

Psychotherapy and Psychosomatics

Publisher: S. Karger AG
P.O. Box CH-4009
Basel, Switzerland

Editor: Giovanni A. Fava, MD
Dipartimento di Psicologia
Universita di Bologna
Viale Berti Pichat 5
I-40127 Bologna
Italy

Editorial Policy: *Psychotherapy and Psychosomatics* publishes research articles, reviews (special articles), clinical notes and letters to the editor on psychotherapy and/or psychosomatic research.

Selective Notes on Submissions: Instructions to authors included in each issue of the journal. Submit three (3) copies of the manuscript to the editor.

Journal Frequency: Bimonthly

Articles/Pages Published per Year: 64/640

Total Subscribers: 1,000

Book Reviews Accepted: NA

Rejection Rate: NA

Notes From Publisher: Official organ of the International Federation for Medical Psychotherapy. No page charge for papers of 7 or fewer printed pages; each additional page $196.

Psychotherapy Research

Publisher: Guilford Publications, Inc.
72 Spring Street
New York, NY 10012

Editors: Robert Elliott
Department of Psychology
University of Toledo
Toledo, OH 43606

Hans H. Strupp
Department of Psychology
Vanderbilt University
Nashville, TN 37203

Bernhard Strauss
University of Kiel
Niemannsweg 147
D24105 Kiel
Germany

Editorial Policy: *Psychotherapy Research* seeks to encourage the development of psychotherapy research, to foster the utilization of research findings in training, practice and policy information, and to enhance the scientific quality and social relevance of psychotherapy research.

Addressed to an international audience, the journal publishes empirical, review, and methodological articles, as well as theoretical articles of direct relevance to psychotherapy research. The journal encourages submission of innovative or controversial research representing diverse research paradigms, including both quantitative and qualitative approaches. Examples include traditional outcome, clinical trials, and outcome-prediction research; process, change process, and process-outcome investigations; systematic case studies; measure development studies; and meta-analyses. Studies of clinical training and practice will also be considered. The journal covers diverse theoretical orientations (e.g., psychodynamic, cognitive–behavioral, humanistic–experiential, and systems approaches) and treatment modalities (e.g., individual, group, couple, and family). The journal emphasizes the integration of research and practice, highlighting the utility of research results to the practitioner.

Selective Notes on Submissions: Instructions to authors included in each issue of the journal. Authors to prepare manuscripts according to the *Publication Manual of the American Psychological Association* (4th ed.). Submit three (3) copies of the manuscript as follows:

Manuscripts in English whose first author resides in North America should be sent to: Robert Elliott, Department of Psychology, University of Toledo, Toledo, OH 43606.

Manuscripts in German, Spanish or French, and English manuscripts whose first author resides outside North America should be sent to: Bernhard Strauss, Klinikum der Friedrich-Schiller-Universitat, Institut fur Medizinishe Psychologie Stoystrasse 2, D 07740 Jena, Germany.

Journal Frequency: Quarterly

Articles/Pages Published per Year: 30/384

Total Subscribers: 1,500

Book Reviews Accepted: Yes

Rejection Rate: 64%

Notes From Publisher: Journal of the Society for Psychotherapy Research.

Quarterly Journal of Experimental Psychology Section A: Human Experimental Psychology

Publisher: Psychology Press
27 Palmeira Mansions
Church Road
Hove, BN3 2FA
England

Editor: Stephen Monsell
Department of Experimental
Psychology
University of Cambridge
Downing Street
Cambridge CB2 3EB
England

Editorial Policy: Publishes original papers in all branches of human experimental psychology without limitation. Areas of work featured in recent volumes include: cognitive neuropsychology, language comprehension, motor skills, reasoning, and work recognition.

Selective Notes on Submissions: Instructions to authors included in each issue of the journal. Authors to prepare manuscripts according to the *Publication Manual of the American Psychological Association* (4th ed.). Submit four (4) copies of the manuscript to the editor.

Journal Frequency: Quarterly

Articles/Pages Published per Year: 45/832

Total Subscribers: 1,561

Book Reviews Accepted: Yes

Rejection Rate: NA

Notes From Publisher: Book reviews may be submitted to the book review editor: Philip T. Smith, Department of Psychology, University of Reading, Earley Gate, White Knights, Reading RG6 2AL, UK.

Quarterly Journal of Experimental Psychology Section B: Comparative and Physiological Psychology

Publisher: Psychology Press
27 Palmeira Mansions
Church Road
Hove, BN3 2FA
England

Editor: Geoffrey Hall
Department of Psychology
University of York
Heslington, York Y01 5DD
England

Editorial Policy: This publication features articles on any topic within the field of animal psychology, including such traditional topics as conditioning, learning, and motivation; any aspect of animal behavior, comparative psychology, and ethology; and work employing physiological and pharmacological techniques.

Selective Notes on Submissions: Instructions to authors included in each issue of the journal. Authors to prepare manuscripts according to the *Publication Manual of the American Psychological Association* (4th ed.). Submit four (4) copies of the manuscript to the editor.

Journal Frequency: Quarterly

Articles/Pages Published per Year: 24/384

Total Subscribers: 1,316

Book Reviews Accepted: Yes

Rejection Rate: 50%

Notes From Publisher: Book reviews may be submitted to the book review editor: Dr. J. Bolhuis, Department of Zoology, University of Cambridge, Downing Street, Cambridge CB2 3EJ, UK.

Reading Psychology

Publisher: Taylor & Francis
1 Gunpowder Square

London EC4A 3DE
England

Editors: Executive Editor:
Lance M. Gentile
Department of Elementary
    Education
San Francisco State University
San Francisco, CA 94132

William H. Rupley
Department of Educational
    Curriculum
Texas A&M University
College Station, TX 77843

Editorial Policy: *Reading Psychology* publishes original papers in the fields of reading and related psychological disciplines. The focus of this journal is on the psychology of reading, the reader, and reading instruction, and it presents papers the editorial advisors consider to be of major importance. Manuscripts in the form of completed research, practitioner-based "experiential" methods or philosophical statements, teacher and counselor preparation services for guiding all levels of reading skill development, attitudes and interests, programs or materials, and literary or humorous material are welcome. Timely reviews of learning resources, either books or instructional packages and programs, of significance to scholars, practitioners, or lay personnel interested in the fields of reading, and various psychological components of the reading process will be considered.

Selective Notes on Submissions: Instructions to authors included in each issue of the journal. Authors to prepare manuscripts according to the *Publication Manual of the American Psychological Association* (4th ed.). Submit two (2) copies of the manuscript to the editor.

Journal Frequency: Quarterly

Articles/Pages Published per Year: 32/400

Total Subscribers: 300

Book Reviews Accepted: No

Rejection Rate: NA

Reading and Writing Quarterly: Overcoming Learning Difficulties

Publisher: Taylor & Francis
1101 Vermont Avenue, NW
Suite 200
Washington, DC 20005

Editor: Howard Margolis
Department of Educational and
    Community Programs
051 Powdermaker Hall
Queen College
City University of New York
Flushing, NY 11367-0904

Editorial Policy: *Reading and Writing Quarterly: Overcoming Learning Difficulties* is a refereed journal, and manuscripts are reviewed anonymously. The journal aims at disseminating information to improve instruction for regular and special education students who have trouble learning to read and write. This interdisciplinary journal contains information regarding the causes, diagnosis, prevention, evaluation, and remediation of reading and writing difficul-

ties in regular and special education settings. It addresses the needs of regular and special educators, including university instructors and researchers, learning consultants, teachers, and school psychologists. The journal provides direction in educating a mainstreamed population for literacy.

The journal encourages manuscripts on teaching the reading and writing processes to students experiencing difficulties in these areas. Possible topics include adjustments for language-learning style, literature-based reading programs, approaches to teaching reading in the mainstream, study strategies specific to various content areas, language-centered computer writing, direction insruction reading, curriculum-based assessment, the impact of environmental factors on instructional effectiveness, and the improvement of self-esteem.

Selective Notes on Submissions: Authors to prepare manuscripts according to the *Publication Manual of the American Psychological Association* (4th ed.). Submit the original and four (4) copies of the manuscript to Dr. Patrick Mc Cabe, Associate Editor, RWQ, Nova Southeastern University, Education and Behavioral Science, 3301 College Avenue, Ft. Lauderdale, FL 33314-7796.

Journal Frequency: Quarterly

Articles/Pages Published per Year: 28/400

Total Subscribers: NA

Book Reviews Accepted: No

Rejection Rate: NA

Rehabilitation Counseling Bulletin

Publisher: American Association for
Counseling and
Development
5999 Stevenson Avenue
Alexandria, VA 22304

Editor: Randall M. Parker
Department of Special
Education
University of Texas at Austin
Austin, TX 78712

Editorial Policy: This research oriented
journal is edited specifically for practitioners, educators, and researchers who serve
individuals with disabilities or other special
needs. Every issue contains articles on
contemporary topics such as psychological
and social aspects of disability, psychiatric
rehabilitation, developmental disabilities,
career development and job placement of
persons with special needs.

Selective Notes on Submissions: Instructions
to authors included in each issue of the
journal. Authors to prepare manuscripts
according to the *Publication Manual of the
American Psychological Association* (4th
ed.). Submit four (4) copies of the manuscript to the editor.

Journal Frequency: Quarterly

Articles/Pages Published per Year: 25/300

Total Subscribers: NA

Book Reviews Accepted: NA

Rejection Rate: NA

Rehabilitation Education

Publisher: Elliott & Fitzpatrick
1135 Cedar Shoals Drive
Athens, GA 30605

Editors: Brian Bolton and Daniel Cook
University of Arkansas
West Avenue Annex
Fayetteville, AR 72701

Editorial Policy: *Rehabilitation Education* is
designed to bridge the gap between researchers, trainers, and service providers
and features original contributions dealing
with all aspects of rehabilitation education.
Topics include advancements of curriculum
development and innovations, information
about instruction materials and educational
media, the significance of enrollment and
employment trends, identification of professional competency, the role of continuing
education for the rehabilitation professional,
and issues related to licensing, certification
and accreditation.

Selective Notes on Submissions: Instructions
to authors included in each issue of the
journal. Authors to prepare manuscripts
according to the *Publication Manual of the
American Psychological Association* (4th
ed.). Submit three (3) copies of the manuscript to the editors.

Journal Frequency: Quarterly

Articles/Pages Published per Year: 24/400

Total Subscribers: NA

Book Reviews Accepted: NA

Rejection Rate: NA

Notes From Publisher: Free sample copy available upon request.

Rehabilitation Psychology

Publisher: Educational Publishing
                Foundation
                750 First Street, NE
                Washington, DC 20002-4242

Editor: Myron G. Eisenberg, PhD
                Psychology Service (116B)
                VA Medical Center
                Hampton, VA 23667

Editorial Policy: *Rehabilitation Psychology* is an interdisciplinary journal of relevance to all concerned with psychological perspectives in rehabilitation. To this end, the journal will publish articles that address the psychological and behavioral aspects of rehabilitation in a wide range of settings and from a number of perspectives. Manuscripts detailing sound empirical research, theory, clinical practice, and policy issues in rehabilitation psychology are invited along with reviews of pertinent topics. Manuscripts concerned with issues of chronic illness and physical, mental, or emotional disability throughout the entire life span are considered appropriate. Suggestions for special issues devoted to a topic of particular importance or interest are welcomed by the editor. (This is a publication of APA's Division 22.)

Selective Notes on Submissions: Instructions to authors included in each issue of the journal. Authors to prepare manuscripts according to the *Publication Manual of the American Psychological Association* (4th

ed.). Submit four (4) copies of the manuscript to the editor.

Journal Frequency: Quarterly

Articles/Pages Published per Year: 22/269

Total Subscribers: 1,500

Book Reviews Accepted: Yes

Rejection Rate: 54%

Research on Aging

Publisher: Sage Publications, Inc.
                2455 Teller Road
                Thousand Oaks, CA 91320

Editor: Rhonda J. V. Montgomery
                Gerontology Center
                University of Kansas
                4089 Dole Human Development
                Center
                Lawrence, KS 66045

Editorial Policy: *Research on Aging* is an interdisciplinary journal designed to reflect the expanding role of research in the field of social gerontology. The journal exists to provide for the publication of research in the broad range of disciplines concerned with aging. Scholars from the disciplines of sociology, geriatrics, history, psychology, anthropology, public health, economics, political science, criminal justice, and social work are encouraged to contribute articles to the journal. Emphasis will be on materials of broad scope and cross-disciplinary interest. Assessment of the current state of knowledge is important as a provision of an outlet for new knowledge, so critical and review articles are welcome. Systematic attention to particular topics will also be featured. Suggestions for special-topic coverage are welcome. The journal will present knowledge about the aging process and the aged—knowledge that can be used in the development of better practices and the formulation of better policies.

Selective Notes on Submissions: Instructions to authors included in each issue of the journal. Authors to prepare manuscripts according to the ASA style manual. Submit four (4) copies of the manuscript to the editor.

Journal Frequency: Quarterly

Articles/Pages Published per Year: 20/400

Total Subscribers: 1,375

Book Reviews Accepted: No

Rejection Rate: 75%

Research in Developmental Disabilities

Publisher: Elsevier Science
660 White Plains Road
Tarrytown, NY 10591-5153

Editor: Johnny L. Matson, PhD
Department of Psychology
Louisiana State University
Baton Rouge, LA 70803-5501

Editorial Policy: *Research in Developmental Disabilities* is aimed at publishing original research of an interdisciplinary nature that has a direct bearing on the remediation of problems associated with developmental disabilities. Articles are primarily empirical studies, although an occasional position paper or review is accepted. The aim of the journal is to publish articles on all aspects of research with the developmentally disabled, with any methodologically sound approach being acceptable. A list of topic areas that is illustrative but not inclusive is applied behavior analysis, pharmacotherapy, traditional assessment, behavioral assessment, speech training, and occupational therapy.

Selective Notes on Submissions: Instructions to authors included in each issue of the journal. Authors to prepare manuscripts according to the *Publication Manual of the American Psychological Association* (4th ed.). Submit five (5) high-quality copies of the manuscript to the editor.

Journal Frequency: Bimonthly

Articles/Pages Published per Year: 600 pp.

Total Subscribers: NA

Book Reviews Accepted: Yes

Rejection Rate: NA

Notes From Publisher: Free sample copy available upon request. In order to speed publication, authors are requested to submit a computer disk containing the final version of their manuscript.

Review of General Psychology

Publisher: Educational Publishing
Foundation
750 First Street, NE
Washington, DC 20002-4242

Editor: Peter Salovey
Department of Psychology
Yale University
P.O. Box 208205
New Haven, CT 06520-8205

Editorial Policy: *Review of General Psychology,* the official journal of APA Division 1, seeks to publish innovative theoretical, conceptual, or methodological articles that cross-cut the traditional subdisciplines of psychology. *Review of General Psychology* contains articles that advance theory, evaluate and integrate research literatures, provide a new historical analysis, or discuss new methodological developments in psychology as a whole. Of special interest are papers that bridge gaps between subdisciplines in psychology as well as related fields or that focus on topics that transcend traditional subdisciplinary boundaries. Intellectual risk taking is encouraged. Some of the most exciting work in psychology is at the edges of subdisciplines, and traditional journals accommodate such articles only with difficulty; *Review of General Psychology* invites these kinds of manuscripts. Papers devoted primarily to reporting new empirical findings are generally not appropriate for this journal.

The target audience for the *Review of General Psychology* consists of those psychologists who appreciate both generalism and specialization and who share a vision of psychology as a unified discipline with common theoretical, methodological, and substantive values. Authors are encouraged to write their manuscripts from the perspective of more than one subdiscipline and to review literature that spans at least two subdisciplines in order to attract a broad readership.

Selective Notes on Submissions: Instructions to authors included in each issue of the journal. Authors to prepare manuscripts according to the *Publication Manual of the American Psychological Association* (4th ed.). Submit five (5) copies of the manuscript to the editor. New in 1997.

Journal Frequency: Quarterly

Articles/Pages Published per Year: NA

Total Subscribers: NA

Book Reviews Accepted: No

Rejection Rate: NA

School Counselor

Publisher: American Association for
Counseling and
Development
5999 Stevenson Avenue
Alexandria, VA 22304

Editor: Stanley B. Baker
520 Poe Hall, Box 7801
North Carolina State University
Raleigh, NC 27695-7801

Editorial Policy: This journal will keep you on top of your field with new ideas on how to deal with current issues such as teen suicide, alcohol and drug abuse, and legal rights of teens. In addition to regular articles on both theoretical issues and applied practices, a new section covers various aspects of the use of microcomputers in counseling.

Selective Notes on Submissions: Instructions to authors included in each issue of the journal. Authors to prepare manuscripts according to the *Publication Manual of the American Psychological Association* (4th ed.). Submit three (3) copies of the manuscript to the editor.

Journal Frequency: 5 issues per year

Articles/Pages Published per Year: 70/400

Total Subscribers: 17,000

Book Reviews Accepted: Yes

Rejection Rate: 65%

School Psychology International

Publisher: Sage Publications, Ltd.
6 Bonhill Street
London EC2A 4PU
England

Editors: R. L. Burden
School of Education
University of Exeter
Exeter EX1 2LU
England

C. S. McLoughlin
School Psychology Program
412 White Hall

Kent State University
Kent, OH 44242

Editorial Policy: *School Psychology International* publishes critical and descriptive review articles and empirical contributions of international interest in all practical and academic areas of school and educational psychology. Many issues will contain review articles based on defined themes. Review article manuscripts should normally be between 3,000 and 6,000 words in length, including tables, figures, and references, and will be evaluated by anonymous referees. Book reviews will also be published.

Selective Notes on Submissions: Instructions to authors included in each issue of the journal. Authors to prepare manuscripts according to the style manual of the British Psychological Society or the *Publication Manual of the American Psychological Association* (4th ed.). Submit three (3) copies of the manuscript to the editor.

Journal Frequency: Quarterly

Articles/Pages Published per Year: 24/400

Total Subscribers: NA

Book Reviews Accepted: Yes

Rejection Rate: 25%

Suggested Index Terms: Education, School Psychology, Educational Psychology

School Psychology Quarterly

Publisher: Guilford Publications, Inc.
72 Spring Street
New York, NY 10012

Editor: Joseph C. Witt, PhD
Department of Psychology
236 Audubon Hall
Louisiana State University
Baton Rouge, LA 70803

Editorial Policy: As the official publication of APA Division 16, this quarterly has kept school psychologists at the cutting edge of the field for the past seven years. It focuses primarily on scientific research and includes a separate section for professional issues. Manuscripts are sought that fall primarily into empirical research and studies broadly emphasizing methods to advance scientific understanding of research, theory, and practice in school psychology, including a range of methodologies that contribute new knowledge to enhancing the life experiences of children, families, and schools. Qualitative research designs and single case experiments will also be appropriate.

Selective Notes on Submissions: Instructions to authors included in each issue of the journal. Authors to prepare manuscripts according to the *Publication Manual of the American Psychological Association* (4th ed.). Submit three (3) copies of the manuscript to the editor.

Journal Frequency: Quarterly

Articles/Pages Published per Year: 24/363

Total Subscribers: 3,000

Book Reviews Accepted: Yes

Rejection Rate: 77%

School Psychology Review

Publisher: National Association of School Psychologists
4340 East-West Highway
Suite 402
Bethesda, MD 20814

Editor: Patti L. Harrison
Educational and School Psychology Program
University of Alabama
P.O. Box 870231
303 Carmichael
Tuscaloosa, AL 35487-0231

Editorial Policy: The primary purpose of the *Review* is to provide a means for communicating scholarly advances in research, training, and practice which can affect the delivery of school psychological services. The review publishes original research, reviews of theoretical and applied topics, case studies, and descriptions of intervention techniques useful to psychologists working in educational settings. Scholarly reviews of books, tests, and other psychological or educational materials also are published occasionally. Portions of two or three issues each year are reserved for guest edited mini-series on themes deemed by the editorial board to be of major interest to practitioners of school psychology. The majority of journal space, however, is open for unsolicited manuscripts covering a wide range of topics. All articles are subject to a masked review process involving members of the Editorial Advisory Board. Ad hoc reviewers also are utilized frequently.

Selective Notes on Submissions: Instructions to authors included in each issue of the

journal. Authors to prepare manuscripts according to the *Publication Manual of the American Psychological Association* (4th ed.). Submit five (5) copies of the manuscript to the editor.

Journal Frequency: Quarterly

Articles/Pages Published per Year: 56/600

Total Subscribers: 20,000

Book Reviews Accepted: No

Rejection Rate: 80%

Notes From Publisher: Sample copies available for review.

Sex Roles

Publisher: Plenum Publishing Corporation
                   233 Spring Street
                   New York, NY 10013-1578

Editor: Sue R. Zalk, PhD
                   Graduate School and University
                     Center
                   Office of the Vice President for
                     Student Affairs
                   CUNY
                   33 West 42nd Street
                   New York, NY 10036-8099

Editorial Policy: *Sex Roles* is a forum for the publication of original research articles and theoretical manuscripts concerned with the basic processes underlying gender-role socialization in children and its consequences. The journal is cross-disciplinary,

and pertinent investigations from the areas of psychology, psychiatry, sociology, anthropology, education, political science, and social work are welcomed. Topics covered include: sex-role stereotypes and childrearing practices; gender roles and political socialization; effects of contemporary social change upon sex-role perceptions and attitudes; effects of parental behavior and type of child care on children's development and adult life styles; gender-role socialization and sexual behavior; factors maintaining sex-role attitudes; sex-role attitudes in work and social relationships. In addition to empirical investigations, the journal also publishes critical reviews of research and book reviews.

Selective Notes on Submissions: Instructions to authors included in each issue of the journal. Authors to prepare manuscripts according to the *Publication Manual of the American Psychological Association* (4th ed.). Submit two (2) copies of the manuscript to the editor.

Journal Frequency: Monthly

Articles/Pages Published per Year: 48/680

Total Subscribers: 996

Book Reviews Accepted: Yes

Rejection Rate: NA

Sexual Abuse: A Journal of Research and Treatment

Publisher: Plenum Publishing Corporation
                   233 Spring Street
                   New York, NY 10013

Editor: Barry M. Maletzky, MD

Editorial Policy: *Sexual Abuse: A Journal of Research and Treatment* provides a vehicle by which clinical and theoretical research in sexual abuse—its causes, treatment, and consequences—can be presented to a professional audience. The journal strives to make available to professionals across a variety of disciplines the most recent thinking and research relating to the assessment and treatment of the sexual offender and to the effects of sexual abuse upon victims and families as such effects relate to sexual offending. The journal aims to foster a better understanding of sexual abuse and to advance the scientific framework within which professionals must operate in addressing issues of clinical and theoretical importance. As such, original peer-reviewed contributions from all academic disciplines are published.

Selective Notes on Submissions: Instructions to authors included in each issue of the journal. Authors to prepare manuscripts according to the *Publication Manual of the American Psychological Association* (4th ed.). Submit four (4) copies of the manuscript to the editor. Send manuscripts to the managing editor: Connie Isaac, 10700 SW Beaverton-Hillsdale Highway, Suite 26, Beaverton, OR 97005-3035.

Journal Frequency: Quarterly

Articles/Pages Published per Year: 24/340

Total Subscribers: 1,300

Book Reviews Accepted: No

Rejection Rate: 30%

Sexual and Marital Therapy

Publisher: Carfax Publishing Company
P.O. Box 25
Abingdon, Oxfordshire OX14 3UE
England

Editor: Patricia d'Ardenne
Department of Psychological Medicine
William Harvey House
61 Saint Bartholomew's Close
London EC1A 7BE
England

Editorial Policy: *Sexual and Marital Therapy* is an international journal for everyone professionally concerned with sexual and marital function. Its readers include academics and researchers, clinicians, therapists and counselors. Sexual and marital difficulties, and their alleviation, are an increasing part of the workload of professionals from many different disciplines, including medicine, psychology, psychotherapy, nursing, counseling and social work. The scope of the journal reflects this diversity of professional interests, and articles will communicate across disciplines without loss of excellence. *Sexual and Marital Therapy* combines transmission of clinical experience with a critical stance towards much of the current literature. The results of original research, subject reviews, accounts of therapeutic and counseling practice, case studies, short communications and book reviews all feature in the journal. *Sexual and Marital Therapy* is the official journal of the British Association for Sexual and Marital Therapy.

Selective Notes on Submissions: Instructions to authors included in each issue of the

journal. Authors to prepare manuscripts according to the Harvard style. Submit three (3) copies of the manuscript to the editor. Send manuscripts to co-editor: Patricia d'Ardenne.

Journal Frequency: Quarterly

Articles/Pages Published per Year: 24/420

Total Subscribers: 1,000

Book Reviews Accepted: No

Rejection Rate: 50%

Small Group Research: An International Journal of Theory, Investigation, and Application

Publisher: Sage Publications, Inc.
2455 Teller Road
Thousand Oaks, CA 91320

Editors: Charles Garvin
School of Social Work
University of Michigan
Ann Arbor, MI 48109-1285

Richard B. Polley
George Fox College

Editorial Policy: *Small Group Research* is an international and interdisciplinary journal presenting research and theory about all types of small groups, including but not limited to therapy and treatment groups. It is the long-term goal of *Small Group Research* to encourage the development of a comparative social science of group work. *Small*

Group Research is a broadly conceived information channel for all group work professionals and includes book reviews, up-to-date bibliographic listings, and news of significant professional activities, meetings, research centers, and the like.

Selective Notes on Submissions: Authors to prepare manuscripts according to the *Publication Manual of the American Psychological Association* (4th ed.). Submit four (4) copies of the manuscript to the first editor.

Journal Frequency: Quarterly

Articles/Pages Published per Year: 32/576

Total Subscribers: 1,338

Book Reviews Accepted: No

Rejection Rate: 75%

Social Cognition

Publisher: Guilford Publications, Inc.
72 Spring Street
New York, NY 10012

Editor: Donal E. Carlson
Department of Psychological Services
Purdue University
West Lafayette, IN 47907-1364

Editorial Policy: *Social Cognition* publishes reports of empirical research, conceptual analyses, and critical reviews on the role of cognitive processes in the study of personality, development, and social behavior. The journal emphasizes three broad concerns:

the ways people perceive, code, manipulate, and remember socially relevant stimuli; the effects of social, cultural, and affective factors on the processing of information; and the behavioral and interpersonal consequences of cognitive processes. Among the areas covered are person perception, self-perception, self-concept, memory for social events and people, social schemata, personal constructs, the development of social cognition, and the role of affect in memory and perception. Also encouraged are articles about cultural influences on cognition, the role of cognitive processes in psychopathology, aquisition of communication skills, and cognitive aspects of psychology and law. The journal welcomes substantive empirical and nonempirical contributions. Reports of original research are judged according to traditional criteria of methodological adequacy and statistical rigor. Authors are especially encouraged to set their research problems in a strong conceptual framework and to discuss fully the theoretical implications of their work.

Selective Notes on Submissions: Instructions to authors included in each issue of the journal. Authors to prepare manuscripts according to the *Publication Manual of the American Psychological Association* (4th ed.). Submit five (5) copies of the manuscript to the editor.

Journal Frequency: Quarterly

Articles/Pages Published per Year: 20/400

Total Subscribers: 700

Book Reviews Accepted: No

Rejection Rate: NA

Social Psychology Quarterly

Publisher: American Sociological Association
1722 N Street, NW
Washington, DC 20036

Editor: Edward J. Lawler
Department of Sociology
University of Iowa
Iowa City, IA 52242

Editorial Policy: NA

Selective Notes on Submissions: Instructions to authors included in each issue of the journal. Authors to prepare manuscripts according to the *Publication Manual of the American Psychological Association* (4th ed.). Submit five (5) copies of the manuscript to the editor.

Journal Frequency: Quarterly

Articles/Pages Published per Year: 28/440

Total Subscribers: 3,250

Book Reviews Accepted: NA

Rejection Rate: NA

Sport Psychologist

Publisher: Human Kinetics Publishers, Inc.
1607 North Market Street
Champaign, IL 61820-2200

Editor: Graham Jones
                   Department of Physical
                        Education
                   Loughborough University
                   Loughborough, Leicestershire
                        LE11 3TU
                   England

Editorial Policy: *Sport Psychologist* is published for educational sport psychologists (those who teach psychological skills to coaches and athletes) and for clinical sport psychologists (those who have provided clinical services to athletes and coaches with psychological dysfunctions). The journal is also intended for those who teach sport psychology in academic institutions and for coaches who have training in sport psychology. *Sport Psychologist* focuses on the professional interest of sport psychologists as these pertain to the delivery of psychological services to coaches and athletes. It is international in scope, receptive to nonscientific methodologies, and refereed. In particular, the journal has sections on applied research and on professional practice.

Selective Notes on Submissions: Instructions to authors included in each issue of the journal. Authors to prepare manuscripts according to the *Publication Manual of the American Psychological Association* (4th ed.). Submit three (3) copies of the manuscript to the editor.

Journal Frequency: Quarterly

Articles/Pages Published per Year: 28/400

Total Subscribers: 1,123

Book Reviews Accepted: Yes

Rejection Rate: 75%

Substance Use and Misuse

Previous Title: International Journal of the Addictions

Publisher: Marcel Dekker, Inc.
                   270 Madison Avenue
                   New York, NY 10016

Editor: Stanley Einstein, PhD
                   Building 113/41
                   East Talpiot
                   Jerusalem, Israel

Editorial Policy: This journal is a comprehensive medium for worldwide communication among both concerned laymen and professionals in policy making, research, training, and treatment in the field of addiction and substance misuse.

Selective Notes on Submissions: Instructions to authors included in each journal. Send original and one (1) duplicate to the editor.

Journal Frequency: 14 issues per year

Articles/Pages Published per Year: 110/ 1600

Total Subscribers: 700

Book Reviews Accepted: Yes

Rejection Rate: 50%

Suicide and Life-Threatening Behavior

Publisher: Guilford Press
72 Spring Street
New York, NY 10012

Editor: Ronald Maris, PhD
Department of Sociology
228 Calcott Building
University of South Carolina
Columbia, SC 29208

Editorial Policy: This journal is devoted to emergent approaches in theory and practice related to self-destruction, other-destructive, and life-threatening behaviors. It is multidisciplinary and concerned with a variety of topics: suicide, suicide prevention, death, accidents, subintentioned destruction, partial death—threats to life's length and breadth from within and without.

Selective Notes on Submissions: Instructions to authors included in each issue of the journal. Authors to prepare manuscripts according to the *Publication Manual of the American Psychological Association* (4th ed.). Submit four (4) copies of the manuscript to the editor.

Journal Frequency: Quarterly

Articles/Pages Published per Year: 36/448

Total Subscribers: 2,000

Book Reviews Accepted: Yes

Rejection Rate: 65%

Notes From Publisher: Official publication of the American Association of Suicidology.

Teaching of Psychology

Publisher: Lawrence Erlbaum Associates, Inc.
10 Industrial Avenue
Mahwah, NJ 07430-2262

Editor: Randolph A. Smith, PhD
Department of Psychology
Ouachita Baptist University
Arkadelphia, AR 71998-0001

Editorial Policy: The *Teaching of Psychology* is devoted to improvement of the teaching/learning process at all educational levels from the secondary school through college and graduate school to continuing education. The journal includes empirical research on teaching and learning: studies of teacher or student characteristics; subject matter or content reviews for class use; investigations of student, course, or teacher assessment; professional problems of teachers; essays on teaching; innovative course descriptions and evaluations; curriculum designs; bibliographic material; demonstrations and laboratory projects; book and media reviews; news items; and reader's commentary. Topical Articles include a range of content from broader to more specialized applicability. Articles may vary in length from 2,500 to 7,000 words. The editor may solicit manuscripts deemed to be of significance to the readership. Methods and Techniques papers are those describing demonstrations, laboratory projects, other learning/teaching devices, or instrumentation (1,000–2,000 words). Topical Articles and Methods and Techniques papers should include empirical assessment of the contribution whenever applicable. Faculty Forum items may cover the full range of the journal's content policy, including commentary, criticism, or opinion.

Brief contributions of methodology, innovative procedures, courses, or other materials in the Forum need not include evaluations (1,200 words or less). (This is a publication of APA's Division 2.)

Selective Notes on Submissions: Instructions to authors included in each issue of the journal. Authors to prepare manuscripts according to the *Publication Manual of the American Psychological Association* (4th ed.). Submit two (2) copies. Submit manuscripts on Methods and Techniques to Linda M. Noble, PhD, Kennesaw State University, 1000 Chastain Road, Kennesaw, GA 30144. Send manuscripts for Computers in Teaching to David J. Pittenger, PhD, Department of Psychology, Marietta College, Marietta, OH 45750. All other manuscripts should be sent to the editor.

Journal Frequency: Quarterly

Articles/Pages Published per Year: 65/272

Total Subscribers: 2,000

Book Reviews Accepted: Yes

Rejection Rate: 86%

Theory and Psychology

Publisher: Sage Publications, Ltd.
6 Bonhill Street
London EC2A 4PU
England

Editor: Henderikus J. Stam
Department of Psychology
University of Calgary
Calgary, Alberta
Canada T2N 1N4

Editorial Policy: *Theory and Psychology* publishes scholarly and expository papers that explore significant theoretical developments within and across such specific sub-areas as cognitive, social, personality, developmental, clinical, perceptual, and biological psychology. It also publishes, and particularly encourages, work with a broader metatheoretical intent, examining such issues as the conceptual frameworks and foundations of psychology, its historical underpinnings, its relation to other human sciences, its methodological commitments, its ideological assumptions, and its political and institutional contexts. Interdisciplinary analyses addressing psychological topics are welcome. These may include (but are not limited to) the philosophy of science and psychology, cognition and intentionality, forms of explanation in psychology, criteria of theory evaluation, the social basis of psychological knowledge, critical theory and methods in psychology, feminist theory and methods in psychology, and rhetoric and argumentation in psychological theory.

Selective Notes on Submissions: Instructions to authors included in each issue of the journal. Authors to prepare manuscripts according to the *Publication Manual of the American Psychological Association* (4th ed.). Submit four (4) copies of the manuscript to the editor.

Journal Frequency: Bimonthly

Articles/Pages Published per Year: 40/864

Total Subscribers: 1,000

Book Reviews Accepted: Yes

Rejection Rate: 75%

Transactional Analysis Journal

Publisher: The International Transactional Analysis Association, Inc.
1772 Vallejo Street
San Francisco, CA 94123-5009

Editor: Howard Douglass, PhD
1772 Vallejo Street
San Francisco, CA 94123

Editorial Policy: The *Transactional Analysis Journal* is published quarterly in January, April, July, and October for the advancement of the theory, principles, and practice of transactional analysis. The editorial board favors the free flow of ideas. Any point of view will be published if it is presented well and contributes something new, no matter how controversial, to the extension and clarification of transactional analysis theory.

Selective Notes on Submissions: Instructions to authors included in each issue of the journal. Authors to prepare manuscripts according to the *Publication Manual of the American Psychological Association* (4th ed.). Submit nine (9) copies of the manuscript to the editor.

Journal Frequency: Quarterly

Articles/Pages Published per Year: 30/300

Total Subscribers: 5,000

Book Reviews Accepted: Yes

Rejection Rate: 30–40%

Vision Research

Publisher: Elsevier Science
P.O. Box 211
1000 AE Amsterdam
The Netherlands

Editor: Chaiman: H. Spekreijse
Netherlands Opthalmic Research Institute
University of Amsterdam
P.O. Box 12011
1100 AA Amsterdam
The Netherlands

Editorial Policy: *Vision Research* is a journal devoted to the functional aspects of human, vertebrate, and invertebrate vision and publishes experimental and observational studies, reviews, and theoretical papers firmly based on the current facts of visual science. The purpose of theoretical papers is to give a higher sense of order to the facts as they are presently known or to point to new observations from which emergent knowledge may arise.

Vision Research also accepts experimental studies in which clinical material has been used to address an issue of basic research interest, or where basic research methods have been used to address an issue of clinical importance, or where basic research may have, as yet unapplied, clinical relevance. The words *clinical* and *vision sciences* should be interpreted in the broadest sense, as represented by the areas of expertise of the members of the editorial board.

Vision Research is also prepared to publish minireviews. A minireview is not intended to be a comprehensive history of the subject but a survey of recent developments in fast-growing and active areas of vision research covered over the past few years.

Selective Notes on Submissions: Instructions to authors included in each issue of the journal. Submit five (5) copies of the manuscript: one copy to the section editor of the appropriate subject area (consult the journal) and the original and three (3) copies to Vision Research, P.O. Box 12011, 1100 AA Amsterdam-Zuidoost, The Netherlands.

Journal Frequency: 24 issues per year

Articles/Pages Published per Year: 620/3500

Total Subscribers: NA

Book Reviews Accepted: NA

Rejection Rate: NA

Visual Neuroscience

Publisher: Cambridge University Press
               40 West 20th Street
               New York, NY 10011-4211

Editor: James McIlwain
               Brown University
               Box G-M416
               Providence, RI 02912

Editorial Policy: This international journal is devoted to the publication of research and theoretical articles in basic visual neuroscience, with primary emphasis on retinal and brain mechanisms that underlie visually guided behaviors and visual perception. The major goal of *Visual Neuroscience* is to bring together in one journal a broad range of studies which reflect the existing diversity and originality of contemporary research in basic visual neuroscience. Methodologies will be drawn from neuroanatomy, neurophysiology, neurochemistry, neuroimmunology, and behavioral science, as well as computational models and computer-assisted formulations. Molecular, cellular, local-circuit, and systems-level analyses in both vertebrate and invertebrate species will be presented.

Selective Notes on Submissions: Submit original and two (2) copies of the manuscript to the editor.

Journal Frequency: Bimonthly

Articles/Pages Published per Year: 45/600

Total Subscribers: NA

Book Reviews Accepted: NA

Rejection Rate: NA

Voices: The Art and Science of Psychotherapy

Publisher: American Academy of
               Psychotherapists

Editor: Monica Savlin
               2751 Ridge
               Evanston, IL 60201

Editorial Policy: Reflecting the aims of the American Academy of Psychotherapists, *Voices* provides a meeting ground for experienced psychotherapists of widely different orientations where they can share both professionally and personally. It is a theme-centered quarterly which prefers the personal essay—therapists writing about their day-to-day struggles with the process of therapy. A unique quarterly in many ways, *Voices* features poetry and reviews as well as clinical articles. Contributors have included poets, politicians, and novelists, as well as Carl Rogers, Rollo May, Virginia Satir, Martin Grotjahn, Carl Whitaker, and Jay Haley. Interdisciplinary in focus, *Voices* will be of interest to a wide variety of professionals including psychologists, psychiatrists, clinical social workers, marriage and family counselors, and pastoral counselors.

Selective Notes on Submissions: Instructions to authors included in each issue of the journal. Authors to prepare manuscripts according to the *Publication Manual of the American Psychological Association* (4th ed.). Submit three (3) copies of the manuscript to the editor.

Journal Frequency: Quarterly

Articles/Pages Published per Year: 40/384

Total Subscribers: 1,500

Book Reviews Accepted: Yes

Rejection Rate: NA

Women & Therapy

Publisher: Haworth Press, Inc.
10 Alice Street
Binghamton, NY 13904-1580

Editors: Ellen Cole, PhD
Department of Psychology and
Human Services
Alaska-Pacific University

Esther D. Rothblum, PhD
Department of Psychology
John Dewey Hall
University of Vermont
Burlington, VT 05405

Editorial Policy: This journal explores the unique multidisciplinary relationship between women and therapy. Feminist in orientation, the journal publishes descriptive, theoretical, clinical, and empirical perspectives on the topic and the therapeutic process.

Selective Notes on Submissions: Authors to prepare manuscripts according to the *Publication Manual of the American Psychological Association* (4th ed.). Submit four (4) copies of the manuscript to Esther D. Rothblum.

Journal Frequency: Quarterly

Articles/Pages Published per Year: 28/320

Total Subscribers: 1,000

Book Reviews Accepted: Yes

Rejection Rate: 80%

Work and Stress

Publisher: Taylor & Francis, Ltd.
1 Gunpowder Square
London EC4A 3DE
England

Editor: Tom Cox, Managing Editor
Centre for Organizational Health
Department of Psychology
University of Nottingham
University Park, Nottingham
NG7 2RD
England

Editorial Policy: The policy of *Work and Stress* is to attract as broad a range of contributions as possible. These are essentially of two types: (a) academic papers relating to stress, health, safety, and performance and associated areas (empirical reports, reviews, case studies, and theoretical papers) and (b) scholarly articles of concern to the policymakers, managers, and trade unionists who have to deal with such issues. Papers should be of interest to ergonomists, human factors engineers, occupational health specialists, industrial sociologists, occupational physicians, medical sociologists, industrial safety officers, personnel managers, occupational hygienists, and trade union representatives.

Selective Notes on Submissions: Instructions to authors included in each issue of the journal. Authors to prepare manuscripts according to the *Publication Manual of the American Psychological Association* (4th ed.). Submit four (4) copies of the manuscript to the editor.

Journal Frequency: Quarterly

Articles/Pages Published per Year: 40/400

Total Subscribers: 1,000

Book Reviews Accepted: Yes

Rejection Rate: 45%

Notes From Publisher: U.S. Editor: Donald Tedai, Psychology, University of Connecticut, Storrs, CT 06268.

Suggested Index Terms: Work psychology, occupational health and safety

World Psychology

Publisher: International Council of
Psychologists
ICP Secretariat
Department of Psychology
Southwest Texas State
University
San Marcos, TX 78666-4616

Editor: Uwe P. Gielen
Department of Psychology
Saint Francis College
Brooklyn Heights, NY 11201

Editorial Policy: *World Psychology* covers issues such as:

1. Developments in international psychology; general discussions of the status of psychology in specific regions of the world; worldwide trends in psychology; cultural and political aspects of psychology; 2. Professional and ethical issues; 3. The training of psychologists around the world; critical discussions of the role of psychologists; 4. The teaching of psychology around the world; 5. Broad research reviews of major topics with an emphasis on applied aspects. The reviews should be written for nonspecialists and reflect an international perspective; 6. Broad review papers of cross-cultural research; 7. Sharply focused

debates; 8. Special issues developed by guest editors; 9. Book reviews; 10. Interdisciplinary papers of interest to psychologists around the world; 11. Historically oriented papers showing the growth of international psychology; 12. Interviews with some of the world's leading psychologists.

The journal will not publish narrowly focused research papers, although papers with broad applications would be appropriate. Authors are especially encouraged to submit papers dealing with psychology or psychological topics in non-western countries.

Selective Notes on Submissions: Instructions to authors included in each issue of the journal. Authors to prepare manuscripts according to the *Publication Manual of the American Psychological Association* (4th ed.). Submit four (4) copies of the manuscript to the editor. If you are unsure whether your manuscript is appropriate for *World Psychology,* send a preliminary inquiry together with a 2-3 page abstract to the editor.

Journal Frequency: Quarterly

Articles/Pages Published per Year: 20/500

Total Subscribers: 1,010

Book Reviews Accepted: Yes

Rejection Rate: 70%